15TH ANNIVERSARY EDITION

SECRETS of POWER NEGOTIATING

UPDATED FOR THE 21ST CENTURY

Inside Secrets From a Master Negotiator

ROGER DAWSON

POMPTON PLAINS, NJ

SECRETS OF POWER NEGOTIATING, 15TH ANNIVERSARY EDITION
EDITED BY JODI BRANDON
TYPESET BY EILEEN MUNSON
Cover design by Jeff Piasky
Printed in the U.S.A.

To order this title, please call toll-free 1-800-CAREER-1 (NJ and Canada: 201-848-0310) to order using VISA or MasterCard, or for further information on books from Career Press.

The Career Press, Inc.
220 West Parkway, Unit 12
Pompton Plains, NJ 07444
www.careerpress.com

Library of Congress Cataloging-in-Publication Data

Dawson, Roger, 1940-
Secrets of power negotiating : inside secrets from a master negotiator / by Roger Dawson. -- 15th anniversary ed.
p. cm.
Rev. ed. of: Secrets of power negotiating : inside secrets from a master negotiator. 2nd ed. 2001.
Includes bibliographical references and index.
ISBN 978-1-60163-139-8 -- ISBN 978-1-60163-688-1 (ebook)
1. Negotiation in business. I. Title.

HD58.6.D39 2011
658.4'052--dc22

2010034222

Dedicated to:

My beautiful wife,
Gisela,
who brought love back into my life.

And to all the attendees of my seminars,
readers of my books,
and listeners to my audio programs,
who shared their negotiating stories with me.

And to my three amazing children:
Julia, Dwight, and John.

And to my beautiful grandchildren:
Astrid and Thomas.

Contents

Section Six
Developing Power Over the Other Side

Introduction

What Is Power Negotiating?

A lot has happened since Career Press published the first edition of this book 15 years ago. A great deal has happened to me, and there has been a great deal of change in the world. The big change that affected us all, of course, was the Internet. It is so much easier to communicate with each other than it used to be. These days, I get up in the morning and answer e-mails that come in from around the world overnight because they work when I sleep. These days, I'm just as likely to be teaching Power Negotiating in Shanghai as I am in Seattle.

This third edition very much reflects the brave new world in which we live. You'll find expanded chapters on negotiating with people from other cultures. It's what I've learned from conducting Power Negotiating seminars around the world, from Kuwait to Nigeria to China, and New Zealand to Iceland. As different as we are, I find that most people want the same thing from a negotiation: They want a fair deal for both sides. They want to use their new negotiating skills to improve their position. They want to be skilled enough to stop the other side from taking advantage of them.

This third edition includes chapters on two subjects that seem to fascinate attendees at my seminars: body language and hidden meanings in Conversation. Remember the high-tech/high-touch theory? It said that the more we contact each other by machine, the more important those rare face-to-face meetings become. The more we are isolated by e-mail and texting of increasingly brief messages, the more we yearn to understand people better.

You'll also find expanded chapters on mediation and arbitration. That's a big shift in our new world, and a very welcome one. Taking the other party to court is a very expensive and time-consuming way to resolve issues. The trend to replace that with mediation (when people of good faith, guided by a trained mediator, search for a solution acceptable to both sides) makes so much more sense.

In this edition, you'll find the new ***Key Points to Remember*** invaluable. If you are reading this book on your iPad or Kindle, you'll find these points valuable as a last-minute brush up before you go into a negotiation. Search for the phrase "Key Points," and go through them on the plane as you fly to your negotiations. If you're reading this as a good old-fashioned book, you'll find Key Points to Remember at the end of nearly every chapter.

A lot has changed in the last 15 years, but much has stayed the same. The objective of a negotiation is still to create a win-win solution, which is a creative way that both you and the other person can walk away from the negotiating table feeling that you've won.

Win-win negotiators always talk about the two people who have only one orange, but both want it. They decide that the best they can do is split the orange down the middle, and each settle for half of what they really need. To be sure that it's fair, they decide that one will cut and the other will choose.

As they discuss their underlying needs in the negotiation, however, they find that one wants the orange to make juice, and the other needs it for the rind because he wants to bake a cake. They have magically found a way that both of them can win, and neither has to lose.

Oh, sure! That could happen in the real world, but it doesn't happen enough to make the concept meaningful. Let's face it: When you're sitting down in a negotiation, chances are that the other side wants the same thing that you do. There's not going to be a magical win-win solution. If they're buying, they want the lowest price and you want the highest price. If they're selling, they want the highest price and you want the lowest. They want to take money out of your pocket and put it right into theirs.

Power Negotiating takes a different position. It teaches you how to win at the negotiating table, but leave the other person feeling that he or she won. I'll teach you how to do this and do it in such a way that the other side permanently feels that they won. They don't wake up the next morning thinking, "Now I know what that person did to me. Wait until I see her again." No! They'll be thinking what a great time they had negotiating with you and how they can't wait to see you again.

The ability to make others feel that they won is so important that I'd almost give you that as a definition of a Power Negotiator. Two people might enter a negotiation in which the circumstances were the same. Perhaps they're buying or selling real estate or equipment. Both might conclude the negotiation at exactly the same price and terms, but the

Power Negotiator leaves the table with the other person feeling that he or she won. The poor negotiator comes away with the other person feeling that he or she lost.

If you learn and apply the secrets of Power Negotiation that I'll teach you in this book, you'll never again feel that you lost to the other person. You'll always come away from the negotiating table knowing that you won, and knowing that you have improved your relationship with the other person.

If you have any comments, suggestions, stories to share, complaints to register, or questions to ask, please e-mail the author at *Roger@RogerDawson.com.*

Section One

Playing the Power Negotiating Game

You play Power Negotiating by a set of rules, just like the game of chess. The big difference between negotiating and chess is that, in negotiating, the other person doesn't have to know the rules. The other person will respond predictably to the moves that you make—not because of metaphysical magic, but because thousands of my students have told me their negotiating experience over the years, and from this feedback we know how the other person will react to any Power Negotiating move you make. Not every time of course, but the likelihood is so high that we now know that negotiating is more of a science than an art.

If you play chess, you know that the strategic moves of the game are called gambits. When I tell you about negotiating gambits, I'm talking about a strategic move that involves some risk. I'll teach you how to select the appropriate gambit. Your skill in selecting the right gambit and using it at the right time will minimize the risk. ***Beginning Gambits*** get the game started in your direction. ***Middle Gambits*** keep the game moving in your direction. You use ***Ending Gambits*** when you get ready to checkmate the other person or, in sales parlance, close the sale.

In the first section of this book, I'll teach you the Gambits of Power Negotiating. You'll learn the Beginning Gambits: the things that you do in the early stages of your contact with the other person, to be sure that you're setting the stage for a successful conclusion. As the negotiation progresses, you'll find that every advance will depend on the atmosphere that you create in the early stages. You should determine the demands that you make, and the attitude you present with a carefully made plan that encompasses all elements of the negotiation.

Your Opening Gambits will win or lose the game for you. You must base their use on a careful evaluation of the other person, the market, and the other side's company.

Next, I'll teach you the Middle Gambits that keep the momentum going in your favor. During this phase, different things come into play. The moves made by each side create currents that swirl around the participants and push them in different directions. You'll learn how to respond to these pressures and continue to master the game.

Finally, I'll teach you Unethical Gambits, Negotiating Principles, and the Ending Gambits that conclude the negotiation with your getting what you want, and with the other person still feeling that he or she won. The last few moments can make all the difference. Just as in a horse race, there's only one point in the contest that counts, and that's the finish line. As a Power Negotiator, you'll learn how to smoothly control the process right down to the wire. Let's get started learning the Gambits of Power Negotiating!

But first, a word (or two) about gender. A lot has happened to the use of gender in American English since I came here from England. John F. Kennedy would no longer be allowed to say, "(Our goal is) to land a *man* on the Moon...and returning *him* safely to the Earth." Bobby Kennedy wouldn't win a California primary election with his slogan "Some *men* see things as they are and say why? I dream things that never were and say, why not?"

In this book, the politically correct thing is to refer to every human as he or she, him or her. With these new-fangled computers on which we write books these days, it would only take me five minutes to have it read that way. But, trust me: You would hate it. It would be like walking barefoot through hot pebbles as you stumbled around trying to make sense of it all. Even my brilliant editor Jodi Brandon, who won't let me get away with a thing, tells me, "Use either he or she, and let the readers know at the start that one could mean the other." So that's what you'll find here. (If you're still unhappy, I encourage you to e-mail me at *Roger@RogerDawson.com*)

Beginning Negotiating Gambits

Chapter 1

Ask for More Than You Expect to Get

One of the cardinal rules of Power Negotiating is you should ask the other side for more than you expect to get. Henry Kissinger went so far as to say, "Effectiveness at the conference table depends upon overstating one's demands." Some reasons why you should do this are:

- Why should you ask the store for a bigger discount than you think you have a chance of getting?
- Why should you ask your boss for an executive suite, although you think you'll be lucky to get a private office?
- If you're applying for a job, why should you ask for more money and benefits than you think they'll give you?
- If you're dissatisfied with a meal in a restaurant, why should you ask the maitre'd to cancel the entire bill, even though you think they will take off only the charge for the offending item?

If you have thought about this, you probably came up with a few good reasons to ask for more than you expect to get. The obvious answer is it gives you some negotiating room. If you're selling, you can always come down, but you can never go up in price. If you're buying, you can always go up, but you can never come down. (When we get to Chapter 14, I'll show you how to nibble for more. Some things are easier to get at the end of the negotiation than they are at the beginning.) What you should be asking for is your MPP—your maximum plausible position. This is the most you can ask for and still have the other side see some plausibility in your position.

The less you know about the other side, the higher your initial position should be, for two reasons:

1. You may be off in your assumptions. If you don't know the other person or his needs well, he may be willing to pay more than you think. If he's selling, he may be willing to take far less than you think.
2. If this is a new relationship, you'll appear more cooperative if you're able to make larger concessions. The better you know the other person and his needs, the more you can modify your position. If the other side doesn't know you, their initial demands may be more outrageous.

If you're asking for more than your maximum plausible position, imply some flexibility. If your initial position seems outrageous to the other person and your attitude is "take it or leave it," you may not even get the negotiations started. The other person's response may be, "Then we don't have anything to talk about." You can get away with an outrageous opening position if you imply some flexibility.

If you're buying real estate directly from the seller, you might say, "I realize that you're asking $200,000 for the property and, based on everything you know, it may seem like a fair price to you. Perhaps you know something that I don't know, but based on all the research that I've done, it seems to me that we should be talking something closer to $160,000." At that point the seller may be thinking, "That's ridiculous. I'll never sell it for that, but he does seem to be sincere, so what do I have to lose if I spend some time negotiating with him, just to see how high I can get him to go?"

If you're a salesperson, you might say to the buyer, "We may be able to modify this position once we know your needs more precisely, but based on what we know so far about the quantities you'd be ordering, the quality of the packaging, and not needing just-in-time inventory, our best price would be in the region of $2.25 per widget." At that the other person will probably be thinking, "That's outrageous, but there does seem to be some flexibility there, so I think I'll invest some time negotiating with her and see how low I can get her to go."

Unless you are already an experienced negotiator, here is the problem you will have with this. Your real MPP is probably much higher than you think it is. We all fear being ridiculed by the other person (something that I'll talk more about later when we discuss Coercive Power in Chapter 55). We're all reluctant to take a position that will cause the other person to laugh at us or put us down. Because of this intimidation, you will probably feel like modifying your MPP to the point where you're asking for less than the maximum amount that the other person would think is plausible.

Another reason for asking for more than you expect to get will be obvious to you if you're a positive thinker: You might just get it. You don't know how the universe is aligned that day. Perhaps your patron saint is leaning over a cloud looking down at you and thinking, "Wow, look at that nice person. She's been working so hard for so long now. Let's just give her a break." You might just get what you ask for and the only way you'll find out is to ask for it.

In addition, asking for more than you expect to get increases the perceived value of what you are offering. If you're applying for a job and asking for more money than you expect to get, you implant in the personnel director's mind the thought that you are worth that much. If you're selling a car and asking for more than you expect to get, it positions the buyer into believing that the car is worth more.

Another advantage of asking for more than you expect to get is it prevents the negotiation from deadlocking. Look at the Persian Gulf War. What were we asking Saddam Hussein to do? (Perhaps asking is not exactly the right word.) President George Bush, in his State of the Union address, used a beautiful piece of alliteration, probably written by Peggy Noonan, to describe our opening negotiating position. He said, "I'm not bragging, I'm not bluffing, and I'm not bullying. There are three things this man has to do. He has to get out of Kuwait. He has to restore the legitimate government of Kuwait (don't do what the Soviets did in Afghanistan and install a puppet government), and he has to make reparations for the damage that he's done."

That was a very clear and precise opening negotiating position. The problem was that this was also our bottom line. It was also the least for which we were prepared to settle. No wonder the situation deadlocked. It had to deadlock because we didn't give Saddam Hussein room to have a win. If we'd have said, "Okay. We want you and all your cronies exiled. We want a non-Arab neutral government installed in Baghdad. We want United Nations supervision of the removal of all military equipment. In addition, we want you out of Kuwait, the legitimate Kuwaiti government restored, and reparation for the damages that you did." Then we could have gotten what we wanted and still given Saddam Hussein a win.

I know what you're thinking. You're thinking, "Roger, Saddam Hussein was not on my Christmas card list last year. He's not the kind of guy I want to give a win to." I agree with that. However, it creates a problem in negotiation. It creates deadlocks.

Sometimes You Want to Create a Deadlock

From the Persian Gulf scenario, you could draw one of two conclusions. The first is that our State Department negotiators are idiots. The second possibility is that this was a situation where we wanted to create a deadlock, because it served our purpose. We had no intention of settling for the three things that George Bush demanded in his State of the Union address. General Schwarzkopf, in his biography, *It Doesn't Take a Hero*, said, "The minute we got there, we understood that anything less than a military victory was a defeat for the United States." We couldn't let Saddam Hussein pull 600,000 troops back across the border, leaving us wondering when he would choose to do it again. We needed a reason to go in and take care of him militarily.

The Persian Gulf War was a situation where it served our purpose to create a deadlock. What concerns me is that, when you're involved in a negotiation, you are inadvertently creating deadlocks, because you don't have the courage to ask for more than you expect to get. A final reason why Power Negotiators say you should ask for more than you expect to get is that it's the only way you can create a climate where the other person feels that he or she won.

If you go in with your best offer up front, there's no way you can negotiate with the other side and leave them feeling that they won. These are the inexperienced negotiators always wanting to start with their best offer. This is the job applicant who thinks, "This is a tight job market, and if I ask for too much money, they won't even consider me."

This is the person who's selling a house or a car and thinking, "If I ask for too much, they'll just laugh at me." This is the salesperson who is saying to her sales manager, "I'm going out on this proposal today, and I know it's going to be competitive. I know they're getting bids from people all over town. Let me cut the price up front, or we won't stand a chance of getting the order." Negotiators know the value of asking for more than you expect to get.

Let's recap the reasons for asking for more than you expect to get:

- You might just get it.
- It gives you some negotiating room.
- It raises the perceived value of what you're offering.

- It prevents the negotiation from deadlocking.
- It creates a climate in which the other side feels that they won.

In highly publicized negotiations, such as when the football players or airline pilots go on strike, the initial demands both sides make are outlandish. I remember being involved in a union negotiation in which the initial demands were unbelievably outrageous. The union's demand was to triple the employees' wages. The company's opening was to make it an open shop—in other words, a voluntary union that would effectively destroy the union's power at that location.

When Sudanese rebels took three Red Cross workers hostage, they demanded $100 million for their release. Fortunately, nobody took this seriously, and they quickly dropped their demand to $2.5 million. Congressman Bill Richardson, who would later ride his negotiating skills all the way to being our ambassador to the United Nations, sat under a tree, ignoring the rebels who were waving guns at him. He eventually secured their release for five tons of rice, four old jeeps, and some radios from Red Cross relief supplies.

I remember being in Beijing, China, when they first started admitting visitors. I wanted a pedishaw ride to my hotel that was only two blocks away. (A pedishaw is like a rickshaw, but it has a bicycle on the front.) When the pedishaw drivers realized that I was an American, they went wild with delight. They all gathered around, apparently oblivious to my presence, and advised the lucky driver how to handle the negotiations with me. One of them told him to ask me for $10, another said $20, and finally, they agreed that $50 would be an appropriate place to start the negotiations. I eventually gave him $1, which was more than a day's wages, and he was very happy.

Power Negotiators know that the initial demands in these types of negotiations are always extreme, so they don't let it bother them. They know that as the negotiations progress, they will work their way toward the middle, where they will find a solution that both sides can accept. Then they can both call a press conference and announce that they won in the negotiations.

How Attorneys Ask for More

An attorney friend of mine, John Broadfoot, from Amarillo, Texas, tested this theory for me. He was representing a buyer of a piece of real estate, and even though he had a good deal worked out, he thought, "I'll see how Roger's rule of 'Asking for More Than You Expect to Get,' works." He dreamed up 23 paragraphs of requests to make of the seller. Some of them were ridiculous. He felt sure that at least half of them would be thrown out right away. To his amazement, he found that the seller of the property took strong objection to only one of the sentences in one of the paragraphs. Even then John, as I had taught him, didn't give in right away. He held out for a couple of days before he finally and reluctantly conceded. Although he had given away only one sentence in 23 paragraphs of requests, the seller still felt that he had won in the negotiation.

Bracketing

The next question has to be: If you're asking for more than you expect to get, for how much more than you expect to get should you ask? The answer is that you should bracket your objective. Your initial proposal should be an equal distance on the other side of your objective as their proposal.

Let me give you some simple examples:

- The car dealer is asking $15,000 for the car. You want to buy it for $13,000. Make an opening offer of $11,000.
- One of your employees is asking if she can spend $400 on a new desk. You think that $325 is reasonable. You should tell her that you don't want her to exceed $250.
- You're a salesperson, and the buyer is offering you $1.60 for your widgets. You can live with $1.70. Bracketing tells you that you should start at $1.80. Then if you end up in the middle, you'll still make your objective.

Of course it's not always true you'll end up in the middle, but that is a good assumption to make if you don't have anything else on which to base your opening position. Assume you'll end up in the middle, between the two opening negotiating positions. If you track this, I think that you'll be amazed at how often it happens.

In little things. Your son comes to you and says he needs $20 for a fishing trip he's going on this weekend. You say, "No way. I'm not going to give you $20. Do you realize that when I was your age I got 50 cents a week allowance and I had to work for that? I'll give you $10 and not a penny more."

Your son says, "I can't do it for $10, Dad."

Now you have established the negotiating range. He's asking for $20. You're willing to pay $10. See how often you end up at $15. In our culture, splitting the difference seems fair.

Bracketing in a Large International Negotiation

In big things. In 1982, we (the United States) were negotiating the payoff of a huge international loan with the government of Mexico. They were about to default on an $82 billion loan. Their chief negotiator was Jesus Herzog, their finance minister. Treasury Secretary Donald Regan and Federal Reserve Board Chairman Paul Volcker represented our side. In a creative solution, we asked Mexico to contribute huge amounts of petroleum to our strategic petroleum reserve, which Herzog agreed to do. That didn't settle it, however. We proposed to the Mexicans that they pay us a $100 million negotiating fee, which was a politically acceptable way for them to pay us accrued interest. When President Lopez Portillo heard what we were asking for, he went ballistic. He said the equivalent of, "You tell Ronald Reagan to drop dead. We're not paying the United States a negotiating fee. Not one peso." Now we had the negotiating range established. We asked for $100 million dollars. They're offering zero. Guess what they ended up paying us? That's right: $50 million dollars.

In little and in big things, we end up splitting the difference. With bracketing, Power Negotiators are assured that if that happens, they still get what they want. To bracket, you get the other person to state his or her position first. If the other person can get you to state your position first, then he or she can bracket you so that, if you end up splitting the difference, as so often happens, the other person ends up getting what he or she wanted. That's an underlying principle of negotiating to which I'll return later (in Chapter 26). Get the other person to state his or her position first. It may not be as bad as you fear, and it's the only way you can bracket a proposal.

Conversely, don't let the other person trick you into committing first. If the status quo is fine with you, and there is no pressure on you to make a move, be bold enough to say to the other person, "You're the one who approached me. The way things are satisfies me. If you want to do this, you'll have to make a proposal to me."

Another benefit of bracketing is that it tells you how big your concessions can be as the negotiation progresses. Let's take a look at how this would work with the three situations I described earlier. The car dealer is asking $15,000 for the car. You want to buy it for $13,000. You made an opening offer of $11,000. Then if the dealer comes down to $14,500, you can go up to $11,500 and you will still have your objective bracketed. If the dealer's next move is to $14,200, you can also shift your position by $300 and go to $11,800.

One of your employees is asking if she can spend $400 on a new desk. You think $325 is reasonable. You suggest $250. If the employee responds by saying she may be able to get what she needs for $350, you can respond by telling her that you'll be able to find $300 in the budget. Because you've both moved $50, your objective will still be in the middle.

Remember the buyer offering you $1.60 for your widgets? You told the buyer that your company would be losing money at a penny less than $1.80. Your goal is to get $1.70. The buyer comes up to $1.63. You can now move down to $1.77 and your goal will still be in the middle of the two proposals that are on the negotiating table. In that way, you can move in on your target and know if the other side offers to split the difference, you can still make your goal.

There is a danger in bracketing, however. You should not become so predictable with your responses that the other side can detect your pattern of concessions. I illustrated this with mathematically computed concessions to make my point clear, but you should vary your moves slightly so your reason for making a move cannot easily be determined. Later (in Chapter 16), I'll go into more detail on patterns of concessions.

A Fable About Asking for More

There was once a very old couple who lived in a dilapidated thatched hut on a remote Pacific Island. One day, a hurricane blew through the village and demolished their home. Because they were much too old and poor to rebuild the hut, the couple moved in with their daughter and her husband. This arrangement precipitated an unpleasant domestic situation, as the daughter's hut was barely big enough for herself, her husband, and their four children, let alone the in-laws.

The daughter went to the wise person of the village, explained the problem and asked, "Whatever will we do?"

The wise person puffed slowly on a pipe and then responded, "You have chickens, don't you?"

"Yes," she replied, "we have 10 chickens."

"Then bring the chickens into the hut with you."

This seemed ludicrous to the daughter, but she followed the wise person's advice. The move naturally exacerbated the problem, and the situation was soon unbearable, for feathers as well as hostile words flew around the hut. The daughter returned to the wise person, pleading again for advice.

"You have pigs, do you not?"

"Yes, we have three pigs."

"Then you must bring the pigs into your hut with you."

That seemed to be ridiculous advice, but to question the wise person was unthinkable, so she brought the pigs into the hut. Life was now truly unlivable, with eight people, 10 chickens, and three pigs sharing one tiny, noisy hut. Her husband complained that he couldn't hear the radio over the racket.

The next day the daughter, fearing for her family's sanity, approached the wise person with a final desperate plea. "Please," she cried, "we can't live like this. Tell me what to do and I'll do it, but please help us."

This time, the wise person's response was puzzling, but easier to follow. "Remove the chickens and the pigs from your hut." She quickly evicted the animals, and the entire family lived happily together for the rest of their days. The moral of the story is that a deal always looks better after something has been thrown out.

Ask for more than you expect to get. It seems like such an obvious principle, but it's something that you can count on in a negotiation. In thousands of workshop situations, and in tens of thousands of traceable real-life situations, this is something participants have proven repeatedly. The more you ask for, the more you're going to get.

Your objective should be to advance your MPP—your maximum plausible position. If your initial proposal is extreme, imply some flexibility. This encourages the other side to negotiate with you. The less you know about the other side, the more you should ask for. A stranger is more likely to surprise you, and you can build goodwill by making bigger concessions. Bracket the other side's proposal, so that if you end up splitting the difference, you still get what you want. You can bracket only if you get the other person to state his or her position first. Continue bracketing as you zero in on your objective with concessions.

Ask for more than you expect to get, for five reasons:

1. You might just get it.
2. It gives you some negotiating room.
3. It raises the perceived value of what you're offering.
4. It prevents the negotiation from deadlocking.
5. It creates a climate in which the other side feels they won.

Chapter 2

Never Say Yes to the First Offer

The reason that you should never say yes to the first offer (or counter-offer) is that it automatically triggers two thoughts in the other person's mind. Let's say that you're thinking of buying a second car. The people down the street have one for sale, and they're asking $10,000. That is such a terrific price on the perfect car for you that you can't wait to get down there, and snap it up before somebody else beats you to it. On the way there you start thinking that it would be a mistake to offer them what they're asking, so you decide to make a super-low offer of $8,000 just to see their reaction. You show up at their house, look the car over, take it for a short test drive, and then say to the owners, "It's not what I'm looking for, but I'll give you $8,000."

You're waiting for them to explode with rage at such a low offer, but what actually happens is that the husband looks at the wife and says, "What do you think, dear?"

The wife says, "Let's go ahead and get rid of it."

Does this exchange make you jump for joy? Does it leave you thinking, "Wow, I can't believe what a deal I got. I couldn't have gotten it for a penny less"?

I don't think so—you're probably thinking: "I could have done better. Something must be wrong." Now let's consider a more sophisticated example and put you in the other person's shoes for a moment. Let's say that you're a buyer for a maker of aircraft engines and you're about to meet with a salesperson who represents the manufacturer of engine bearings, something that's a vital component for you.

Your regular supplier has let you down, and you need to make an emergency purchase from this new company. It is the only company that can supply within 30 days what you need to prevent a shutdown of your assembly line. If you can't supply the engines on time, it will invalidate your contract with the aircraft manufacturer, who provides 85 percent of your business.

Under these circumstances, the price of the bearings you need is definitely not a high priority. As your secretary announces the arrival of the salesperson, however, you think to yourself, "I'll be a good negotiator. Just to see what happens, I'll make him a super-low offer."

The salesperson makes his presentation and assures you that he can ship on time to your specifications. He quotes you a price of $250 each for the bearings. This surprises you because you have been paying $275 for them. You manage to mask your surprise and respond with, "We've been paying only $175" (in business, we call this a lie, and it is done all the time), to which the salesperson responds, "Okay. We can match that."

At this point, you almost certainly have two responses: 1) "I could have done better," and 2) "Something must be wrong." In the thousands of seminars that I've conducted over the years, I've posed a situation like this to audiences and can't recall getting anything other than these two responses. Sometimes people reverse them, but usually the response is automatic: "I could have done better," and "Something must be wrong." Let's look at each of these responses separately.

First reaction: I could have done better. The interesting thing about this is that it doesn't have a thing to do with the price. It has to do only with the way the other person reacts to the proposal. What if you'd offered $7,000 for the car, or $6,000, and they told you right away that they'd take it? Wouldn't you still think you could have done better? What if that bearing salesperson had agreed to $150 or $125? Wouldn't you still think you could have done better?

"I Could Have Done Better" in a Land Purchase

Many years ago, I bought 100 acres of land in Eatonville, Washington, a beautiful little town just west of Mount Rainier. The seller was asking $185,000 for the land. I analyzed the property and decided that if I could get it for $150,000, it would be a terrific buy. I bracketed that price and asked the real estate agent to present an offer to the seller at $115,050. (Specific numbers build credibility, so you're more likely to get them to accept an offer like this than to counter it. More about this later.)

I went back to my home in La Habra Heights, California, leaving the agent to present the offer to the seller. Frankly, I thought I'd be lucky if they came back with any kind of counteroffer on a proposal this low. To my amazement, I got the offer back in the mail a few days later, accepted at the price and terms that I had proposed. I'm sure that I got a terrific buy on the land. Within a year, I'd sold 60 of the acres for more than I paid for the whole hundred. Later, I sold another 20 acres for more than I paid for the whole hundred. When they accepted my offer, I should have been thinking, "Wow. That's terrific, I couldn't have gotten a lower price." That's what I should have been thinking, but I wasn't. I was thinking, "I could have done better."

Second reaction: Something must be wrong. My second reaction when I received the accepted offer on the land was, "Something must be wrong. I'm going to take a thorough look at the preliminary title report. Something must be going on that I don't understand, if they're willing to accept an offer that I didn't think they would."

The second thought you'd have when the seller of that car said yes to your first offer is that something must be wrong. The second thought that the buyer of the bearings will have is, "Something must be wrong. Maybe something's changed in the market since I last negotiated a bearing contract. Instead of going ahead, I think I'll tell this salesperson that I've got to check with a committee and then talk to some other suppliers."

These two reactions will go through anybody's mind if you say yes to the first offer. Let's say your son came to you and said, "Could I borrow the car tonight?" and you said, "Sure, Son, take it. Have a wonderful time." Wouldn't he automatically think, "I could have done better. I could have gotten $10 for the movie out of this"? And wouldn't he automatically think, "What's going on here? Why do they want me out of the house? What's going on that I don't understand"?

This is a very easy negotiating principle to understand, but it's very hard to remember when you're in the thick of a negotiation. You may have formed a mental picture of how you expect the other side to respond, and that's a dangerous thing to do. Napoleon Bonaparte once said, "The unforgivable sin of a commander is to 'form a picture'—to assume that the enemy will act a certain way in a given situation, when in fact his response may be altogether different." You're expecting them to counter at a ridiculously low figure, and to your surprise, the other person's proposal is much more reasonable than you expected it to be.

Here's an example: You have finally plucked up the courage to ask your boss for an increase. You've asked for a 15-percent increase in pay, but you think you'll be lucky to get 10 percent. To your astonishment, your boss tells you that he or she thinks you're doing a terrific job, and would love to give you the increase in pay. Do you find yourself thinking about what a wonderfully generous company you work for? I don't think so. You're probably wishing you'd asked for a 25-percent increase.

Your son asks you for $100 to take a weekend hiking trip. You say, "No way. I'll give you $50 and not a penny more." In reality, you have bracketed his proposal (see Chapter 1) and expect to settle for $75. To your surprise your son says, "That would be tight, Dad, but okay. $50 would be great." Are you thinking how clever you were to get him down to $50? I don't think so. You're probably wondering how much less he would have settled for.

You're selling a piece of real estate that you own. You're asking $100,000. A buyer makes an offer at $80,000, and you counter at $90,000. You're thinking that you'll end up at $85,000, but to your surprise, the buyer immediately accepts the $90,000 offer. Admit it—aren't you thinking that if they jumped at $90,000, you could have gotten them up more?

Power Negotiators are careful that they don't fall into the trap of saying yes too quickly, which automatically triggers in the other person's mind the following: "I could have done better, and next time I will." A sophisticated person won't tell you that he felt that he lost in the negotiation, but he will tuck it away in the back of his mind, thinking, "the next time I deal with this person, I'll be a tougher negotiator. I won't leave any money on the table next time."

Something Must Be Wrong

Turning down the first offer may be tough to do, particularly if you've been calling on the person for months, and just as you're about to give up, she comes through with a proposal. It will tempt you to grab what you can. When this happens, be a Power Negotiator—remember not to say yes too quickly.

Many years ago, I was president of a real estate company in southern California that had 28 offices and 540 sales associates. One day, a magazine salesman came in, trying to sell me advertising space in his magazine. I was familiar with the magazine, and knew it to be an excellent opportunity, so I wanted my company to be in it. He made me a very reasonable proposal that required a modest $2,000 investment.

Because I love to negotiate, I started using some Gambits on him and got him down to the incredibly low price of $800. You can imagine what I was thinking at that point. Right. I was thinking, "Holy cow. If I got him down from $2,000 to $800 in just a few minutes, I wonder how low I can get him to go if I keep on negotiating?" I used a Middle Gambit on him called Higher Authority (see Chapter 7). I said, "This looks fine. I do just have to run it by my board of directors. Fortunately, they're meeting tonight. Let me run it by them and get back to you with the final okay."

A couple of days later, I called him back and said, "You'll never know how embarrassed I am about this. You know, I really felt that I wouldn't have any problem at all selling the board of directors on that $800 price you quoted me, but they're so difficult to deal with right now. The budget has been giving everyone headaches lately. They did come back with a counteroffer, but it's so low that it embarrasses me to tell you what it is."

There was a long pause, and he finally said, "How much did they agree to?"

"$500."

"That's okay. I'll take it," he said. I felt cheated. Although I'd negotiated him down from $2,000 to $500, I still felt that I could have done better.

There's a postscript to this story. I'm always reluctant to tell stories such as this at my seminars, for fear that it may get back to the person with whom I was negotiating. However, several years later, I was speaking at the huge California Association of Realtors convention being held that year in San Diego. I told this story in my talk, never imagining that the magazine salesman was standing in the back of the room. As I finished my presentation, I saw him pushing his way through the crowd. I braced myself for what I expected to be a verbal assault. However, he shook my hand and said with a smile, "I can't thank you enough for explaining that to me. I had no idea the impact that my tendency to jump at a quick deal was having on people. I'll never do that again."

At Times You Should Say Yes to the First Offer

I used to think that it was a 100-percent rule that you should never say yes to the first offer—until I heard from Tim Rush, a real estate executive in Los Angeles, who told me, "I was driving down Hollywood Boulevard last night, listening to your cassette tapes in my car. I stopped at a gas station to use the rest room. When I came back to my car, somebody stuck a gun in my ribs and said, 'Okay, buddy. Give me your wallet.' Well, I'd just been listening to your tapes, so I said, 'I'll give you the cash, but let me keep the wallet and the credit cards. Fair enough?' And he said, 'Buddy, you didn't listen to me, did you? Give me the wallet!'" In this litigious age, that's my disclaimer: Sometimes you should say yes to the first offer, but it's almost a 100-percent rule that you should never jump at the first offer.

Key Points to Remember

1. Never say yes to the first offer or counteroffer from the other side. It automatically triggers two thoughts: "I could have done better (next time I will)," and "Something must be wrong."
2. The big danger is when you have formed a mental picture of how the other person will respond to your proposal and he or she comes back much higher than you expected. Prepare for this possibility so it won't catch you off guard.

Chapter 3

Flinch at Proposals

Power Negotiators know you should always flinch—react with shock and surprise at the other side's proposals. Let's say you're in a resort area and you stop to watch a charcoal sketch artist. He doesn't have the price posted, so you ask him how much he charges, and he tells you $15. If that doesn't appear to shock you, his next words will be, "And $5 extra for color." If you still don't appear shocked, he will say, "And we have shipping cartons here. You'll need one of these, too."

Perhaps you know someone who would never flinch like that because it's beneath his or her dignity, the kind of person who would walk into a store, and say to the clerk, "How much is the coat?"

The clerk would respond, "$2,000."

And this person would respond with, "That's not bad!" You should be having a heart attack in the background. I know it sounds dumb and ridiculous, but the truth of the matter is that when people make a proposal to you, they are watching for your reaction. They may not think for a moment that you'll go along with their request. They've just thrown it out to see what your reaction will be.

For example:

- You sell computers and the buyer asks you to include an extended warranty.
- You're buying a car and the dealer offers you only a few hundred dollars for your trade-in.
- You sell contractor supplies and the buyer asks you to deliver it to the job site at no extra charge.
- You're selling your house and the buyer wants to move in two weeks before the transaction closes.

In each of these situations, the other side may not have thought for a moment that you would go along with the request, but if you don't flinch, he or she will automatically think, "Maybe I will get them to go along with that. I didn't think they would, but I think I'll be a tough negotiator and see how far I can get them to go."

It's very interesting to observe a negotiation when you know what both sides are thinking. Wouldn't that be fascinating for you? Wouldn't you love to know what's going on in the other person's mind when you're negotiating with her? When I conduct the one- or two-day Secrets of Power Negotiating seminars, we break up into groups and do some negotiating to practice the principles that I teach. I create a workshop and customize it to the industry in which the participants are involved. If they are medical equipment salespeople, they may find themselves negotiating the sale of laser surgery equipment to a hospital. If they are owners of print shops, the workshop may involve the acquisition of a smaller printing company in an outlying town.

I break the audience up into buyers, sellers, and referees. The referees are in a very interesting position because they have been in on the planning sessions of both the buyers and the sellers. They know each side's negotiating range. They know what the opening offer is going to be, and they know how far each side will go. The sellers of the printing company would go as low as $700,000, but they may start as high as $2 million. The buyers may start at $400,000, but they're prepared to go to $1.5 million if they must. The negotiating range is $400,000 to $2 million, but the acceptance range is $700,000 to $1.5 million.

The acceptance range embraces the price levels at which the buyers' and the sellers' negotiating ranges overlap. If they do overlap and there is an acceptance range, it's almost certain that the final price to which they agree will fall within this range. If the top of the buyers' negotiating range is lower than the bottom of the sellers' negotiating range, then one or both sides will have to compromise their objectives.

The negotiation starts with each side trying to get the other side to put their offer on the table first. Someone has to break the ice, so the sellers may suggest the $2 million (which is the top of their negotiating range). They believe $2 million is ridiculously high, and they barely have the nerve to propose it. They think they're going to be laughed out of the room the minute they do. To their surprise, the buyers don't appear to be that shocked. The sellers expect the buyers to say, "You want us to do what? You must be out of your minds." What they actually respond with is much milder, perhaps, "We don't think that we'd be prepared to go that high." In an instant, the negotiation changes its tune. A moment ago, the $2 million had seemed to be an impossible goal. Now the sellers are thinking that perhaps they're not as far apart as they previously thought they were. Now they're thinking, "Let's hang in and be tough negotiators. Maybe we will get this much."

Flinching is critical because most people believe what they see more than what they hear. The visual overrides the auditory in most people. It's safe for you to assume that at least 70 percent of the people with whom you negotiate will be visuals. What they see is more important than what they hear. I'm sure you've been exposed to some neuro-linguistic programming. You know that people are either visual, auditory, or kinesthetic (what they feel is paramount). There are a few gustatory (taste) and olfactory (smell) people around, but not many, and they're usually chefs or perfume blenders.

If you'd like to know what you are, close your eyes for 10 seconds and think of the house in which you lived when you were 10 years old. You probably saw the house in your mind; you're a visual. Perhaps you didn't get a visual picture, but you heard what was going on, perhaps trains passing by or children playing. That means you're an auditory. Neil Berman is a psychotherapist friend of mine in Santa Fe, New Mexico. He can remember every conversation he's ever had with a patient, but if he meets them in the supermarket, he doesn't remember them. The minute they say good morning to him, he thinks, "Oh yes, that's the bipolar personality with antisocial tendencies."

The third possibility is that you didn't so much see the house, or hear what was going on, but you just got a feeling for what it was like when you were 10. That makes you a kinesthetic. Assume that people are visual, unless you have something else to go on. Assume that what they see has more impact than what they hear. That's why it's so important to respond with a flinch to a proposal from the other side. Don't dismiss flinching as childish or too theatrical until you've had a chance to see how effective it can be. It's so effective that it usually surprises my students when they first use it. A woman told me that she flinched when selecting a bottle of wine in one of Boston's finest restaurants, and the wine steward immediately dropped the price by five dollars. A man told me that a simple flinch caused the salesperson to take $2,000 off the price of a Corvette. A speaker friend of mine attended my seminar in Orange County, California, and decided to see if he could use it to get his speaking fees up. At the time, he was just getting started and was charging $1,500. He went to a company and proposed that they hire him to do some in-house training. The training director said, “We might be interested having you work for us, but the most we can pay you is $1,500.”

In the past, he would have said, “That’s what I charge.” But now he gasped in surprise and said, “$1,500? I couldn’t afford to do it for just $1,500.”

The training director frowned thoughtfully. “Well,” he said, “the most we’ve ever offered any speaker is $2,500, so that’s the best we can do.” That meant $1,000 in additional bottom-line profit dollars per speech to my friend, and it took him 15 seconds to do. Not bad pay.

Key Points to Remember

1. Flinch in reaction to a proposal from the other side. They may not expect to get what they are asking for; however, if you do not show surprise, you’re communicating that it is a possibility.
2. A concession often follows a flinch. If you don’t flinch, it makes the other person a tougher negotiator.
3. Assume that the other person is a visual unless you have something else on which to go.
4. Even if you’re not face-to-face with the other person, you should still gasp in shock and surprise. Telephone flinches can be very effective also.

Chapter 4

Avoid Confrontational Negotiation

What you say in the first few moments of a negotiation often sets the climate of the negotiation. The other person quickly gets a feel for whether you are working at a win-win solution, or whether you are a tough negotiator who is out for everything you can get. That is one problem that I have with the way attorneys negotiate—they're very confrontational negotiators. You get that white envelope in the mail with black, raised lettering in the top left-hand corner and you think, "Oh, no! What is it this time?" You open the letter, and what is the first communication from them? It is a threat—what they're going to do to you if you do not give them what they want.

Attorneys Are Confrontational Negotiators

I was conducting a negotiating seminar for 50 attorneys who litigated medical malpractice lawsuits, or, as they prefer to call them, physician liability lawsuits. I have never met an attorney who was eager to go to a negotiating seminar, although that is what they do, and these people were no exception to the rule. The organization that was giving the attorneys their business told them that they were expected to attend my seminar if they wanted to receive any more cases and work from the organization.

The attorneys gave in, but weren't too happy about having to spend Saturday with me in the first place. However, once we got started, they became involved and were having a good time. I got them absorbed in a workshop involving a surgeon being sued over an unfortunate incident involving a nun. I couldn't believe how confrontational they were being. Most of them started with a vicious threat and then became more abusive from that point on. I had to stop the exercise and tell them that if they wanted to really settle the case without expensive litigation (and I seriously doubted their motives on that idea) that they should never be confrontational in the early stages of the negotiation.

Be careful what you say at the beginning. If the other person takes a position with which you totally disagree, don't argue. Arguing always intensifies the other person's desire to prove himself or herself right. You're much better off agreeing with the other person initially and then turning around using the Feel, Felt, Found formula.

Respond with, "I understand exactly how you feel about that. Many other people have felt exactly the same way as you do right now. [Now you have diffused that competitive spirit. You're not arguing with them, you're agreeing with them.] But you know what we have always found? When we take a closer look at it, we have always found that.... " Let's look at some examples.

You are selling something, and the other person says, "Your price is way too high." If you argue with him, he has a personal stake in proving you wrong and himself right. Instead, you say, "I understand exactly how you feel about that. Many other people have felt exactly the same way as you do when they first hear the price. When they take a closer look at what we offer, however, they have always found that we offer the best value in the marketplace."

Negotiating salary contracts is something I cover in detail in my Career Press book *Secrets of Power Salary Negotiating.* Let's say that you are applying for a job, and the human resources director says, "I don't think you have enough experience in this field." If you respond with, "I've handled much tougher jobs than this in the past," it may come across as "I'm right and you're wrong." It's just going to force her to defend the position she's taken. Instead, say, "I understand exactly how you feel about that. Many other people would feel exactly the same way as you do right now. However, there are some remarkable similarities between the work I've been doing and what you're looking for, that are not immediately apparent. Let me tell you what they are."

You're a salesperson and the buyer says, "I hear that you people have problems in your shipping department." Arguing with him will make him doubt your objectivity. Instead, say, "I understand how you could have heard that because I've heard it, too. I think that rumor may have started a few years ago when we relocated our warehouse, but now major companies such as General Motors and General Electric trust us with their inventories, and we never have a problem."

The other person says, "I don't believe in buying from offshore suppliers. I think we should keep the jobs in this country." The more you argue, the more you'll force him into defending his position. Instead, say, "I understand exactly how you feel about that, because these days many other people feel exactly the same way as you do. But do you know what we have found? Because the initial assembly has been done in Thailand, we have actually been able to increase our American workforce by more than 42 percent and this is why.... " Instead of arguing up front, which creates confrontational negotiation, get in the habit of agreeing and then turning it around.

At my seminars, I sometimes ask a person in the front row to stand. As I hold my two hands out, with my palms facing toward the person I've asked to stand, I ask him to place his hands against mine. Having done that, and without saying another word, I gently start to push against him. Automatically, without any instruction, he always begins to push back. People shove when you shove them. Similarly, when you argue with someone, it automatically makes him or her want to argue back.

The other great thing about Feel, Felt, Found is that it gives you time to think. Similarly, you sometimes catch other people at a bad moment. You may be a salesperson who is calling to get an appointment, and the buyer says to you, "I don't have any time to waste talking to some lying scum-sucking salesperson." You haven't heard anything like this before. It shocks you. You don't know what to say; but if you have Feel, Felt, Found in the back of your mind, you can say, "I understand exactly how you feel about that. Many other people have felt exactly the same way. However, I have always found.... " By the time you get there, you'll have thought of something to say. You calmly say, "I understand exactly how you feel about that. Many other people have felt exactly the same way. However...." Feel, Felt, Found gives you time to recover your composure, and you will know exactly what to say.

Key Points to Remember

1. Don't argue with people in the early stages of the negotiation because it creates confrontation.
2. Use the Feel, Felt, Found formula to turn the hostility around.
3. Having Feel, Felt, Found in the back of your mind gives you time to think when the other side throws some unexpected hostility your way.

Chapter 5

The Reluctant Seller and the Reluctant Buyer

Imagine for a moment that you own a sailboat, and you are desperate to sell it. It was fun when you first got it, but now you hardly ever go out on the boat, and the maintenance and slip fees are eating you alive. It's early Sunday morning, and you've given up a chance to play golf with your buddies because you need to be down at the marina cleaning your boat. You're scrubbing away and cursing your stupidity for having bought the boat in the first place. Just as you're thinking, "I'm going to give this turkey away to the next person who comes along," you look up and see an expensively dressed man with a young woman on his arm coming down the dock. He's wearing Gucci loafers, white slacks, and a blue Burberry blazer topped off with a silk cravat. His young girlfriend is wearing high heels, a silk sheath dress, big sunglasses, and huge diamond earrings.

They stop at your boat, and the man says, "That's a fine-looking boat, young man. By any chance is it for sale?"

His girlfriend snuggles up to him and says, "Oh, let's buy it, Poopsy. We'll have so much fun."

You feel your heart start to burst with joy, and your mind is singing, "Thank you, Lord! Thank you, Lord!"

Expressing that sentiment is not going to get you the best price for your boat, is it? How are you going to get the best price? Playing Reluctant Seller. You keep on scrubbing and say, "You're welcome to come aboard, although I hadn't thought of selling the boat." You give them a tour of the boat, and at every step of the way, you tell them how much you love the boat and how much fun you have sailing her. Finally you tell them, "I can see how perfect this boat would be for you and how much fun you'd have with it, but I really don't think I could ever bear to part with it. However, just to be fair to you, what is the very best price you would offer me?"

Power Negotiators know that this Reluctant Seller technique expands the negotiating range before the negotiating begins. If you've done a good job of building the other person's desire to own the boat, he will have formed a range in his own mind. He may be thinking, "I would be willing to go to $30,000, $25,000 would be a fair deal, and $20,000 would be a bargain." Therefore, his negotiating range is from $20,000 to $30,000. Just by playing the Reluctant Seller, you will have moved him up through that range. He may even offer you $40,000. If you had appeared eager to sell, he may have offered you only $20,000. By playing the Reluctant Seller, you may move him to the mid-point, or even beyond the high point of his negotiating range, before the negotiations even start.

One of my Power Negotiators is an extremely rich and powerful investor, a man who owns real estate all over town. He is very successful—what you could justifiably call a heavy hitter. He likes wheeling and dealing.

Like many investors, his strategy is simple: Buy a property at the right price and on the right terms, hold onto it and let it appreciate, then sell it at a higher price. Many smaller investors bring him purchase offers for one of his holdings, eager to acquire one of his better-known properties. That's when this well-seasoned investor knows how to use the Reluctant Seller Gambit.

He reads the offer quietly, and when he's finished, he slides it back across the table and scratches above one ear, saying something such as, "I don't know. Of all my properties, I have very special feelings for this one. I was thinking of keeping it and giving it to my daughter for her college graduation present, and I really don't think I would part with it for anything less than the full asking price. Please understand that this particular property is worth a great deal to me. But look, it was good of you to bring in an offer for me, and in all fairness, so that you won't have wasted your time, what is the very best price that you feel you could give me?" Many times, I saw him make thousands of dollars in a few seconds using the Reluctant Seller philosophy. Power Negotiators always try to edge up the other side's negotiating range before the real negotiating ever begins.

When You're Desperate, Play Reluctant Seller

A few years back, Donald Trump was in trouble. He was very highly leveraged in real estate, and the New York real estate market was about to collapse. He needed to raise cash quickly so that he could survive the coming crunch. His best opportunity was to sell the St. Moritz hotel. He had bought it three years before from the

> Helmsleys for $79 million. It was just around the corner from his recently acquired flagship Plaza Hotel, so he didn't need it anymore. Alan Bond, a brash Australian billionaire, expressed an interest. As desperately as Trump needed to sell, he still played Reluctant Seller.
>
> "Oh, Alan, not the St. Moritz. That's my favorite property. I'm never going to sell that. I'm going to put that in trust for my grandchildren. Anything else I have is for sale; you can make me an offer, but not the St. Moritz. But look, Alan, just to be fair to you—what is the very best price you would give me?"
>
> Unless you realize what they are doing to you, you'll go from the low point of your negotiating range, to the mid-point, maybe even the high point, before the negotiation even starts. Alan Bond paid Trump $160 million for the St. Moritz. It gave Trump the cash he needed to survive the subsequent real estate recession.

I remember an oceanfront condominium I bought as an investment. The owner was asking a fair price for it. It was a hot real estate market at the time, and I wasn't sure how eager the owner was to sell, or if she had any other offers on it. I wrote up three offers, one at the low end of my negotiating range, one at the mid-point, and one at the high end of what I was willing to pay. I made an appointment to meet with the seller, who had moved out of the condominium in Long Beach and was living in Pasadena.

After talking to her for a while, I determined she hadn't had any other offers and was eager to sell. I reached into my briefcase, where I had the three offers filed, and pulled out the lowest of them. She accepted it, and when I sold the condominium a year later, it fetched more than twice what I had paid for it. (Be aware you can do this only with a "For Sale by Owner." If a real estate agent has listed the property, that agent is working for the seller, and is obligated to tell the seller if he's aware that the buyer would pay more. This is another reason why you should always list property with an agent when you're selling.)

Power Negotiators play Reluctant Seller when they're selling. Even before the negotiation starts, it squeezes the other side's negotiating range. Turn this around and consider the Reluctant Buyer. Put yourself on the other side of the desk for a moment. Let's say you're in charge of buying new computer equipment for your company. How would you get a salesperson to give you the lowest possible price? I would let the salesperson come in and have her go through her entire presentation. I would ask all the questions I could possibly think of, and when I finally couldn't think of another thing to ask, I would say, "I really appreciate all the time you've taken. You've obviously put a lot of work into this presentation, but unfortunately it's just not the way we want to go; however, I sure wish you the best of luck."

I would pause to examine the crestfallen expression on the salesperson's face. I'd watch her slowly package her presentation materials. Then at the very last moment, just as her hand hit the doorknob on the way out, I would come back with a magic expression. There are some magic expressions in negotiating. If you use them at exactly the right moment, the predictability of the other person's response is amazing.

I'd say, "You know, I really do appreciate the time you took with me. Just to be fair to you, what is the very lowest price you'd take?"

Would you agree with me that it's a good bet that the first price the salesperson quoted is not the real bottom line? Sure, it's a good bet. The first price a salesperson quotes is what I call the "wish number." This is what she is wishing the other person would agree to. If the other person agreed, she would probably burn rubber back to her sales office and run in screaming, "You can't believe what just happened to me. I was over at XYZ Company to make a bid on the computer equipment they need for their new headquarters. I went over the proposal and they said, 'What's your absolute bottom-line price?' I was feeling good so I said, 'We never budge off list price less a quantity discount, so the bottom line is $225,000,' and held my breath. The president said, 'It sounds high, but if that's the best you can do, go ahead and ship it.' I can't believe it. Let's close the office and go celebrate."

Somewhere out there, there's a "walk-away" price, a price at which the salesperson will not or cannot sell. The other person doesn't know what the walk-away price is, so he or she has to do some probing, some seeking of information. The buyer has to try some negotiating Gambits to see if he or she can figure out the salesperson's walk-away price.

When you play Reluctant Buyer, the salesperson is not going to come all the way from the wish price to the walk-away price. Here's what will happen. When you play Reluctant Buyer, the salesperson will typically give away half of his or her negotiating range. If that computer salesperson knows the bottom line is $175,000, $50,000 below the list price, she will respond to the Reluctant Buyer Gambit with, "Well, I tell you what. It's the end of our quarter, and we're in a sales contest. If you'll place the order today, I'll give it to you for the unbelievably low price of $200,000." She'll give away half her negotiating range, just because you played Reluctant Buyer.

When people do this to you, it's merely a game that they're playing. Power Negotiators don't get upset about it. They just learn to play the negotiating game better than the other side. When the other person does it to you, the correct response to this Gambit is to go through the following sequence of Gambits:

"I don't think that there is any flexibility in the price, but if you'll tell me what it would take to get your business (getting the other side to commit first), I'll take it to my people (Higher Authority—a middle negotiating Gambit that I'll cover later), and I'll see what I can do for you with them (Good Guy/Bad Guy—an ending negotiating Gambit)."

Key Points to Remember

1. Always play Reluctant Seller.
2. Look out for the Reluctant Buyer.
3. Playing this Gambit is a great way to squeeze the other side's negotiating range before the negotiation even starts.
4. The other person will typically give away half of his or her negotiating range just because you use this.
5. When it's used on you, get the other person to commit, go to Higher Authority, and close with Good Guy/Bad Guy.

Chapter 6

Use the Vise Technique

The Vise is another very effective negotiating Gambit and what it will accomplish will amaze you. It is the simple little expression, "You'll have to do better than that." Here's how Power Negotiators use it: Let's say you own a small steel company that sells steel products in bulk. You are calling on a fabricating plant where the buyer has listened to your proposal and your pricing structure. You ignored his insistence that he's happy with his present supplier and did a good job of building desire for your product.

Finally, the other person says to you, "I'm really happy with our present vendor, but I guess it wouldn't do any harm to have a backup supplier to keep them on their toes. I'll take one carload if you can get the price down to $1.22 per pound."

You respond with the Vise Gambit by calmly saying, "I'm sorry. You'll have to do better than that."

An experienced negotiator will automatically respond with the Counter Gambit, which is, "Exactly how much better than that do I have to do?" In this, the negotiator is trying to pin you down to a specific. However, it will amaze you how often inexperienced negotiators will concede a big chunk of their negotiating range simply because you did that.

What's the next thing you should do, once you've said, "You'll have to do better than that"? You have it. Shut up! Don't say another word. The other side may just make a concession to you. Salespeople call this the silent close, and they all learn it during the first week that they are in the business. You make your proposal and then shut up. The other person may just say yes, so it's foolish to say a word until you find out if he or she will or won't.

I once watched two salespeople do the silent close on each other. There were three of us sitting at a circular conference table. The salesman on my right wanted to buy a piece of real estate from the salesman on my left. He made his proposal and then shut up, just as they taught him in sales training school. The more experienced salesperson on my left must have thought, "Son of a gun. I can't believe this. He's going to try the silent close on *moi*? I'll teach him a thing or two. I won't talk, either."

I was sitting between two strong-willed people who were both silently daring the other to be the next one to talk. There was dead silence in the room, except for the grandfather clock ticking away in the background. I looked at each of them, and obviously they both knew what was going on. Neither one was willing to give in to the other. I didn't know how this was ever going to get resolved. It seemed as though half an hour went by, although it was probably more like five minutes, because silence seems like such a long time in our culture (see Section Four to learn how people from other cultures will use this against us).

Finally, the more experienced salesperson broke the impasse by scrawling "*decizion?*" on a pad of paper and sliding it across to the other. He had deliberately misspelled the word decision. The younger salesperson looked at it and without thinking said, "You misspelled decision." And once he started talking, he couldn't stop. (Do you know a salesperson like that? Once they start talking, they can't stop?) He went on to say, "If you're not willing to accept what I offered you, I might be willing to come up another $2,000, but not a penny more." He renegotiated his own proposal before he found out if the other person would accept it or not.

To use the Vise technique, Power Negotiators simply respond to the other side's proposal or counter-proposal with, "I'm sorry. You'll have to do better than that," and then shut up.

A client called me up after a *Secrets of Power Negotiating* seminar that I had conducted for their managers, and told me, "Roger, I thought you might like to know we just made $14,000 using one of the Gambits that you taught us. We are having new equipment put into our Miami office. Our standard procedure has been to get bids from three qualified vendors and then take the lowest bid. I was sitting here going over the bids and was just about to okay the one I'd decided to accept. Then I remembered what you taught me about the Vise technique. I thought, 'What have I got to lose?' and scrawled across it, 'You'll have to do better than this,' and mailed it back to them. Their counter-proposal came back $14,000 less than the proposal that I was prepared to accept."

You may be thinking, "Roger, you didn't tell me whether that was a $50,000 proposal, in which case it would have been a huge concession, or a multi-million dollar proposal, in which case $14,000 wouldn't have been that big a deal." Don't fall into the trap of negotiating percentages when you should be negotiating dollars. The point was that he made $14,000 in the two minutes that it took him to scrawl that counter-proposal across the bid, which meant that while he was doing it, he was generating $420,000 per hour of bottom-line profits. That's pretty good money, isn't it?

This is another trap into which attorneys fall. When I work with attorneys, it's clear that if they're negotiating a $50,000 lawsuit, they might send a letter back and forth over $5,000. If it's a million-dollar lawsuit, they'll kick $50,000 around as though it doesn't mean a thing, because they're mentally negotiating percentages, not dollars.

If you make a $2,000 concession to a buyer, it doesn't matter if it got you a $10,000 sale or a million-dollar sale. It's still $2,000 that you gave away. Therefore, it doesn't make any sense for you to come back to your sales manager and say, "I had to make a $2,000 concession, but it's a $100,000 sale." What you should have been thinking was, "$2,000 is sitting in the middle of the negotiating table. How long should I be willing to spend negotiating further to see how much of it I could get?"

Have a feel for what your time's worth. Don't spend half an hour negotiating a $10 item (unless you're doing it just for the practice). Even if you got the other side to concede all of the $10, you'd be making money only at the rate of $20 an hour for the half-hour you invested in the negotiation. To put this in perspective for you, if you make $100,000 a year, you're making about $50 an hour. You should be thinking to yourself, "Is what I'm doing right now generating more than $50 per hour?" If so, it's part of the solution. If you're aimlessly chatting with someone at the water cooler, or talking about last night's television movie, or anything else that is not generating $50 an hour, it's part of the problem.

Here's the point. When you're negotiating with someone—when you have a deal in front of you that you could live with—but you're wondering if you could hang in a little bit longer and do a little bit better, you're not making $50 an hour. No, sir. No, ma'am. You're making $50 a minute and probably $50 a second.

If that's not enough, remember that a negotiated dollar is a bottom-line dollar. It's not a gross-income dollar. This means that the $2,000 you may have conceded in seconds because you thought it was the only way you could get the sale, is worth many times that in gross sales dollars. I've trained executives at discount retailers and health maintenance organizations (HMOs) where the profit margin is only 2 percent. They do a billion dollars' worth of business a year, but they bring in only 2 percent in bottom-line profits. At their company, a $2,000 concession at the negotiating table has the same impact on the bottom line as getting a $100,000 sale.

You're probably in an industry that does better than that. I have trained people at some companies where the bottom line is an incredible 25 percent of the gross sales, but that's the exception. In this country, the average profit margin is about 5 percent of gross sales, which means that probably the $2,000 concession you made is the equivalent of making a $40,000 sale. Let me ask you something. How long would you be willing to work to get a $40,000 sale? An hour? Two hours? All day? I've had many sales managers tell me, "For a $40,000 sale, I expect my salespeople to work as long as it takes."

However fast paced your business, you're probably willing to spend several hours to make a $40,000 sale. Why are you so willing to make a $2,000 concession at the negotiating table? It has the same impact on the bottom line as a $40,000 sale if you're in a business that generates the typical 5 percent bottom-line profit.

A negotiated dollar is a bottom-line dollar. You'll never make money faster than you will when you're negotiating! Power Negotiators should respond to a proposal with, "You'll have to do better than that." When the other person uses it on them, they automatically respond with the Counter Gambit, "Exactly how much better than that do I have to do?"

☑ Key Points to Remember

1. Respond to a proposal or counter-proposal with the Vise technique: "You'll have to do better than that."
2. If it's used on you, respond with the Counter Gambit, "Exactly how much better than that do I have to do?" This will pin the other person down to a specific.
3. Concentrate on the dollar amount that's being negotiated. Don't be distracted by the gross amount of the sale and start thinking in percentages.
4. A negotiated dollar is a bottom-line dollar. Be aware of what your time is worth on an hourly basis.
5. You will never make money faster than you will when you're Power Negotiating.

Middle Negotiating Gambits

Chapter 7

Handling the Person Who Has No Authority to Decide

One of the most frustrating situations you can experience in negotiating is trying to negotiate with the person who claims that he or she does not have the authority to make a final decision. Unless you realize that this is simply a negotiating tactic that is being used, you have the feeling that you will never get to talk to the real decision-maker.

When I was president of the real estate company in California, I would use the board of directors as my higher authority. I had salespeople visiting the office all the time in hopes of selling me things, including advertising, photocopy machines, computer equipment, and so on. I would always negotiate the very lowest price that I could, using all of these Gambits. Then I would say to them, "This looks fine. I do just have to run it by my board of directors, but I'll get back to you tomorrow with the final okay."

The very next day, I would get back to them and say, "Boy, are my directors tough to deal with right now. I felt so positive that I could sell it to them, but they just won't go along with it unless you can shave another couple of hundred dollars off the price." Invariably, I would get it. There was no approval needed by the board of directors, and it never occurred to me that this deception was underhanded. The people with whom you deal see it as well within the rules by which one plays the game of negotiating.

When the other person says to you that they have to take it to some committee, director, or the legal department, it's probably not true; however, it is a very effective negotiating tactic that they're using on you. Let's first look at why this is such an effective tactic, and then I'll tell you how to handle it when the other side decides to use it on you.

The Other Side Loves to Use Higher Authority

You would think that if you were going out to negotiate something, you would want to have the authority to make a decision. At first glance, it would seem you would have more power if you were to say to the other person, "I have the power to make a deal with you."

You have a tendency to say to your manager, "Let me handle this. Give me the authority to cut the best possible deal." Power Negotiators know that you put yourself in a weakened negotiating position when you do that. You should always have a higher authority with whom you have to check before you can change your proposal or make a decision. Any negotiator who presents himself as the decision-maker has put himself at a severe bargaining disadvantage. You have to put your ego on the back-burner to do this, but you'll find it very effective.

The reason that this is so effective is simple. When the other person knows that you have the final authority to make a deal, he knows that he has only to convince you. He doesn't have to work quite as hard to give you the benefits of his proposal if you're the final authority. Once you've given your approval, he knows that he has consummated the deal. This is not so if you are telling him that you have to answer to a higher authority. Whether you have to get approval from a region, head office, management, partners, or a board of directors, the other person has to do more to convince you. He must make an offer that you can take to your higher authority and get approved. He knows that he must completely win you over to his side so that you will want to persuade your higher authority to agree to his proposal.

Higher Authority works much better when the higher authority is a vague entity, such as a committee or a board of directors. For example, have you ever actually met a loan committee at a bank? I never have. Bankers at my seminars have consistently told me that for loans of $500,000 or less, somebody at that bank can make a decision without having to go to a loan committee. However, the loan officer knows that if she said to you, "Your package is on the president's desk," you would say, "Well, let's go talk to the president right now. Let's get it resolved." You can't do that with the vague entity.

If you use the Higher Authority Gambit, be sure that your higher authority is a vague entity, such as a pricing committee, the people back at corporate, or the marketing committee. If you tell the other person that your manager would have to approve it, what's the first thought that they are going to have? It is going to be, "Then why am I wasting time talking to you? If your manager is the only one who can make a decision, get your manager down here." When your higher authority is a vague entity, it appears to be unapproachable. In all the years I told salespeople I had to run it by my board of directors, I only once had a salesperson say to me, "When does your board of directors meet? When can I make a presentation to them?" The use of Higher Authority puts pressure on people without confrontation.

A Real Estate Investor Uses Higher Authority

Back when I had the time to do it, I invested in apartment buildings and houses. When I first bought the buildings, it felt great to tell the tenants that I owned the property. It was an ego trip for me. However, when my portfolio became substantial, I realized that it wasn't that much fun anymore, because the tenants assumed that the owner of the property was made of money, so why would it be a problem to replace the carpeting in their unit because of a small cigarette burn, or to replace the drapes because of a small tear? Why would it be a problem if the rent was late that month? In their eyes, I was rich. I must be because I had all that property. Why was this upsetting me?

The moment I learned the power of the Higher Authority Gambit and started a company that I called Plaza Properties, many of these problems went away. I became the president of that company that was, to the tenants, a property management company handling their building for a vague group of investors out there somewhere.

Then when they said, "We've got this cigarette burn in the carpet, and it needs to be replaced," I'd say, "I don't think I can get the owners to do that for you just yet. I'll tell you what, though: You keep the rent coming in on the first of the month, and in about six months, I'll go to bat for you with the owners. Let me see what I can do for you with them at that time." (That's Good Guy/Bad Guy, an Ending Gambit I'll teach you in Chapter 14.) If they would say, "Roger, we're not going to have the rent until the 15th of the month," I would say, "Wow, I know exactly how it goes. Sometimes it can get difficult, but on this property, I just don't have any leeway. The owners of this property told me that if the rent is not in by the fifth of the month, I just have to file an eviction notice. What can we do to get the rent in on time?"

The Higher Authority Gambit is a very effective way of pressuring people without any confrontation on either side's part. I'm sure that you can see why the other person loves using it on you. Let's look at the benefits to the other side when they tell you that they have to get your proposal approved by a committee, director, or boss. This allows them to put pressure on you without confrontation. "We'd be wasting our time taking a proposal that high to the committee." It unbalances you as a negotiator because it's so frustrating to feel that you're not able to present to the real decision-maker.

By inventing a higher authority with whom they must first seek approval, they can set aside the pressure of making a decision for as long as it takes to review the negotiations. When I was a real estate broker, I would teach our agents that before they put buyers into their cars to show them any property, they should say to them, "Just to be certain that I understand, if we find exactly the right home for you today, is there any reason why you wouldn't make a decision today?"

The buyer may have interpreted this action as putting pressure on them to decide quickly. What it really accomplished here was that it eliminated their right, under the pressure of the closing situation, to delay by inventing a higher authority. If the agent did not do this, they would very often defer the decision by saying, "We can't decide today because Uncle Harry is helping us with the down payment, and we have to run it by him."

It sets them up for using the Vise technique: "You'll have to do better than that if you want to get it past the committee." It puts you in the position of needing the other person to be on your side if it's to be approved by the committee. They can make suggestions to you without implying it's something to which they'd agree: "If you can come down another 10 percent, you may have a chance of the committee approving it."

Higher Authority can be used to force you into a bidding war. "The committee has asked me to get five bids, and they'll take the lowest one." Also, the other person can squeeze your price without revealing what you're up against: "The committee is meeting tomorrow to make a final decision. I know they've already gotten some really low bids, so there may not be any point in your submitting one, but there's always a chance if you can come in with a super-low proposal."

It sets the other person up to use Good Guy/Bad Guy: "If it were up to me, I'd love to keep on doing business with you, but the bean counters on the committee care only about the lowest price." At this point, you may be thinking, "Roger, I can't use this. I own a small company that manufactures patio furniture, and everybody knows that I own it. They know that I don't have anybody above me with whom I have to check."

Sure you can use it. I own my own company, too, but there are decisions that I won't make unless I've checked with the people to whom I've delegated that area of responsibility. If somebody asks me about doing a seminar for their company, I'll say, "Sounds good to me, but I have to check with my marketing people first. Fair enough?" If you own your own company, your higher authority becomes the people in your organization to whom you've delegated authority.

In international negotiations, the president is careful to protect himself by maintaining the position that he cannot make a decision until he has gotten the approval of his negotiators and the Senate.

The Counter Gambits to Higher Authority

I'm sure that you can see why people love to use the Higher Authority Gambit on you. Fortunately, you can learn how to handle this challenge smoothly and effectively. Your first approach should be trying to remove the other person's resort to higher authority before the negotiations even start, by getting him to admit that he could make a decision if the proposal were to be irresistible.

It's exactly the same thing that the car dealer will do to you when, before he lets you take it for a test drive, he says, "Let me be sure I understand, if you like this car as much as I know you're going to like it, is there any reason why you wouldn't make a decision today?" Because they know that if they don't remove the resort to higher authority up front, then there's a danger that under the pressure of asking for a decision, the other person will invent a higher authority as a delaying tactic, such as "Look, I'd love to give you a decision today, but I can't because my father-in-law has to look at the property (or the car), or Uncle Joe is helping us with the down payment and we need to talk to him first."

One of the most frustrating things that you encounter is taking your proposal to the other person and having her say to you, "Well, that's fine. Thanks for bringing me the proposal. I'll talk to our committee (or our attorney or the owners) about it, and if it interests us we'll get back to you." Where do you go from there? If you're smart enough to counter the Higher Authority Gambit before you start, you can remove yourself from that dangerous situation.

Before you present your proposal to the other person, before you even get it out of your briefcase, you should casually say, "Let me be sure I understand. If this proposal meets all of your needs (That's as broad as any statement can be, isn't it?), is there any reason why you wouldn't give me a decision today?"

It's a harmless thing for the other person to agree to because the other person is thinking, "If it meets all of my needs? No problem; there's loads of wiggle room there." However, look at what you've accomplished if you can get them to respond with, "Well, sure. If it meets all of my needs, I'll give you an okay right now."

- You've eliminated their right to tell you that they want to think it over. If they say that, you say, "Well, let me go over it one more time. There must be something I didn't cover clearly enough because you did indicate to me earlier that you were willing to make a decision today."
- You've eliminated their right to refer it to a higher authority. You've eliminated their right to say, "I want our legal department to see it, or the purchasing committee to take a look at it."

What if you're not able to remove their resort to Higher Authority? I'm sure that many times you'll say, "If this proposal meets all of your needs, is there any reason why you wouldn't give me a decision today?" and the other person will reply, "I'm sorry, but on a project of this size, everything has to get approved by the specifications committee. I'll have to refer it to them for a final decision." Here are the three steps that Power Negotiators take when they're not able to remove the other side's resort to Higher Authority:

Step 1—Appeal to their ego. With a smile on your face, say, "They always follow your recommendations, don't they?" With some personality styles that is enough of an appeal to his ego that he'll say, "Well, I guess you're right. If I like it, then you can count on it." Often they'll still say, "Yes, they usually follow my recommendations, but I can't give you a decision until I've taken it to the committee." If you realize that you're dealing with egotistical people, try preempting their resort to Higher Authority early in your presentation by saying, "Do you think that if you took this to your supervisor, she'd approve it?" Often an ego-driven person will make the mistake of proudly telling you that he doesn't have to get anybody's approval.

Step 2—Get their commitment that they'll take it to the committee with a positive recommendation. Say, "You will recommend it to them—won't you?" Hopefully, you'll get a response similar to "Yes, it looks good to me. I'll go to bat for you with them." Getting the other side's commitment that they're going to recommend it to the higher authority is very important because it's at this point that they may reveal that there really isn't a committee. They really do have the authority to make a decision and saying they had to check with someone else was just a negotiating Gambit they were using on you.

How Higher Authority Was Used Against Me

I remember when I first came to this country in 1962; I went to work for Bank of America in Menlo Park, California. After nine months, I found that I couldn't stand the excitement of working in the banking industry, so I looked around for something else. I applied for a position as a management trainee at Montgomery Ward, the department store chain.

Before I could go to work for them, the manager to whom they would assign me for training had to approve. They sent me up to Napa, California, to interview with the local store manager, Lou Johnson. For whatever reason, the interview didn't go well. I knew that I wasn't going to get the job—probably because I was so new in the country that Lou didn't believe that I was here to stay. I had no intention of going back to England, but I could understand his concern. Finally, he said to me, "Roger, thank you for coming in for the interview. I'll report back to the committee at the head office, and you'll be hearing from them."

I said to him, "You will recommend me to them, won't you?" That's step number two: asking for a commitment that they'll go in with a positive recommendation. I saw his mind swinging from one side to the other. He apparently didn't want to recommend me to his committee. On the other hand, he didn't want the confrontation of telling me that he wasn't going to recommend me. His mind went from one side to the other for a few minutes, and finally he said, "Well, yes, I guess I'm willing to give you a try." With this, he immediately revealed that there was no higher authority. There was no committee. He was the one making the decision.

In step two, Power Negotiators get the other person's commitment that she will go to the higher authority with a positive recommendation. There are only two things that can happen now. Either she'll say yes, she will recommend it to them, or she'll say no, she won't, because.... Either way you've won. Her endorsement would be preferable, of course, but any time you can draw out an objection you should say, "Hallelujah," because objections are buying signals. People are not going to object to your price unless buying from you interests them. If buying from you doesn't interest them, they don't care how high you price your product or service.

When You Don't Care What They Charge

For a while, I dated a woman who was really into interior decorating. One day she excitedly dragged me down to the Orange County Design Center to show me a couch covered in kidskin. The leather was as soft and as supple as anything I'd ever felt. As I sat there, she said, "Isn't that a wonderful couch?"

I said, "No question about it. This is a wonderful couch."

She said, "And it's only $12,000."

I said, "Isn't that amazing? How can they do it for only $12,000?"

She said, "You don't have a problem with the price?"

"I don't have a problem with the price at all." Why didn't I have a problem with the price? Because I had no intention of paying $12,000 for a couch, regardless of what they covered it with. Let me ask you this: If buying the couch interested me, would I have a problem with the price? Oh, you'd better believe I'd have a problem with the price!

Objections are buying signals. We knew in real estate that if we were showing property, and the people were "oooohing and aaahing" all over as if they loved everything about it, they weren't going to buy. The serious buyers were the ones who were saying, "Well, the kitchen's not as big as we like. Hate that wallpaper. We'd probably end up knocking out that wall." Those were the people who buy.

If you're in sales, think about it. Have you ever in your life made a big sale where the person loved your price up front? Of course not. All serious buyers complain about the price. Your biggest problem is not an objection; it's indifference. I would rather they said to you, "I wouldn't buy widgets from your company if you were the last widget vendor in the world, because..." than have them say to you, "I've been using the same source of widgets for the past 10 years, and they do a fine job. I am just not interested in taking the time to talk to anyone else about making a change." Indifference is your problem, not objections, because there is always a reason for objections and people just may change their minds.

Let me prove this to you. Give me the opposite of the word love. If you said hate, think again. As long as they are throwing plates at you, you have something there you can work with. It is indifference that's the opposite of love. When they're saying to you, like Rhett Butler in *Gone with the Wind,* "Frankly, my dear, I don't give a damn"—that's when you know the movie is about over. Indifference is your problem, not objections. Objections are buying signals.

When you say to them, "You will recommend it to them, won't you?" they can either say yes, they will, or no, they won't. Either way you've won. Then you can move to the next step.

Step 3—Use the qualified "subject to" close. The "subject to" close is the same one that your life insurance agent uses on you when he or she says, "Quite frankly, I don't know if we can get this much insurance on someone your age. It would be 'subject to' you passing the physical anyway, so why don't we just write up the paperwork 'subject to' you passing the physical?" The life insurance agent knows that if you can fog a mirror during that physical, he or she can get you that insurance. Then it doesn't sound as though you're making as important a decision as you really are.

The qualified "subject to" close in this instance would be: "Let's just write up the paperwork 'subject to' the right of your specifications committee to reject the proposal within a 24-hour period for any specifications reason." Or, "Let's just write up the paperwork 'subject to' the right of your legal department to reject the proposal within a 24-hour period for any legal reasons." Notice now that you're not saying subject to their acceptance. You are saying subject to their right to decline it for a specific reason. If they are going to refer it to an attorney, it would then be a legal reason. If they're going to refer it to their CPA, it would be a tax reason, and so on and so forth. Try to get it nailed down to a specific reason.

To recap, the three steps to take if you are not able to get the other person to waive his or her resort to Higher Authority are:

1. Appeal to the other person's ego.
2. Get the other person's commitment that he will recommend it to the higher authority.
3. Use the qualified "subject to" close.

What's the counter to the Counter Gambit? What if someone was trying to remove your resort to Higher Authority like that? If the other person says to you, "You do have the authority to make a decision, don't you?" you should say, in so many words, "It depends on what you're asking. There's a point at which I have to go to my marketing committee."

Let's say you're selling aluminum garden sheds to a chain of warehouse hardware centers, and they're asking you to participate in their holiday weekend mailer. Your sales manager has set aside $30,000 for this, but the buyer at the chain is asking you to commit to $35,000. You should shake your head and say, "Wow. That's a lot more than I expected. I'd have to take that to the advertising committee. I'd feel comfortable giving you the go ahead at $25,000, but anything above that I'd have to hold off until I find out what the committee has to say."

Without creating a confrontation, you've put the other person in a position in which he might prefer to go with the $25,000, rather than have the entire mailer on hold until you can get back to him. Note that you've also bracketed his proposal. Assuming you end up splitting the difference, then you'll still be within budget.

One more thing about the Higher Authority Gambit. What if you have somebody trying to force you to a decision before you're ready to make it? Let's say you're an electrical subcontractor, and you're negotiating a shopping center bid. The general contractor is pressuring you to commit to a price and start date, and wants a decision right now. He's saying, "Harry, I love you like a brother, but I'm running a business, not a religion. Give me what I need on this one right now, or I'll have to go with your competitor." (I'll show you in Chapter 37 how a person under time pressure tends to become much more flexible.)

How do you handle it? Very simply. You say, "Joe, I'm happy to give you a decision. In fact, I'll give you an answer right now if you want it. But I have to tell you—if you force me to a decision now, the answer has to be no. Tomorrow, after I've had a chance to talk to my estimating people, the answer might be yes. Why don't you wait until tomorrow and see what happens. Fair enough?"

You may find yourself in a situation in which escalating authority is being used on you. You think you have cut a deal, only to find that the head buyer has to approve it and won't. You sweeten the deal only to find the vice president won't give approval. Escalating authority is, in my mind outrageously unethical, but you do run into it. I'm sure that you've experienced it when trying to buy a car. After some preliminary negotiation, the salesperson surprises you by immediately accepting your low offer. After getting you to commit to a price (which sets you up psychologically to accept the idea that you will buy that car), the salesperson will say something like, "Well, this looks good. All I have to do is run this by my manager and the car is yours."

You can feel the car keys and ownership certificate in your hands already, and you are sitting there in the closing room congratulating yourself on getting such a good deal, when the salesperson returns with the sales manager. The manager sits down and reviews the price with you. He says, "You know, Fred was a little out of line here." Fred looks properly embarrassed. "This price is almost $500 under our factory invoice cost." He produces an official-looking factory invoice. "Of course, you can't possibly ask us to take a loss on the sale, can you?"

Now, you feel embarrassed yourself. You're not sure how to respond. You thought you had a deal, and Fred's higher authority just shot it down. Unaware that the dealer could sell you the car for 5 percent under invoice and still make money because of factory incentives, you fall for the sales manager's appeal to your being a reasonable person and nudge your offer up by $200.

Again, you think you've bought the car, until the sales manager explains that at this incredibly low price, he needs to get his manager's approval. And so it goes. You find yourself working your way through a battalion of managers, each one able to get you to raise your offer by a small amount. If you find the other side using escalating authority on you, remember the Counter Gambits. You can play this game also, by bringing in your escalating levels of authority. The other person will quickly catch on to what you're doing and call a truce. At each escalating level of authority, you should go back to your opening negotiating position. Don't let them "salami close" you by letting each level of authority cut off another slice of your markup.

Don't think of it as a firm deal until you have final approval and the ink is dry on the contract. If you start mentally spending the profits or mentally driving the car, you'll be too emotionally involved in the sale to walk away. Don't get so frustrated that you lose your temper with them and walk away from what could be a profitable transaction for everybody. Sure, the tactic is unfair and unethical, but this is a business and not a religion. You're there to grease the wheels of commerce, not to convert the sinners. Being able to use and handle the resort to Higher Authority is critical to you when you're Power Negotiating. Always maintain your own resort to Higher Authority. Always try to remove the other person's resort to a higher authority.

☑ Key Points to Remember

1. Don't let the other side know you have the authority to make a decision.
2. Your higher authority should be a vague entity and not an individual.
3. Even if you own your own company, you can still use this by referring down through your organization.
4. Leave your ego at home when you're negotiating. Don't let the other person trick you into admitting that you have authority.
5. Attempt to get the other person to admit that he could approve your proposal if it meets all of his needs. If that fails, go through the three Counter Gambits: Appeal to his ego, get his commitment that he'll recommend to his higher authority, and go to a qualified "subject to" close.
6. If they are forcing you to make a decision before you're ready to do so, offer to decide, but let them know that the answer will be no, unless they give you time to check with your people, and if they're using escalating authority on you, revert to your opening position at each level, and introduce your own levels of escalating authority.

Chapter 8

The Declining Value of Services

Here's something you can expect when dealing with another person: Any concession you make to him or her will quickly lose its value. The value of any material object you buy may go up in value over the years, but the value of services always appears to decline rapidly after you have performed those services. Power Negotiators know that, any time you make a concession to the other side in a negotiation, you should ask for a reciprocal concession right away. The favor you did the other side loses value very quickly. Two hours from now, the value of it will have diminished rapidly.

Real estate salespeople are very familiar with the principle of the declining value of services. When a seller has a problem getting rid of a property, and the real estate salesperson offers to solve that problem for a 6-percent listing fee, it doesn't sound as though it's an enormous amount of money.

However, the minute the realtor has performed the service by finding the buyer, suddenly that 6 percent starts to sound like a tremendous amount of money. "Six percent. That's $12,000," the seller is saying. "For what? What did they do? All they did was put it in a multiple listing service." A Realtor did much more than that to market the property and negotiate the contract, but remember the principle. The value of a service always appears to diminish rapidly after you have performed that service.

I'm sure you've experienced that, haven't you? A person with whom you do a small amount of business has called you. He is in a state of panic because the supplier from whom he receives the bulk of his business has let him down on a shipment. Now his entire assembly line has to shut down tomorrow, unless you can work miracles and get a shipment to them first thing in the morning. Sound familiar? You work all day and through the night, rescheduling shipments all over the place. Against all odds, you're able to get a shipment there just in time for the assembly line to keep operating. You even show up at their plant and personally supervise the unloading of the shipment, and the buyer loves you for it. He comes down to the dock, where you are triumphantly wiping the dirt off your hands, and says, "I can't believe you were able to do that for me. That is unbelievable service. You are incredible. Love you, love you, love you."

You reply, "Happy to do it for you, Joe. That's the kind of service we can give when we have to. Don't you think it's time we looked at my company being your main supplier?"

He replies, "That does sound good, but I don't have time to talk about it now because I've got to get over to the assembly line and be sure that it's running smoothly. Come to my office Monday morning at 10 o'clock and we'll go over it. Better yet, come by at noon and I'll buy you lunch. I really appreciate what you did for me. You are fantastic. Love you, love you, love you." All weekend long, you think to yourself, "Boy. Have I got this one made. Does he owe me." Monday rolls around, however, and negotiating with him is just as hard as ever. What went wrong? The declining value of services came into play. The value of a service always appears to decline rapidly after you have performed the service.

If you make a concession during a negotiation, get a reciprocal concession right away. Don't wait. Don't be sitting there thinking that because you did them a favor, they owe you and that they will make it up to you later. With all the goodwill in the world, the value of what you did goes down rapidly in their mind.

For the same reason, consultants know that you should always negotiate your fee up front, not afterward. Plumbers know this, don't they? They know that the time to negotiate with you is before they do the work, not after. I had a plumber out to my house. After looking at the problem, he slowly shook his head and said, "Mr. Dawson, I have identified the problem, and I can fix it for you. It will cost you $150."

You know how long it took him to do the work? Five minutes. I said, "Now wait a minute. You're going to charge me $150 for five minutes of work? I'm a nationally known speaker, and I don't make that kind of money."

He replied, "I didn't make that kind of money either—when I was a nationally known speaker."

☑ Key Points to Remember

1. The value of a material object may go up, but the value of services always appears to go down.
2. Don't make a concession and trust that the other side will make it up to you later.
3. Negotiate your fee before you do the work.

Chapter 9

Never Offer to Split the Difference

In this country, we have a tremendous sense of fair play. This dictates to us that if both sides give equally, then it's fair. If Fred puts his home up for sale at $200,000, Susan makes an offer at $190,000, and both Fred and Susan are eager to compromise, both tend to be thinking, "If we settled at $195,000 that would be fair, because it's equal." Fairness depends on the opening negotiating positions Fred and Susan took. If the house is worth $190,000 and Fred was holding to his over-inflated price only to take advantage of Susan having fallen in love with his house, then it's not fair. If the house is worth $200,000 and Susan is willing to pay that, but is taking advantage of Fred's financial problems, then it isn't fair.

Splitting the difference is not necessarily fair. It depends on the opening negotiating positions that each side took. With that misconception removed, let me point out that Power Negotiators know that splitting the difference does not mean splitting it down the middle. Just split the difference twice, and the split becomes 75/25 percent; furthermore, you may be able to get the other side to split the difference three or more times.

Splitting Doesn't Always Mean Down the Middle

I once negotiated with a bank that had a blanket encumbrance over several properties I owned. I had sold one property out from under the blanket, and our contract entitled them to a $32,000 pay-down of the loan. I offered them $28,000. I got them to offer to split the difference at $30,000. Over a period of weeks until this four-unit building closed, I was able to get them to offer to split the difference again at $29,000 and at $28,500, and finally they agreed to $28,250.

Here's how this Gambit works: The first thing to remember is you shouldn't offer to split the difference yourself, but always encourage the other person to offer to split the difference. Let's say that you're a building contractor. You have been working on getting a remodeling job that you bid at $86,000, and for which they offered $75,000. You've been negotiating for a while, during which time you've been able to get the owners of the property up to $80,000, and you've come down to $84,000 with your proposal. Where do you go from there? You have a strong feeling that if you offered to split the difference, they would agree to do so, which would mean agreeing at $82,000.

Instead of offering to split the difference, here's what you should do. You should say, "Well, I guess this is just not going to fly. It seems like such a shame though, when we've both spent so much time working on this proposal." (In Chapter 37 I'll teach you how people become more flexible in relationship to how long they've been negotiating.) "We've spent so much time on this proposal, and we've come so close to a price with which we could both live. It seems like a shame that it's all going to collapse, when we're only $4,000 apart."

If you keep stressing the time that you've spent on it and the small amount of money that you're apart on the price, eventually the other people will say, "Look, why don't we split the difference?"

You act a little dumb and say, "Let's see, splitting the difference, what would that mean? I'm at $84,000 and you're at $80,000. What you're telling me is you'd come up to $82,000? Is that what I hear you saying?"

"Well, yes," they say. "If you'll come down to $82,000, then we'll settle for that." In doing this, you have immediately shifted the negotiating range from $80,000 to $84,000. The negotiating range is now $82,000 to $84,000, and you have yet to concede a dime.

You say, "$82,000 sounds a lot better than $80,000. Tell you what: Let me talk to my partners [or whatever other higher authority you've set up] and see how they feel about it. I'll tell them you came up to $82,000, and we'll see if we can't put it together now. I'll get back to you tomorrow."

The next day, you get back to them and you say, "Wow, are my partners tough to deal with right now. I felt sure that I could get them to go along with $82,000, but we spent two hours last night going over the figures again, and they insist that we'll lose money if we go a penny below $84,000. But my goodness. We're only $2,000 apart on this job now. Surely, we're not going to let it all fall apart when we're only $2,000 apart?" If you keep that up long enough, eventually they'll offer to split the difference again.

If you are able to get them to split the difference again, this Gambit has made you an extra $1,000 of bottom-line profit. However, even if you can't get them to split the difference again, and you end up at the same $82,000 that you would have done if you had offered to split the difference, something very significant happened here. What was the significant thing that happened? Right. They think they won because you got them to propose splitting the difference at $82,000. Then you got your partners to reluctantly agree to a proposal the other side had made. If you had suggested splitting the difference, then you would have been putting a proposal on the table and forcing them to agree to a proposal that you had made.

That may seem like a very subtle thing to you, but it's very significant in terms of who felt they won and who felt they lost. Remember that the essence of Power Negotiating is to always leave the other side thinking he or she won. The rule is this: Never offer to split the difference, but always encourage the other person to offer to split the difference.

Key Points to Remember

1. Don't fall into the trap of thinking that splitting the difference is the fair thing to do.
2. Splitting the difference doesn't mean down the middle, because you can do it more than once.
3. Never offer to split the difference yourself, but encourage the other person to offer to split the difference.
4. By getting the other side to offer to split the difference, you put them in a position of suggesting the compromise. Then you can reluctantly agree to their proposal, making them feel that they won.

Chapter 10

Handling Impasses

In extended negotiations, you will frequently encounter impasses, stalemates, and deadlocks with people. Here's how I define those three terms:

- **Impasse:** You are in complete disagreement on one issue, and it threatens the negotiations.
- **Stalemate:** Both sides are still talking, but seem unable to make any progress toward a solution.
- **Deadlock:** The lack of progress has frustrated both sides so much that they see no point in talking to each other anymore.

It's easy for an inexperienced negotiator to confuse an impasse with a deadlock. For example, you manufacture auto parts, and the purchasing agent at the automobile manufacturer in Detroit says, "You'll have to cut your price by 5 percent a year for the next five years, or we'll have to resource." You know it's impossible to do that and still make a profit, so it's easy to think you've deadlocked, when you've really reached only an impasse.

You're a contractor and a building owner says to you, "I'd love to do business with you, but you charge too much. I have three other bids that are way below what you're asking." Your firm policy is that you won't participate in bid shopping, so it's easy to think you've deadlocked when you've really reached only an impasse.

You own a retail store and a customer is yelling at you, "I don't want to talk about it. Take it back and give us credit, or the next person you hear from will be my attorney!" You know that the item would work properly if the customer would permit you to teach them how to use it. However, they're so upset that you think you've reached a deadlock.

You manufacture bath fixtures and the president of a plumbing supply company in New Jersey pokes his cigar in your face and growls, "Let me tell you the facts of life, buddy boy. Your competition will give me 90 days' credit, so if you won't do that, we don't have anything to talk about."

You know that your company hasn't made an exception to their 30 days' net rule in the 72 years they've been in business, so it's easy to think you've deadlocked, when you've really reached an impasse.

All of these may sound like deadlocks to the inexperienced negotiator, but to the Power Negotiator, they're only impasses. You can use a very easy Gambit whenever you reach an impasse. It's called the Set-Aside Gambit.

The Set-Aside Gambit is what you should use when you're talking to a buyer and she says to you, "We might be interested in talking to you, but we have to have a prototype from you by the first of the month for our annual sales meeting in New Orleans. If you can't move that quickly, let's not waste time even talking about it."

Even if it's virtually impossible for you to move that quickly, you can still use the Set-Aside Gambit. "I understand exactly how important that is to you, but let's just set that aside for a minute and talk about the other issues. Tell me about the specs on the job. Do you require us to use union labor? What kind of payment terms are we talking about?"

When you use the Set-Aside Gambit, you resolve many of the little issues first to establish some momentum in the negotiation before leading up to the big issues. As I'll teach you in Chapter 64, don't narrow it down to just one issue. (With only one issue on the table, there has to be a winner and there has to be loser.)

By resolving the little issues first, you create momentum that will make the big issues much easier to resolve. Inexperienced negotiators always seem to think that you need to resolve the big issues first. "If we can't get together on the major things like price and terms, why waste much time talking to them about the little issues?" Power Negotiators that understand the other side will become much more flexible after you've reached agreement on the small issues.

☑ Key Points to Remember

1. Don't confuse an impasse with a deadlock. True deadlocks are very rare, so you've probably reached only an impasse.
2. Handle an impasse with the Set-Aside Gambit: "Let's just set that aside for a moment and talk about some of the other issues, may we?"
3. Create momentum by resolving minor issues first, but don't narrow the negotiation down to only one issue. (See Chapter 64.)

Chapter 11

Handling Stalemates

Somewhere between an impasse and a deadlock, you will sometimes encounter a stalemate. That's when both sides are still talking to each other, but seem unable to make any progress toward a solution. Being in a stalemate is similar to being "in irons," which is a sailing expression meaning that the boat has stalled with its head into the wind. A boat will not sail directly into the wind. It will sail almost into the wind, but it won't sail directly into it. To sail into the wind, you must sail about 30 degrees off course to starboard, and then tack across the wind 30 degrees to port. It's hard work to keep resetting the sails that way, but eventually you'll get where you want to go.

To tack across the wind, you must keep the bow of the boat moving through the wind. If you hesitate, you can get stuck with your bow in the wind. If you lose momentum as you tack, there's not enough wind to move the bow around. When a skipper is "in irons," he or she has to act to correct the problem. This could include resetting the sails, backing up the jib sail to pull the bow around, waggling the tiller or wheel, or anything that will regain momentum. Similarly, when negotiations stall, you must change the dynamics to reestablish momentum. Here are some things that you can do, other than changing the monetary amount involved:

- Change the people in the negotiating team. A favorite expression that attorneys use is "I have to be in court this afternoon, so my partner Charlie will be taking my place." The court may be a tennis court, but it's a tactful way of changing the team.
- Change the venue by suggesting that you continue the discussion over lunch or dinner.
- Remove a member who may have irritated the other side. A sophisticated negotiator won't take offense at being asked to

leave because he or she may have played a valuable role as a Bad Guy. Now it's time to alternate the pressure on the other side by making the concession of removing him or her from your team.

- Ease the tension by talking about their hobbies or a piece of gossip that's in the news, or by telling a funny story.
- Explore the possibility of a change in finances, such as extended credit, a reduced deposit with the order, or restructured payments. Any of these may be enough to change the dynamics and move you out of the stalemate. Remember that the other side may be reluctant to raise these issues for fear of appearing to be in poor financial condition.
- Discuss methods of sharing the risk with the other side. Taking on a commitment that may turn sour might concern them. Try suggesting that one year from now, you'll take back any unused inventory that is in good condition for a 20-percent restocking fee. Perhaps a weasel clause in the contract that applies should the market change will assuage their fears.
- Try changing the ambiance in the negotiating room. If the negotiations have been low-key with an emphasis on win-win, try becoming more competitive. If the negotiations have been hard driving, try switching to more of a win-win mode.
- Suggest a change in specifications, packaging, or delivery method to see if this shift will make the people think more positively.

It may be possible to get them to overlook any difference of opinion, provided you agree to a method of arbitrating any dispute, should it become a problem in the future.

When a sailboat is "in irons" the skipper may know exactly how to reset the sails, but sometimes he simply has to try different things to see what works. If negotiations stalemate, you have to try different things to see what will regain momentum for you. It reminds me of something I was told many years ago about a road construction crew in India busily digging a tunnel through the side of a hill. It seemed like a very primitive operation; there were thousands of workers armed with picks and shovels, and it was amazing that they would even attempt such an undertaking with nothing but laborers.

A tourist walked up to the foreman and asked him, "How in the world do you go about this?"

"It's very simple, really," he answered. "I blow a whistle and all the workers on this side start digging through the hill. On the other side of the hill, we have another crew of workers, and we tell them to start digging through the hill toward us. If the two crews meet in the middle, then we have a tunnel. If they don't meet, then we have two tunnels."

Handling a stalemate is like that. Something will happen when you change the dynamics in an attempt to create momentum, but you're never sure what it will be.

Key Points to Remember

1. Be aware of the difference between an impasse, a stalemate, and a deadlock. In a stalemate, both sides still want to find a solution, but neither can see a way to move forward.
2. The response to a stalemate should be to change the dynamics of the negotiation by altering one of the elements.

Chapter 12

Handling Deadlocks

In the previous two chapters, I've shown you how to handle the first two levels of problems that can occur: the impasse and the stalemate. If things get any worse, you may reach a deadlock, something that I defined as "both sides are so frustrated with the lack of progress, that they see no point in talking to each other any more."

Deadlocks are rare, but if you do reach one, the only way to resolve it is to bring in a third party—someone who will act as a mediator or arbitrator. As you'll see in Chapter 34 and Chapter 35, there is a major difference between an arbitrator and a mediator. In the case of an arbitrator, both sides agree before the process starts that they will abide by the decision of the arbitrator. If a union critical to the public's welfare goes on strike, such as the union of transportation or sanitation workers, the federal government will eventually insist that an arbitrator be appointed, and both sides will have to settle for the solution that the arbitrator thinks is fair. A mediator doesn't have that kind of power. A mediator is simply someone brought in to facilitate a solution. He or she acts as a catalyst, using his or her skills to seek a solution that both sides will accept as reasonable.

Inexperienced negotiators are reluctant to bring in a mediator because they see their inability to resolve a problem as being a failure. "I don't want to ask my sales manager for help because he'll think of me as a poor negotiator" is what is running through their minds. Power Negotiators know that there are many reasons why a third party can resolve a problem, other than that they are better negotiators.

An arbitrator or a mediator can be effective only if both sides see them as reasonably neutral. Sometimes you must go to great lengths to assure this perception. If you bring in your manager to resolve a dispute with a customer, what is the chance that your customer will perceive him or her as neutral? It is somewhere between nil and zero. Your manager must do something to create a feeling of neutrality in the other person's mind. The way to do this is for your manager to make a small concession to the other person early in the mediation process.

Your manager comes in and, even if he's fully aware of the problem, says, "I haven't really had a chance to get into this yet. Why don't you both explain your position and let me see if I can come up with a solution that you can both live with?" The terminology is important here. By asking both sides to explain their positions, he is projecting that he comes to the process without prejudice. Also, note that he's avoiding the use of "we" when he refers to you.

Having patiently heard out both sides, he should then turn to you and say, "Are you being fair pushing that? Perhaps you could give a little on the terms [or some other detail]? Could you live with 60 days?" Don't feel that your manager is failing to support you. What he is trying to do is position himself as neutral in your customer's eyes.

Do not assume you must avoid impasses, stalemates, and deadlocks at all cost. An experienced negotiator can use them as tools to pressure the other side. Once your mind-set is that a deadlock is unthinkable, it means you're no longer willing to walk away, and you have surrendered your most powerful pressure point (your edge), as you'll see in Chapter 17.

☑ Key Points to Remember

1. The only way to resolve a true deadlock is by bringing in a third party.
2. The third party acts as a mediator or an arbitrator. Mediators can only facilitate a solution, but both sides agree up front that they will abide by an arbitrator's final decision.
3. Don't see having to bring in a third person as a failure on your part. There are many reasons why third parties can reach a solution that the parties involved in the negotiation couldn't reach alone.
4. The third party is seen as neutral by both sides. If he or she is not neutral, he or she should position him- or herself as such by making a small concession to the other side early in the negotiation.

5. Keep an open mind about the possibility of a deadlock. You can only develop your full power as a Power Negotiator if you're willing to walk away. By refusing to consider a deadlock, you're giving away a valuable pressure point.
6. You can learn more about the art of mediation and arbitration in Chapter 34 and Chapter 35.

Chapter 13

Always Ask for a Trade-Off

The Trade-Off Gambit tells you that, any time the other side asks you for a concession in the negotiations, you should automatically ask for something in return. The first time you use this Gambit, you'll get back the money you invested in this book many times over. From then on, using it will earn you thousands of dollars every year. Let's look at a couple of ways of using the Trade-Off Gambit.

Let's say that you have sold your house, and the buyers ask you if they could move some of their furniture into the garage three days before closing. Although you wouldn't want to let them move into the house before closing, you see an advantage in letting them use the garage. It will get them emotionally involved and far less likely to create problems for you at closing. With that in mind, you're almost eager to make the concession, but I want you to remember the rule: However small the concession they're asking you for, always ask for something in return. Say to them, "Let me check with my family [vague Higher Authority], and see how they feel about that, but let me ask you this: If we do that for you, what will you do for us?"

Perhaps you sell forklifts and you've sold a large order to a warehouse-style hardware store. They've requested delivery on August 15th—30 days ahead of their grand opening. Then the operations manager for the chain calls you and says, "We're running ahead of schedule on the store construction. We're thinking of moving up the store opening to take in the Labor Day weekend. Is there any way you could move up delivery of those forklifts to next Wednesday?" You may be thinking, "That's great. They're sitting in our local warehouse ready to go, so I'd much rather move up the shipment and get paid sooner. We'll deliver them tomorrow if you want them." Although your initial inclination is to say, "That's fine," I still want you to use the Trade-Off Gambit. I want you to say, "Quite frankly, I don't know whether we can get them there so soon. I'll have to check with my scheduling people [note the use of a vague Higher Authority] and see what they say about it. But let me ask you this: If we can do that for you, what can you do for us?"

The following happens when you ask for something in return: You might just get something. The buyers of your house may be willing to increase the deposit, buy your patio furniture, or give your dog a good home. The hardware store owner may just have been thinking, "Boy, have we got a problem here. What can we give them as an incentive to get them to move this shipment up?" They may just concede something to you. They may just say, "I'll tell accounting to cut the check for you today," or "Take care of this for me, and I'll use you again for the store that we're opening in Chicago in December."

By asking for something in return, you elevate the value of the concession. When you're negotiating, why give anything away? Always make a big deal out of it. You may need it. Later, you may be doing the walk-through with the buyers of the house, and they've found a light switch that doesn't work. You're able to say, "Do you know how it inconvenienced us to let you move your furniture into the garage? We did that for you, and now I want you to overlook this small problem." Later you may need to be able to go to the people at the hardware store and say, "Do you remember last August when you needed me to move that shipment up for you? You know how hard I had to talk to my people to get them to reschedule all our shipments? We did that for you, so don't make me wait for our money. Cut me the check today, won't you?" When you elevate the value of the concession, you set it up for a Trade-Off later.

It stops the grinding-away process. This is the key reason why you should use the Trade-Off Gambit. If they know that every time they ask you for something, you're going to ask for something in return, then it stops them constantly coming back for more. I can't tell you how many times a student of mine has come up to me at seminars, or called my office and said to me, "Roger, can you help me with this? I thought I had a sweetheart of a deal put together. I didn't think I would have any problems at all with this one. But in the very early stages, they asked me for a small concession. I was so happy to have their business that I told them, 'Sure, we can do that.' A week later, they called me for another small concession, and I said, 'All right. I guess I can do that.' Ever since, it's been one darn thing after another. Now it looks as though the whole thing is going to fall apart on me." He should have known up front that when the other person asked him for that first small concession, he should have asked for something in return. "If we can do that for you, what can you do for us?"

A Fortune 50 Company Learns This Lesson

I once trained the top 50 salespeople at a Fortune 50 company. They have a Key Account Division that negotiates their largest accounts with their biggest customers. A salesperson at the seminar had just made a $43 million sale to an aircraft manufacturer. (That's not a record. When I trained people at a huge computer manufacturer's headquarters, a salesperson in the audience had just closed a $3-billion sale, and he was in my seminar taking notes!)

This Key Account Division had its own vice president, and he came up to me afterward to tell me, "Roger, that thing you told us about trading off was the most valuable lesson I've ever learned in any seminar. I've been coming to seminars for years and thought that I'd heard it all, but I'd never been taught what a mistake it is to make a concession without asking for something in return. That's going to save us hundreds of thousands of dollars in the future."

Use these Gambits the way that I'm teaching them to you. If you change even a word, it can dramatically change the effect. If, for example, you change this from "If we can do that for you, what can you do for us?" to "If we do that for you, you will have to do this for us," you have become confrontational. You've become confrontational at a very sensitive point in the negotiations, when the other side is under pressure and is asking you for a favor. Don't do it. It could cause the negotiation to blow up in your face. You may be tempted to ask for a specific concession because you think that you'll get more that way. I disagree. I think you'll get more by leaving the suggestion up to them.

Don't Ask for Something Specific

Jack Wilson, who produced my video training tapes, told me that after I taught him this Gambit, he used it to save several thousand dollars. A television studio called him and said one of their camera operators was sick. Would Jack mind if they called one of the camera operators who Jack had under contract and ask him if he could fill in? It was just a courtesy call, something to which Jack would have said, "No problem" in the past. However, this time he said, "If I do that for you, what will you do for me?" To his surprise, they said, "Tell you what. The next time you use our studio, if you run overtime, we'll waive the overtime charge." They had just conceded several thousand dollars to Jack on something that he never would have asked for in the past, had he not known this gambit.

When you ask what they will give you in return, they may say, "Nothing," or "You get to keep our business. That's what you get." That's fine, because you had everything to gain by asking and haven't lost anything. If necessary, you can always revert to a position of insisting on a Trade-Off by saying, "I don't think I can get my people to agree to it unless you're prepared to accept a charge for expedited shipping," or "unless you're willing to move up the payment date."

Key Points to Remember

1. When asked for a small concession by the other side, always ask for something in return.
2. Use this expression: "If we can do that for you, what can you do for me?" You may just get something in return. It elevates the value of the concession so you can use it as a Trade-Off later. Most importantly, it stops the grinding process.
3. Don't change the wording and ask for something specific in return because that's being too confrontational.

Ending Negotiating Gambits

Chapter 14

Good Guy/Bad Guy

Good Guy/Bad Guy is one of the best-known negotiating gambits. Charles Dickens wrote about it in his book *Great Expectations.* In the opening scene of the story, the young hero, Pip, is in the graveyard when out of the fog comes a large, very frightening man. This man is a convict, and he has chains around his legs. He asks Pip to go into the village and bring back food and a file, so he can remove the chains. The convict has a dilemma, however. He wants to scare the child into doing as he's asked, yet he mustn't put so much pressure on Pip that he'll be frozen in place or bolt into town to tell the policeman.

The solution to the convict's problem is to use the Good Guy/Bad Guy Gambit. Taking some liberty with the original work, what the convict says, in effect, is, "You know, Pip, I like you and I would never do anything to hurt you. But I have to tell you that waiting out here in the mist is a friend of mine and he can be violent, and I'm the only one who can control him. If I don't get these chains off—if you don't help me get them off—then my friend might come after you. You have to help me. Do you understand?" Good Guy/Bad Guy is a very effective way of putting pressure on people, without confrontation.

I'm sure you have seen Good Guy/Bad Guy used in the old police movies. The officers bring a suspect down to the police station for questioning, and the first detective to interrogate him is a rough, tough, mean-looking guy. He threatens the suspect with all kinds of things that they're going to do to him if he doesn't cooperate with them. Then, he's mysteriously called away to take a phone call, and the second detective, who's brought in to look after the prisoner while the first detective is away, is the warmest, nicest guy in the world. He sits down and makes friends with the prisoner. He gives him a cigarette and says, "Listen kid, it's really not as bad as all that. I've rather taken a liking to you. I know the ropes around here.

Why don't you let me see what I can do for you?" It's a real temptation to think the Good Guy's on your side when, of course, he really isn't.

Then the Good Guy would go ahead and close on what salespeople would recognize as a minor point close. "All I think the detectives really need to know," he tells the prisoner, "is where did you buy the gun?" What he wants to know is: "Where did you hide the body?"

Starting out with a minor point like that, and then working up from there, works very well, doesn't it? The car salesperson says to you, "If you did invest in this car, would you get the blue or the gray? Would you want the vinyl upholstery or the leather?" Little decisions lead to big ones. The real estate salesperson who says, "If you did invest in this home, how would you arrange the furniture in the living room?" Or, "Which of these bedrooms would be the nursery for your new baby?" Little decisions grow to big decisions.

A Dictator Attempts Good Guy/Bad Guy

Bill Richardson, our former United Nations ambassador, tells this story about General Cedras, the dictator of Haiti, using Good Guy/Bad Guy in *Fortune* magazine (May 26, 1996): "With General Cedras of Haiti, I learned that he played good guy and that a top general, Philippe Biamby, played bad guy, so I was prepared. During our meeting, Biamby leaped up on the table and started screaming, 'I don't like the U.S. government to call me a thug.... Je ne suis pas un thug.' I remember turning to Cedras as Biamby was doing this and saying, 'I don't think he likes me very much.' Cedras laughed and laughed. He said, 'All right, Biamby, sit down.'"

People use Good Guy/Bad Guy on you much more than you might believe. Look out for it anytime you find yourself dealing with two people. Chances are, you'll see it being used on you, in one form or another. For example, you may sell corporate health insurance plans for an HMO, and have made an appointment to meet with the vice president of human resources at a company that manufactures lawn mowers. When the secretary leads you in to meet with the vice president, you find to your surprise that the president of the company wants to sit in and listen in on your presentation.

That's negotiating two on one (that's not good, and I'll tell you more about why in Chapter 48 on body language), but you go ahead and everything appears to be fine. You feel you have a good chance of closing the sale, until the president looks irritated. He says to his vice president, "Look, I don't think these people are interested in making a serious proposal to us, and I've got things to do." Then he storms out. This really shakes you up if you're not used to negotiating. Then the vice president says, "Wow. Sometimes he gets that way, but I really like the plan you presented, and I think we can still work this out. If you could be more flexible with your price, I think we can still put it together. Tell you what—why don't you let me see what I can do for you with him?" If you don't realize what they're doing to you, you'll hear yourself say something such as, "What do you think the president would agree to?" Then it won't be long before you'll have the vice president negotiating for you—and he or she is not on your side.

If you think I'm exaggerating on this one, consider this: Haven't you, at one time or another, said to a car salesperson, "What do you think you could get your sales manager to agree to?" as if the salesperson is on your side, not on theirs? Haven't we all, at one time, been buying real estate and have found the property we want to buy, so we say to the agent who has been helping us find the property, "What do you think the sellers would take?" Let me ask you something: For whom is your agent working? Who is paying her? It's not you, is it? She is working for the seller, and yet she has effectively played Good Guy/Bad Guy with you. Look out for Good Guy/Bad Guy, because you run into it a lot.

When I was the president of a large real estate company in California, we had one branch that consistently lost money. The branch had been open about a year, but we had signed a three-year lease on the premises, which committed us to try to make it work for two more years. No matter how hard I tried, however, I couldn't find a way to either increase the income, or decrease the expenses of the office. The biggest problem was the lease. We were paying $1,700 a month, and that one expense was killing our profit.

I called the landlord, explained my problem to him, and tried to get him to reduce the rent to $1,400 a month, a figure at which we could have made a small profit. He said, "You have two more years on that lease and will just have to live with it." I used all of the Gambits I knew, but nothing would budge him to change his mind. It looked as though I would have to accept the situation.

Finally, I tried the Good Guy/Bad Guy Gambit combined with a great deal of time pressure. Several weeks later, I called him at 5:50 p.m. "About that lease," I said. "A problem has come up here. I want you to know that I agree with your position. I signed a three-year lease, there are more than two years left on it, and there isn't any question that we should live with it. But here's the problem. I have to go into my board of directors' meeting in half an hour, and they're going to ask me if you've been willing to reduce the lease to $1,400. If I have to tell them no, they'll tell me to close the office."

The landlord protested, "But I'll sue."

"I know. I agree with you entirely," I said. "I'm squarely on your side, but the problem is the board of directors with whom I have to deal. If you threaten to sue, they'll just say, 'Okay, let him sue. This is Los Angeles County, and it will take him two years to get into court.'"

His response demonstrates how effective the Good Guy/Bad Guy Gambit can be. He said, "Would you go into that board meeting and see what you can do for me? I'd be willing to split the difference and reduce the lease to $1,550, but if they won't settle for that, I could drop it as low as $1,500." The Gambit had worked so well that he actually asked me to negotiate for him with my own board of directors.

See how effective it can be in putting pressure on the other person without confrontation? What would have happened if I had said to him, "Go ahead and sue me. It'll take you two years to get into court"? It would have upset him so much that we would have spent the next two years talking to each other through attorneys. By using a vague higher authority as my bad guy, I was able to put incredible pressure on him without having him get upset with me.

Counter Gambits to Good Guy/Bad Guy

The first Counter Gambit is to identify the Gambit. Although there are other ways to handle the problem, this one is so effective that it's probably the only one you need to know. Good Guy/Bad Guy is so well-known it embarrasses people when they are caught using it. When you notice the other person using it you should smile and say, "Oh, come on—you aren't going to play Good Guy/Bad Guy with me, are you? Come on, sit down, and let's work this thing out." Usually their embarrassment will cause them to retreat from the position.

You could respond by creating a bad guy of your own. Tell them that you'd love to do what they want, but you have people back in the head office who are obsessed with sticking to the program. You can always make a fictitious bad guy appear more unyielding than a bad guy who is present at the negotiation.

You could go over their heads to their supervisor. For example, if you're dealing with a buyer and head buyer at a distributorship, you may call the owner of the distributorship and say, "Your people were playing Good Guy/Bad Guy with me. You don't approve, do you?" (Always be cautious of going over someone's head. The strategy can easily backfire because of the bad feelings it can cause.)

Sometimes just letting the bad guy talk resolves the problem, especially if he's being obnoxious. Eventually, his own people will get tired of hearing it and tell him to knock it off.

You can counter Good Guy/Bad Guy by saying to the Good Guy, "Look, I understand what you two are doing to me. From now on, anything that he says, I'm going to attribute to you also." Now you have two bad guys to deal with, so it diffuses the Gambit. Sometimes just identifying them both in your own mind as bad guys will handle it, without your having to come out and accuse them.

If the other side shows up with an attorney or controller who is clearly there to play bad guy, jump right in and forestall his or her role. Say to him or her, "I'm sure you're here to play bad guy, but let's not take that approach. I'm as eager to find a solution to this situation as you are, so why don't we all take a win-win approach? Fair enough?" This really takes the wind out of the other side's sails.

Key Points to Remember

1. People use Good Guy/Bad Guy more than you might believe. Look out for it whenever you're dealing with two or more people. It's an effective way of putting pressure on the other person without creating confrontation. Counter it by identifying it. It's such a well-known tactic that when you catch them using it, they get embarrassed and back off.
2. Don't be concerned that the other side knows what you're doing. Even if they do, it can still be a powerful tactic. When you're Power Negotiating with someone who understands all of these Gambits, it becomes more fun. It's like playing chess with a person of equal skill, rather than with someone you can easily outsmart.

Chapter 15

Nibbling

Power Negotiators know that by using the Nibbling Gambit, you can get a little bit more, even after you have agreed on everything. You can also get the other person to do things that she had refused to do earlier. Car salespeople understand this, don't they? They know that when they get you on the lot, a kind of psychological resistance has built up to the purchase. They know to first get you to the point where you're thinking, "Yes, I'm going to buy a car. Yes, I'm going to buy it here." Even if it means closing you on any make and model of car, even a stripped-down model that carries little profit for them. Then they can get you into the closing room and start adding all the other little extras that really build the profit into the car.

The principle of Nibbling tells you that you can accomplish some things more easily with a Nibble later in the negotiations. Children are brilliant Nibblers. If you have teenage children living at home, you know that they don't have to take any courses on negotiating. But you have to—just to stand a chance of surviving the whole process of bringing them up—because they're naturally brilliant negotiators. Not because they learn it in school, but because when they're little, everything they get, they get with negotiating skills.

How Children Nibble to Get What They Want

When my daughter, Julia, graduated from high school, she wanted to get a great high school graduation gift from me. She had three things on her hidden agenda. Number one, she wanted a five-week trip to Europe. Number two, she wanted $1,200 in spending money. And number three, she wanted a new set of luggage.

She was smart enough not to ask for everything up front. She was a good negotiator to first close me on the trip, then come back a few weeks later and show me in writing that the recommended spending money was $1,200, and she got me to commit to that. (I'll stress the importance of the "in writing" part in Chapter 31.) Then right at the last minute, she came to me and she said, "Dad, you wouldn't want me going to Europe with that ratty old set of luggage, would you? All the kids will be there with new luggage." And she got that, too. Had she asked for everything up front, I would have negotiated out the luggage and negotiated down the spending money.

What's happening here is that a person's mind always works to reinforce decisions that it has just made. Power Negotiators know how this works, and use it to get the other side to agree to something that they wouldn't have agreed to earlier in the negotiation.

Why is Nibbling such an effective technique? To find out why Nibbling works so well, a couple of psychologists did an extensive study at a racetrack in Canada. They studied the attitude of people immediately before they placed the bet, and again immediately after they placed the bet. They found out that before the people placed the bet, they were uptight, unsure, and anxious about what they were about to do. Compare this to almost anyone with whom you negotiate: They may not know you, they may not know your company, and they certainly don't know what's going to come out of this relationship. Chances are they're uptight, unsure, and anxious.

At the racetrack, the researchers found out that once people had made the decision to go ahead and place the bet, they suddenly felt very good about what they had just done and even had a tendency to want to double the bet before the race started. In essence, their minds did a flip-flop until they had finally made the decision. Before they decided, they were fighting it; once they'd made the decision, they supported it.

If you're a gambler, you've had that sensation, haven't you? Watch them at the roulette tables in Atlantic City or Las Vegas. The gamblers place their bets. The croupier spins the ball. At the very last moment, people are pushing out additional bets. The mind always works to reinforce decisions that it has made earlier.

I spoke at a Philadelphia convention when the Pennsylvania lottery prize was $50 million, and many of the people in the audience were holding tickets. To illustrate how people's minds work to reinforce the decisions that they have made, I tried to buy a lottery ticket from somebody in the audience. Do you think he would sell me one? No, he wouldn't—even for 50 times the purchase price. I'm sure that, before he bought that ticket, he was uptight and anxious about betting money on a 100-million-to-one shot.

However, having made the decision, he refused to change his mind. The mind works to reinforce decisions that it has made earlier. One rule for Power Negotiators is that you don't necessarily ask for everything up front. You wait for a moment of agreement in the negotiations, and then go back and Nibble for a little extra.

You might think of the Power Negotiating process as pushing a ball uphill—a large rubber ball that's much bigger than you. You're straining to force it up to the top of the hill. The top of the hill is the moment of first agreement in the negotiations. Once you reach that point, then the ball moves easily down the other side of the hill. This is because people feel good after they have made the initial agreement. They feel a sense of relief that the tension and stress are over. Their minds are working to reinforce the decision that they've just made, and they're more receptive to any additional suggestions you may have. After the other side has agreed to make any kind of purchase from you, it's time for that "second effort."

Vince Lombardi and the Second Effort

Vince Lombardi loved to talk about the second effort. He'd show his players football clips of receivers who almost caught the ball, but it just slipped through their fingers. But instead of giving up, they made the second effort. They dove and caught the ball before it hit the ground. He was also proud of film clips of the running back that the defense almost brought down, but who still wriggled free and made the touchdown. Lombardi used to say that everyone makes the first effort. You wouldn't be on the team if you didn't know how to play the game well, and were doing everything the coach expects you to do when you're on the field. Everybody's doing that. The players on the other team are doing that. The players who would like to replace you on the team are capable of doing that.

Lombardi was fond of pointing out that the difference between the good players and the great players is that the great ones always make the second effort, despite their first failure. Just doing everything their coach expects them to do isn't good enough for the great ones; they must go beyond that.

Let's translate the second-effort philosophy into workplace situations. If you're a receptionist, you need to realize that it isn't enough to know how to do your job and do everything that your boss asks you to do. Your boss expects anyone in your position to do that. You have to look for opportunities to make the extra effort. Perhaps you learn how to hang in with a complaining customer a little longer until you can satisfy her without having to turn her over to your boss.

If you're an architect, you must realize that it isn't enough to create a design that will please your clients. Clients expect any architect in the country to do that. You have to learn a little more about the customer than anyone else would, so that you can come up with a design that will knock his or her socks off.

If you're a salesperson, you must understand that you wouldn't be selling for your company unless you knew how to play the selling game well and were out there doing everything that your company expects you to do. However, everybody's doing that. The people who sell for your competition are doing that. The people who apply for your job every day are capable of doing that. The difference between a good salesperson and a great salesperson is that the great ones always make another effort. Even when they know their sales manager would pat them on the back and tell them not to feel bad because they did everything they could to get the sale, that's not good enough for the superstar salespeople. They always make another effort.

Always go back at the end for that second effort. Perhaps as a receptionist, one of your duties is to sell extended warranty contracts on equipment that customers bring in for repair. You explain the program, but the customer resists. Have the courage before the customer leaves to make that second effort. You might say, "Mr. Jones, could we take one more look at that extended warranty? What you may be overlooking is the preventative maintenance factor. If you know that repair work won't cost you a penny, you'll call us much sooner than you would if you had to pay for it. The sooner you have repairs made, the longer the equipment will last. Yes, it's a good deal for us, but it's an even better deal for you." You have a good chance of Mr. Jones saying, "Well, all right, if you think it's that important, I'll go ahead."

As an architect, you may have some trouble convincing your client that he should put the highest-quality of carpet in the lobby of his new hotel, and you have to back off the topic. After you have reached agreement on the other issues, have the courage to say, "Could we take another look at upgrading the carpet in the lobby? I realize that it's a huge investment, but nothing projects the quality image better than having your guests sink into plush carpeting the moment they get into the door. I don't recommend it for everybody, but with this type of project, I really think it's very, very important." And you have a good chance of your client saying, "Well, all right. If you think it's that important, let's go ahead with it." This is how you talk the client into your way of thinking in negotiating.

Perhaps you sell packaging equipment, and you are trying to convince your customer that he or she should go with the top-of-the-line model, but he or she's balking at that kind of expense. You back off, but come back and Nibble for it before you leave. After you have reached agreement on all the other points, you say, "Could we take another look at the top-of-the-line model? I don't recommend it for everyone, but with your kind of volume and growth potential, I really think it's the way for you to go, and all it means is an additional investment of $500 a month." And you have a good chance of him or her saying, "Well, alright, if you think it's that important, let's go ahead." Always go back at the end of the negotiations to make a second effort on something that you couldn't get them to agree to earlier.

Look Out for People Nibbling on You

There is a point in the negotiation when you are very vulnerable, and that point is when you think that the negotiations are all over. I'd be willing to bet that you have been the victim of a Nibble at one time or another. You've been selling a car or a truck to someone. You're finally feeling good because you've found the buyer. The pressure and the tension of the negotiations have drained away. He's sitting in your office, writing out the check. But just as he's about to sign his name, he looks up and says, "That does include a full tank of gas, doesn't it?" Here, you're at your most vulnerable point in the negotiations because of the following reasons:

- You've made a sale, and are feeling good. When you feel good, you tend to give things away that you otherwise wouldn't.
- You're thinking, "Oh, no. I thought we had resolved everything. I don't want to take a chance on going back to the beginning and renegotiating the whole thing. If I do that, I might lose the entire sale. Perhaps I'm better off just giving in on this little point."

You are at your most vulnerable just after the other person has made the decision to go ahead. Look out for people Nibbling on you. Making a huge sale has excited you so much that you can't wait to call your sales manager and tell her what you've done. The other person tells you that he needs to call purchasing and get a purchase order number for you. While he's on the telephone, he puts his hand over the mouthpiece and says, "By the way, you can give us 60 days on this, can't you? All of your competitors will." Because you've just made a big sale, and you're afraid to reopen the negotiations for fear of losing it, you will have to fight to avoid the tendency to make the concession.

(An aside to sales managers: When your salespeople have this happen to them, they're not going to come back to you and say, "Boy, was that person a good negotiator. He slid that Nibble in on me and before I even knew what he'd done, I'd agreed to 60-day terms." No! Your salesperson is going to come back to you and say, "I got the order, but I had to give them 60-day terms to get it.")

Prevent the Other Side From Nibbling on You

Try to prevent the possibility of being Nibbled by using the following techniques. Show them in writing what any additional concessions will cost them. List extended terms if you ever make them available, but show what it costs them to do that. List the cost of training, installation, extended warranties, and anything else for which they might Nibble. Don't give yourself the authority to make any concessions. Protect yourself with the Higher Authority Gambit (see Chapter 7) and Good Guy/Bad Guy (see Chapter 14). Counter the Nibble when the other person does it to you. The Counter Gambit to the Nibble is to gently make the other person feel cheap. You have to be careful about the way you do this because you're at a sensitive point in the negotiation. You smile and say, "Oh, come on, you negotiated a fantastic price with me. Don't make us wait for our money, too. Fair enough?" That's the Counter Gambit to the Nibble when it's used against you. Be sure that you do it with a big grin on your face, so that they don't take it too seriously.

Consider these points when you go into negotiations: Are there some elements that you are better off to bring up as a Nibble, after you have reached initial agreement? Do you have a plan to make a second effort on anything to which you can't get them to agree the first time around? Are you prepared for the possibility of them Nibbling on you at the last moment?

Preventing Post-Negotiation Nibbles

Sometimes the other person wishes that he had Nibbled on you during the negotiation, so he decides to Nibble on you afterward. This could include certain scenarios. The other person agrees to 30-day terms, but deliberately takes 60 days or more to pay. He pays in 30 days, but still deducts the Net 15 discount. He requests free additional accounting breakdowns, sometimes just to delay payment. He protests a charge for installation, claiming that you didn't cover this with him. He rejects a charge for training, saying that your competition doesn't charge. He contracts for a carload shipment, but calls at the last moment to cut the shipment and insist on the carload price. He refuses to pay or slashes the billing for engineering charges, although during the negotiation, he waived this aside as unimportant. He requests extra certifications, and is unwilling to pay for them.

You can avoid most of this unpleasantness by negotiating all the details up front and getting them in writing. Don't leave anything to "We can work that out later." Don't be lazy and feel that if you avoid an issue, you are closer to making the sale. Use the Gambits to create a climate in which the other person feels that he or she won. If the other side felt they won, then they are much less likely to Nibble—either during the negotiation or afterward. Power Negotiators always take into account the possibility of being able to Nibble. Timing is very critical—catch the other parties when the tension is off, and they're feeling good because they think the negotiations are all over.

On the other hand, look out for the other side Nibbling on you at the last moment, when you're feeling good. At that point, you're the most vulnerable and liable to make a concession, about which half an hour later you'll be thinking, "Why on Earth did I do that? I didn't have to do that. We'd agreed on everything already."

☑ Key Points to Remember

1. With a well-timed Nibble, you can get things at the end of a negotiation that you couldn't have gotten the other side to agree to earlier. It works because the other person's mind reverses itself after it has made a decision. He may have been fighting the thought of buying from you at the start of the negotiation. After he has made a decision to buy from you, however, you can Nibble for a bigger order, upgraded product, or additional services.

2. Being willing to make that additional effort is what separates great salespeople from merely good salespeople.
3. Stop the other person from Nibbling on you by showing her, in writing, the cost of any additional features, services, or extended terms, and by not revealing that you have the authority to make any concessions.
4. When the other person Nibbles on you, respond by making him feel cheap, in a good-natured way.
5. Avoid post-negotiation Nibbling by addressing and tying up all the details and using Gambits that cause them to feel that they won.

Chapter 16

How to Taper Concessions

In extended negotiations over price, be careful that you don't set up a pattern in the way that you make concessions. Let's say that you're selling a used car and you've gone into the negotiation with a price of $15,000, but you would go as low as $14,000. You have a negotiating range of $1,000.

The way in which you give away that $1,000 is very critical. There are several mistakes that you should avoid:

Equal-sized concessions. This means giving away your $1,000 negotiating range in four increments of $250. Imagine what the other person is thinking if you do that. She doesn't know how far she can push you; all she knows is that every time she pushes, she gets another $250. She's going to keep on pushing. In fact, it's a mistake to make any two concessions of equal size. If you were buying the car, and the owner made a $250 concession and when pushed, made another $250 concession, wouldn't you bet that the next concession will be $250 also?

Another mistake is making the final concession a big one. Let's say that you made a $600 concession, followed by a $400 concession. Then you tell the other person, "That's absolutely our bottom line. I can't give you a penny more." The problem is that $400 is too big a concession to be your final concession. If you made a $600 concession, followed by a $400 concession, the other person is probably thinking that he's sure that he can get at least another $100 out of you. He says, "We're getting close. If you can come down another $100, we can talk." You refuse, telling him that you can't even come down another $10, because you've given him your bottom line already. By now, the other person is really upset, because he's thinking, "You just made a $400 concession and now you won't give me another lousy $10. Why are you being so difficult?" Avoid making the last concession a big one, because it can create hostility.

Never give it all away up front. Another variation of the pattern is to give the entire $1,000 negotiating range away in one concession. When I set this up as a workshop at my seminars, it's amazing to me how many participants will turn to the person with whom they're to negotiate and say, "Well, I'll tell you what he told me." Such naiveté is a disastrous way to negotiate. I call it "Unilateral Disarmament." It's what some pacifists would have us do about nuclear arms: dismantle all our nuclear weapons and hope that the Iranians and North Koreans would reciprocate. I don't think that's very smart.

I bet you're thinking, "How on Earth would a person be able to get me to do a stupid thing like that?" It's actually very easy. Someone who looked at your car yesterday calls you up and says, "We've located three cars that we like equally well, so now we're just down to price. We thought the fairest thing to do would be to let all three of you give us your very lowest price, so that we can decide." Unless you're a skilled negotiator, you'll panic and cut your price to the bone, although they haven't given you any assurance that there won't be another round of bidding later.

Another way the other side can get you to give away your entire negotiating range up front is with the "we don't like to negotiate" ploy. Say you're a salesperson trying to get a new account with a company. With a look of pained sincerity on his face, their buyer says, "Let me tell you about the way we do business here. Back in 1926, when he first started the company, our founder said, 'Let's treat our vendors well. Let's not negotiate prices with them. Have them quote their lowest price, and then tell them whether we'll accept it or not.' That's the way we've always done it. Just give me your lowest price, and I'll give you a yes or a no. Because we don't like to negotiate here."

The buyer is lying! He or she loves to negotiate. That is negotiating—seeing if you can get the other side to make all of their concessions before the negotiating even starts.

Another mistake is giving a small concession to test the waters. We're all tempted to do that. You initially tell the other person, "Well, I might be able to squeeze another $100 off the price, but that is about our limit." If they reject that, you might think, "This negotiation is not going to be as easy as I previously thought." You offer them another $200. That still doesn't get them to buy the car, so in the next round you give away another $300 and then you have $400 left in your negotiating range, and you end up giving them the whole thing.

You see what you've done there? You started with a small concession and you built up to a larger concession. You'll never reach agreement doing that, because every time they ask you for a concession, it just gets better and better for them and they'll keep on asking.

These patterns of concession making are wrong, because they create expectations in the other person's mind. The best way to make concessions is first to offer a reasonable concession that might just cinch the deal. Maybe a $400 concession wouldn't be out of line. Then, be sure that if you have to make any future concessions, they are smaller and smaller. Your next concession might be $300, and then $200, and then $100. By reducing the size of the concessions that you're making, you convince the other person that he has pushed you just about as far as you will possibly go.

If you want to test how effective this can be, try it on your children. Wait until the next time they come to you for money for a school outing or a book fair. They ask you for $100. You say, "No way. Do you realize that when I was your age, my weekly allowance was 50 cents? Out of that money, I had to buy my own shoes and walk 10 miles to school in the snow, uphill both ways. I had to take off my shoes and walk barefoot to save money (and other stories that parents all over the world tell their children). No way am I going to give you $100. I'll give you $50, but you have to earn the rest."

"I can't do it on $50," your children protest in horror.

Now you have established the negotiating range with your child. They are asking for $100. You're only offering $50. The negotiations progress at a frenzied pace and you move up to $60. Then it's $65 and finally $67.50. By the time you've reached $67.50, you don't have to tell them that they are not going to do any better; they already know it. By tapering your concessions, you have subliminally communicated that they are not going to do any better than the $67.50 that you are offering them.

However, Power Negotiators know how to do even better than that. Power Negotiators know how to take away a concession that they have already offered the other side, and I'll tell you how to do that in Chapter 17.

☑ Key Points to Remember

1. The way that you make concessions can create a pattern of expectations in the other person's mind.

2. Don't make equal-sized concessions, because the other side will keep on pushing.
3. Don't make your last concession a big one, because it creates hostility.
4. Never concede your entire negotiating range just because the other person calls for your "last and final" proposal, or claims that he or she "doesn't like to negotiate."
5. Taper the concessions to communicate that the other side is getting the best possible deal.

Chapter 17

The Withdrawing an Offer Gambit

In this chapter, I'll teach you how to conclude the negotiations very effectively. You don't have to use it when the other person is negotiating in good faith with you. You use it only when you feel that the other side is simply grinding away to get the last penny off your price. Or when you know that the other person wants to do business with you, but she's thinking, "How much would I be making per hour, if I spent a little more time negotiating with this person?"

Let's say that a group of friends got together and bought a cabin in the mountains to use for a vacation home. There's a whole group of owners, and they're sharing the use of it. One partner drops out of the syndication, and your neighbor comes to you and tells you about the cabin in the mountains. Your initial reaction to this is, "This sounds fantastic. I'd love to do something like that." However, you're smart enough to play the Reluctant Buyer Gambit (see Chapter 5).

You say, "I appreciate your telling me about that, but I just don't think we'd be interested right now. I'm so busy, I don't think we'd have the time to get up there. But look, just to be fair to you, what is the very lowest price that you would sell a share in the home for?"

He's been studying negotiating too, however, and he's learned you should never be the first one to name the price. He says, "We have a committee that decides on the price [the Higher Authority Gambit; see Chapter 7] and I don't know what that price would be. I can take them a proposal, but I don't know what the reaction would be."

When you press him a little more, he finally says, "I'm pretty sure that they're going to be asking $20,000."

This is a lot less than you expected. You were willing to go to $30,000. Your initial reaction is to jump at it right away, but you're smart enough to remember to flinch (see Chapter 3). You exclaim, "$20,000! Oh no, I could never go along with anything like that. That's way too much. Tell you what—$16,000 might interest me. If they're interested at $16,000, let me know and we'll talk about it. "

The next day he returns and decides to bring you into line by using the Withdrawing an Offer Gambit. He says, "I am embarrassed about this. I know we were talking $20,000 yesterday, but the committee decided that they wouldn't sell a share for less than $24,000."

This is psychologically devastating to you for two reasons:

- Because you feel that you created the problem—you say, "Boy, I wish I'd never run into that Roger Dawson and his Power Negotiating, because if I hadn't, I would have nailed him down at $20,000 yesterday."
- You've made the mistake telling your family all about it. They're all excited about the home up in the mountains, and you've passed that critical point in the negotiations when you're prepared to walk away.

You say, "Joe what are you talking about? You said $20,000 yesterday. $24,000 today. Is it going to be $28,000 tomorrow? What's going on here?"

He says, "I do feel bad, but that's what they [Higher Authority] decided."

You say, "Joe, come on."

Joe says, "Well I do feel bad about this. Tell you what, let me go back to them one more time, let me see what I can do for you with them." (That's Good Guy/Bad Guy, isn't it?) "If I can get it for you for the $20,000, are you interested?"

"Of course I'm interested. I want it." He has sold you at full price, and you may not have realized what he's done to you until it's too late.

Let me give you another example, because it's a very powerful negotiating Gambit. Let's say that you sell widgets, and you quote the buyer a price of $1.80; the buyer offers you $1.60. You negotiate back and forth, and finally it looks as though he will agree to $1.72. What's going through the buyer's mind is "I got him down from $1.80 to $1.72. I bet I can squeeze another penny out of him. I bet I can get this salesperson to $1.71." He says, "Look, business is really tough right now. I just can't do business with you on those widgets unless you can bring the order in at $1.71 per widget."

He may be only baiting you, just trying it to see if he can get you down. Don't panic and feel you have to make the concession to stay in the game. The way to stop this grinding away process is to say, "I'm not sure if we can do that or not, but tell you what: If I can possibly get it for you, I will. [That's a subtle form of Good Guy/Bad Guy; see Chapter 14.] Let me go back, we'll figure it out again, and see if we can do it. I'll get back to you tomorrow."

The next day, you come back and pretend to withdraw the concession that you made the day before. You say, "I'm really embarrassed about this, but we've been up all night figuring out the price of widgets. Somebody, somewhere down the line, has made a mistake. We had an increase in the cost of raw materials that the estimator didn't figure in. I know we were talking $1.72 yesterday, but we can't even sell it to you for that—$1.73 is the lowest price that we could possibly offer you on widgets."

What's the buyer's reaction? He's going to get angry and say, "Hey, wait a minute buddy. We were talking $1.72 yesterday, and $1.72 is what I want." And immediately the buyer forgets $1.71. The Withdrawing an Offer Gambit works well when you want to stop the buyer grinding away on you.

Haven't we all had an appliance or car salesperson, when we were trying to force the price a little lower, say, "Let me go to my sales manager, and I'll see what I can do for you with him." Then he comes back and says, "Am I embarrassed about this. You know that advertised special we were talking about? I thought that ad was still in effect, but it ended last Saturday. I can't even sell it to you at the price we were talking about." Immediately, you forget future concessions and want to jump on the bandwagon at the price you'd been talking about. You can also employ this Gambit by withdrawing a feature of the offer, rather than raising the price.

Here are some examples of doing just that: The appliance salesperson says to you, "I know we were talking about waiving the installation charge, but my sales manager is now telling me that at this price we just can't do that; it's such a steal." The air-conditioner salesperson says to you, "I understand that we were talking about including the cost of building permits, but at a price this low, my estimators are telling me we'd be crazy to do that."

You're a sub-contractor and you say to your general contractor, "I know you requested 60-day terms, but at this price, we'd need payment in 30 days."

You market computers, and you tell your customer, "Yes, I told you that we would waive the charge for training your people, but my people are saying that at this price, we'd have to charge."

Don't do it with something big because that could really antagonize the other person.

The Withdrawing an Offer Gambit is a gamble, but it will force a decision and usually make or break the deal. Whenever the other person uses this on you, don't be afraid to counter by insisting that the other side resolve its internal problem first, so that you can then resume the real negotiation.

Key Points to Remember

1. The Withdrawing an Offer Gambit is a gamble, so use it only on someone who is grinding away on you. You can do it by backing off your last price concession, or by withdrawing an offer to include freight, installation, training, or extended terms.
2. To avoid direct confrontation, make the bad guy a vague Higher Authority. Continue to position yourself as on the other person's side.

Chapter 18

Positioning for Easy Acceptance

The Positioning for Easy Acceptance Gambit is important if you're dealing with people who have studied negotiating. If they're proud of their ability to negotiate, you can get ridiculously close to agreement, and the entire negotiation could still fall apart on you. When it does, it's probably not the price or terms of the agreement that caused the problem; it's the ego of the other person as a negotiator.

Let's say that you market advertising specialties, such as rulers with the company's name on it, or custom printed baseball caps and t-shirts. You have made an appointment to meet with the manager at a local appliance store. What you may not realize is that, just before you showed up in his office, the manager said to the owner of the store, "You just watch me negotiate with this advertising specialty representative. I know what I'm doing, and I'll get us a good price."

Now he's not doing as well as he had previously hoped in the negotiation, and he's reluctant to agree to your proposal because he doesn't want to feel he lost to you as a negotiator. That can happen, even when the other person knows that your proposal is fair and it also satisfies his needs. When this happens, you must find a way to make the other person feel good about giving in to you. You must Position for Easy Acceptance. Power Negotiators know that the best way to do this is to make a small concession just at the last moment. The size of the concession can be ridiculously small, and you can still make it work because it's not the size of the concession that's critical, but the timing.

You might say, "We just can't budge another dime on the price, but I tell you what. If you'll go along with the price, I'll personally supervise the installation, just to be sure that it all goes smoothly." Perhaps you were planning to do that anyway, but the point is that you've been courteous enough to position the other person so that he can respond, "Well, all right. If you'll do that for me, we'll go along with the price." Then he doesn't feel that he lost to you in the negotiation, he feels that he traded off. Positioning for Easy Acceptance is another reason why you should never go in with your best offer up front. If you have offered all of your concessions already, before you get to the end of the negotiation, you won't have anything left with which to position the other side.

Here are some concessions you can use to position the other side:

- You're selling a boat, so you offer to take the buyers out and show them how to sail it.
- If you sell office equipment, offer to set up their supplies on an automatic reordering system.
- You're selling a car, so you offer to include the snow chains.
- Hold this price for 90 days in case they want to duplicate the order.
- You're hiring someone and can't pay him or her what he or she asked, but you offer to review it after 90 days.
- Offer 45-day terms instead of 30 days.
- Offer three years for the price of two on an extended service warranty.

Remember that it's the timing of the concession that counts, not the size. The concession can be ridiculously small and still be effective. Using this Gambit, Power Negotiators can make the other person feel good about giving in to them.

Never, ever gloat. Never, when you get through negotiating, say to the other person, "Harry, you know, if you'd hung in there a little bit longer, I was prepared to do this and this and this for you." Harry's going to say unkind things about your mommy when you do that!

I realize in the normal course of business, you'd never be foolish enough to gloat over the other person because you felt you out-negotiated him. However, you get into trouble with this one when you're negotiating with someone you know well. Perhaps you have been playing golf with this person for years. Now you're negotiating something. You're having fun playing the negotiating game. Finally, he says to you, "All right. We're all agreed and we're not going to back out, but just for my own satisfaction, what was your real bottom line there?" Of course you're tempted to brag a little, but don't do it. He will remember that for the next 20 years.

When you're done negotiating, congratulate. However poorly you think the other people may have done, congratulate them. Say, "Wow. Did you do a fantastic job negotiating with me. I realize I didn't get as good a deal as I could have, but frankly, it was worth it because I learned so much about negotiating. You were brilliant." You want the other person to feel he or she won in the negotiations.

Attorneys Don't Need More Trouble

Have you ever watched attorneys in court? They'll cut each other to ribbons inside the courtroom. However, outside you'll see the district attorney go up to the defense attorney and say, "Wow, were you brilliant in there. You really were. True, your guy got 30 years, but I don't think anybody could have done a better job than you did." The district attorney understands that he'll be in another courtroom one day with that same defense attorney, and he doesn't want the attorney to feel that this is a personal contest. Gloating over a victory will just make the attorney more determined than ever to win the rematch. Remember that you will be dealing with that other person again. You don't want her to feel that she lost to you. It would make her only more determined to get the better of you in a rematch.

Key Points to Remember

1. If the other person is proud of his or her ability to negotiate, his or her need to win may stop you from reaching agreement.
2. Position the other person to feel good about giving in to you with a small concession made just at the last moment.
3. Because timing is more important than the size of the concession, the concession can be ridiculously small and still be effective.
4. Always congratulate the other person when you get through negotiating, however poorly you think he or she did.

Unethical Negotiating Gambits

Chapter 19

The Decoy

The other side can use the Decoy Gambit to take your attention away from what is the real issue in the negotiation. Perhaps you are selling custom gears to a large manufacturer of bulldozers located in Houston. You have been calling on this company for two years trying to get your foot in the door, but they have never been willing to budge from their existing supplier. However, today appears to be the day when all your persistence will pay off. The buyer offers to give you a large order, providing that you can complete shipment in a 90-day period. Both of you know that it typically takes 120 days to design, engineer, and manufacture a custom gear. The thought of getting the sale excites you, but you realize that a 90-day ship date is virtually impossible.

You check with the people at your plant, and they confirm that even 120 days would be a scramble and that non-recurring engineering costs will be $22,000. As much as you fight for an accelerated production schedule, you can't get your people to budge. It's going to take 120 days and not a day less, even if you have to lose the order over it.

You return to present the proposal to the other side. You show him a price of $230,000 for the gears, plus $22,000 in nonrecurring engineering costs, F.O.B. (meaning that the customer pays the freight) from your plant in Toledo, with shipment in 120 days.

The buyer insists that he must have delivery in 90 days to complete a large shipment that his company needs to deliver to a construction project in Buenos Aires. The negotiation has taken on an air of two people desperately trying to solve a problem together, but nothing you can come up with seems to solve the problem. The negotiations appear to have stalemated.

Finally, the buyer says, "Maybe there's something that would work. Let me check with my shipping people and see what they have to say.

I'll be right back." He leaves the office for 15 minutes. Your mind is in turmoil, thinking of the commission that you'll lose if you can't put this sale together. By the time the buyer returns, you're almost frantic.

The buyer has a concerned look on his face and says, "I think I've found a way, but I need your help to put it together. My guy in shipping says that we can air freight the gears to Argentina, but we're going to have to pay off some customs people. To do this, I need you to waive the engineering charges and air freight them to us in Houston at your expense."

Unless you're very careful, the relief of finding a solution to the problem will overwhelm you so much that you'll concede the $22,000 engineering charge and agree to pick up a $6,000 airfreight bill. And it may be months before you realize that the buyer used the Decoy Gambit on you. Six months later you're sitting in a hotel coffee shop in Dallas, talking to a friend of yours who sells sheet metal to the bulldozer company. He asks you how you got your foot in the door, and you tell him the story.

Your friend says, "I don't believe what the buyer told you. It doesn't ring true to me. Those people are the best-organized manufacturing plant in the business. They always work at least six months out. No way would they be ordering custom gears only 90 days out." Only then does it dawn on you that the shipment date never was the real issue. They could have lived with 120 days. The ship date was the Decoy issue. The buyer created the issue of an accelerated shipment date simply so that he could trade it off later for the real issue: waiving the engineering charges and the freight.

Several years ago, an association hired me to do a seminar at John Portman's Peachtree Hotel in Atlanta. That's a Westin Hotel and a fabulous place. It's 73 stories high, one of the tallest hotels in the country and possibly the world. It's a round, tall tower with only 15 or so pie-shaped rooms on each floor.

As I walked into the hotel, I was wondering what I could do to provide an illustration to the people who would be in the seminar the following day, to show how effective Power Negotiating can be. A room had been prearranged for me by the organization that had hired me, and I decided to see what I could do about negotiating down the price of the room. Rooms at the Peachtree then typically cost $135. They had given me a very good corporate rate of $75. Nevertheless, I was determined to see what I could do, and within 10 minutes got them to reduce the price of the room to $37.50.

I used the Decoy Gambit on them. They told me that they only had a twin-size room for me. Understand that if they had said they only had a full-size room, I would have asked for a twin bed. It didn't matter what it was, but I said, "The association that hired me booked this room a month ahead of time. I am not going to accept a twin-size room." The desk clerk brought out the manager. He explained that they have 1,074 rooms in the hotel, guests already occupied 1,064 of them, so they only had 10 available, and I would have to settle for a twin-size room.

I used the Trade-Off Gambit (see Chapter 13). I said, "Well, I might be willing to settle for a twin-size room, but if I do that for you, what will you do for me?" I thought they might offer a free breakfast or something like that. However, to my amazement he said, "We might be able to adjust the price of the room a little bit. How would half price be for you?"

I said, "That would be just fine." Then, as they gave me the key to the room, the manager said, "Let me check just a moment. We may be able to do something more for you." They made a telephone call and found out that they did have a queen-size room available. Maintenance had just finished redecorating it, and they weren't sure whether they had released it yet. I ended up getting a $135 queen-size room for only $37.50. (Other than giving me a neat story for the seminar, this didn't benefit me because the organization that hired me was paying for it, and they got the benefit of the reduction.)

The Decoy I used was that they only had twin-size rooms available, not king-sized. That wasn't the real issue at all, of course; what I wanted to accomplish was a reduced room rate. The size of the bed took their attention away from the real issue.

Sometimes the other side will make a big show of appearing hurt or offended by something that you did. When Bill Richardson, our former United Nations ambassador, was negotiating with a Muslim dictator, he was told, "Dictators often try to take advantage of you at the outset. They try to catch you off guard."

Richardson said:

> At the beginning of my meeting with the dictator I crossed my legs and the soles of my feet were visible. He got up and left the room. I asked the interpreter, "What did I do?" He said, "The President was insulted that you crossed your legs. To an Arab that's a nasty insult, and you should apologize." I asked, "Is he coming back?" The interpreter said, "Yes, he'll come back." When he did, I made the decision not to apologize. I wasn't going to grovel, and say, "Hey, I'm real sorry I crossed my legs." I planted my feet and said, "Mr. President, let me resume." And I think he respected that,

because the discussions got better. You try to show that you're a humble person, but at the same time, you can't back down. You can't show weakness. You keep coming at them.

(*Fortune* magazine, May 26, 1996)

Watch out for people who lure you away from the real issue with the Decoy Gambit. Stay focused and isolate the objection. "Is that the only thing that's bothering you?" Then go to Higher Authority and Good Guy/Bad Guy: "Let's get something in writing, and I'll take it to my people and see what I can do for you with them." Then turn the tables: "We may be able to accelerate the shipment, but it's going to increase the non-recurring engineering charges."

Key Points to Remember

1. Watch for issues that the other side declares important.
2. They may be creating a decoy that they will try to trade off later for something they really care about.
3. Don't be thrown off if they appear to be offended by a minor slight.
4. Watch out for people who lure you away from the real issue with the Decoy Gambit. Stay focused and isolate the objection.

Chapter 20

The Red Herring

The Red Herring Gambit is a further twist on the Decoy Gambit. With the Decoy, the other person raises a phony issue to get concessions on a real issue. With the Red Herring, the other person makes a phony demand that he will withdraw, but only in exchange for a concession. If the Red Herring distracts you, it'll deceive you into thinking that it's of major concern to the other side when it may not be. Red Herring is an English fox-hunting expression. England has many vocal animal-rights activists, and their prime target has been fox hunting, a sport Oscar Wilde called "the unspeakable in pursuit of the uneatable."

Herrings that have been dried and salted turn dark red, like smoked salmon. The English call such red herrings "bloaters." Opponents of fox hunting found that if they dragged a bloater across the path of the hunt, its smell would mask the trail of the fox and confuse the dogs. When it happens, the hunt master will cry, "Those blighters have faulted my hounds." The phrase *red herring* became part of the English language and came to mean the raising of an issue that would divert and confuse opponents.

How the North Koreans Used the Red Herring

The classic example of the use of a red herring came during the Korean War armistice talks. Very early in the talks, the parties concerned agreed that officials of three neutral countries, along with their own national negotiators, would represent each side at the table. The South Korean side selected the countries Norway, Sweden, and Switzerland as their three neutral negotiators. The North Koreans chose Poland and Czechoslovakia, but couldn't seem to choose a third. They suggested that the talks start, and they would identify a third country later.

What they were really doing was leaving an opening for the Red Herring Gambit. When the time came and they had set the stage, they announced their selection for the third country: the Soviet Union. The international outcry was unanimous: "The Soviet Union? Now wait a minute. The Soviet Union isn't a neutral country."

The North Koreans responded by saying that the Soviets were not directly involved in the conflict, and there was no reason for them to be considered biased.

They waged the battle of the Red (pardon the pun) Herring for quite a while, until the situation became absurd. What the North Koreans were using, beside the Red Herring Gambit, was a repetitive tactic that children everywhere understand.

"Dad," says Junior, "may I go to the movies tonight?"

Filled with paternal authority, the father says, "No, Son. I don't want you going to the movies tonight."

Junior pleads, "Why not, Dad?"

"Because you went to a movie last week."

"I know that, but why can't I go tonight?"

The father says, "I don't want you going to the movies so much."

"Why not, Dad? I don't understand."

By the time the father has repeated himself 10 or 12 times, he's forgotten why he was making such a big deal about Junior going to the movie in the first place. His reasoning seems to have lost validity, and he begins to think of himself as making a mountain out of a molehill.

That was the tactic the North Koreans were using to support their Red Herring Gambit. They continued to insist that they couldn't understand what the objection was to using the Soviet Union as a neutral third party, until the objections of the South Koreans seemed as ludicrous as the demands of the North Koreans. The negotiations had stalemated.

Just as it seemed that the pointless arguing would continue forever, the North Koreans announced that they would abandon their insistence on having the Soviets at the negotiating table, but they expected a reciprocal concession.

Both sides had agreed earlier that during the negotiations, neither side would rebuild their airstrips. The North Koreans realized later that this left them at a severe disadvantage because the United States could fly planes off aircraft carriers, but North Korea needed their runways. The North Koreans decided that it was time to use the Red Herring Gambit and suggested the Soviet Union as the third neutral country. Now it was time to name the price: They would concede and choose a different country to represent them, but only if the South Koreans would waive the restriction on rebuilding the airfields.

The North Koreans never thought that we would permit the Soviet Union to be part of the negotiations. However, they were able to magically create a bargaining issue out of thin air and then trade it off later for an issue about which they really cared.

Key Points to Remember

1. Be alert to the other side using a Red Herring on you.
2. They may be creating an issue that they will try to trade off later.
3. Keep your eye on the real negotiating issues and don't let them link the Red Herring to a concession you're reluctant to make.

Chapter 21

Cherry Picking

Cherry Picking is a Gambit a buyer can use against a seller with devastating effect, unless the seller is a Power Negotiator and knows his or her options. Imagine that you're getting bids from contractors on a remodeling job at your house. It involves adding a second story office over your garage. You ask three contractors to submit bids and ask each of them to break down their bids by component.

Contractor "A" Bids		Contractor "B" Bids		Contractor "C" Bids	
Framing:	$19,200	Framing:	$17,200	Framing:	$18,400
Flooring:	$2,400	Flooring:	$2,900	Flooring:	$2,800
Roofing:	$6,300	Roofing:	$6,800	Roofing:	$7,300
Carpentry:	$4,300	Carpentry:	$4,100	Carpentry:	$4,100
Carpeting:	$1,750	Carpeting:	$1,950	Carpeting:	$1,950
Plumbing:	$1,800	Plumbing:	$1,600	Plumbing:	$1,600
Painting:	$1,100	Painting:	$1,500	Painting:	$1,300
Total	$36,850	Total	$36,050	Total	$37,650

Which bid should you take? Contractor "A" at $36,850, contractor "B" at $36,050, or contractor "C" at $37,650? If the choice is obvious to you, you are probably obsessed with price. If the workmanship, reliability, start date, completion date, and quality of materials and subcontractors used were of no importance to you, then you'd obviously choose contractor "B." However, there is much more than price for you to consider and the best bid for you may be the highest.

A Cherry Picker can do better than that. He or she would go to Contractor "B" and say, "You are close on your bid, but you're high on flooring by $500 and carpentry by $200. If you'll match contractor "A" on those two items, I'll give you the job." This would cause the general contractor to go back to his flooring and carpentry sub-contractors and get them to rework their bids. You can understand why contractors don't like to break down their bids into components.

You could also Cherry Pick on the terms of a proposal. Let's say that you're buying a piece of land in the country, and the seller is offering it for $100,000 with 20 percent down and the balance due over 10 years with 10 percent interest added. You might ask the owner to quote his or her lowest price for an all-cash deal. He or she might agree to $90,000 for all cash. Then you ask what the lowest interest rate would be for a 50-percent-down transaction. The owner quotes you 7 percent. Then you Cherry Pick the best features of both components of the deal and offer $90,000 with 20 percent down and the balance carried by the owner with 7 percent interest added.

Buyers Love Cherry Picking—Sellers Hate It

There's no question that information is the key to effective Cherry Picking and it takes time. However, if you're thinking of acquiring a new piece of equipment for your company, you should shop around and accumulate information before making a decision. Call up and have other companies' salespeople come in and make a presentation to you. You'll find that one has a good point in a certain area, another has a low price, and a third has a good guarantee. From all these interviews, you piece together the ideal piece of equipment.

Then you go back to the one you like best and say, "I'd like to buy your equipment except, that I want to get the longer guarantee. Or I want to get the faster shipping." In this way, you create the type of deal and the kind of contract that you want. Buyers should push for itemized contracts, whereas sellers should avoid them. Because to me Cherry Picking is an unethical Gambit, the perpetrator is less likely to do it to someone he knows and trusts than he is to a comparative stranger. Sellers can forestall this tactic by building a personal relationship with the buyer.

Another way to handle people who want to Cherry Pick you is to forestall the Gambit. Let's say that you're a contractor who is trying to sell a remodeling job to a homeowner, and you know she's going to talk to all the other contractors in town. How do you forestall it? The answer is to know more about your competition than they'll ever learn. The homeowner says, "I want to check with some other people before I make my final decision."

You respond, "I absolutely agree with you." Always agree up front, right? Salespeople should always agree with any objection however ridiculous it is and then work to turn it around. "I absolutely agree with you. You should check with other companies before you make a decision. But look, let me save you some time. Have you talked to Ted Smith over at ABC Construction? He uses XYZ cabinets that have this feature, this feature, and this feature; but they don't have this. Then if you talk to the national department store company down at the mall, the salesperson who'll come out will be Fred Harrison, and he'll tell you about model number such and such...."

By the time you've gone through letting her know how much you know about the competition, she's going to think, "Why on Earth do I need to waste my time talking to all these other people, when this person knows more than I'll ever learn?"

To defend yourself against Cherry Picking, always consider the alternatives of the other side before making a concession. The fewer alternatives the other side has, the more power you have. If you, as a seller, refuse to budge on your price, then you force the buyer to pay more from another supplier or use multiple suppliers. In the case of the home remodeling job, this would mean that the homeowner would have to bypass you as the general contractor and contract with each subcontractor separately. This may require more knowledge or expertise than the other side possesses, or may create extra work and pressure that are not worth the savings.

Key Points to Remember

1. If you're the buyer, get itemized breakdowns of bids.
2. Try to get them to match the lowest price on each item.
3. If you're the seller, learn so much about your competitors that the buyer doesn't want to waste time talking to them.
4. Also calculate the alternatives available to the other side. You have power in a negotiation when you have more alternatives available to you than they do.

Chapter 22

The Deliberate Mistake

The Deliberate Mistake is a very unethical tactic, and, as with any con job, it requires a victim who also lacks ethics. The seller baits the hook when she prepares a proposal and deliberately leaves out or under-prices one of the elements. This could be the car salesperson who runs a tape on the cost of the car, but includes only the price of a CD player, when the car also has an MP3 auxiliary jack. If the buyer takes the bait, he starts thinking that he now has an opportunity to put one over on the car salesperson. He becomes eager to close the deal before the salesperson spots the mistake. This eagerness makes the buyer a sloppy negotiator, and he may end up paying more for the car than if he had pointed out the mistake. Apart from that, the salesperson still has the option of "discovering" the mistake before the buyer consummates the sale and, with an accusing look, shames the buyer into paying the extra amount.

The Counter Gambit may sound high-minded, but it's obvious: Never try to get away with anything. If your greed doesn't cost you at that moment, it will certainly catch up with you later on down life's road. Instead, point out the mistake and say, "I assume that you're not charging me for the MP3 jack because you're trying to get me to make a decision now?"

A variation of the Deliberate Mistake is the Erroneous Conclusion close. Using this method, the salesperson asks a question of the buyer, but deliberately draws an erroneous conclusion. When the buyer corrects the salesperson, she finds that she has made a commitment to buy. For example, the car salesperson says, "If you did decide today, you wouldn't need to take delivery today, would you?" The buyer responds, "Well, of course we'd want to take it today."

The real estate salesperson says, "You wouldn't want the sellers to include the refrigerator, would you?" The buyers hadn't been thinking of doing that, but the refrigerator looks better than theirs does so they reply, "Do you think they would include it?" The salesperson responds with, "Let's include it in our offer and see what happens."

The boat salesperson says, "You wouldn't expect us to include a GPS, would you?" The buyer sees an opportunity to get something for nothing and responds, "I sure would."

Chapter 23

The Default

The Default Gambit is one that involves a unilateral assumption that obviously works to the advantage of the side proposing it, such as the company that sends a payment check to a vendor after having deducted 2 1/2 percent. Attached is a note that says, "All of our other vendors discount for payment within 15 days, so we assume you will, too." Or the salesperson who writes a potential buyer, "Because I haven't heard from you on your choice of options, I will ship the deluxe model, unless I hear from you within 10 days."

The Default Gambit preys on busy or lazy people; it assumes that rather than take action, the other side will take the easy way out and let you get away with it. Once you have failed to respond, the law of precedent comes into play. When you finally do object the perpetrator is able to say, "But you've never had a problem with it in the past."

As with all unethical Gambits, call the other side on it, and gently explain that you expect to see a higher level of ethics from them in the future. You might e-mail them to say, for example, "I'm disappointed that you deducted 2 1/2 percent from this invoice when that is not what we had agreed to. Please remit balance by return mail."

Chapter 24

Escalation

I once knew a man who became very wealthy after he sold his real estate franchise to a large corporation. He had been one of the original purchasers of a territory when real estate franchising was new, and the founder of the company was running around the country trying to sign up anyone who believed in his concept.

Many years later, a huge New York corporation had bought the master franchise and was starting to buy back the territorial franchises. After attending one of my *Secrets of Power Negotiating* seminars, he asked me to join him for a drink and asked me, "Roger, have you ever heard voices speak to you when you're negotiating?" Not wanting to admit it if I had, I asked him what he was talking about. He told me that after he had agreed to sell his territorial franchise to the new corporate owners for what he first thought was a huge amount of money, he started to have second thoughts.

Because his was the first franchise the corporation was buying back, they flew him to New York for a signing ceremony to be followed by a press conference at which they would announce the corporation's plans to buy back all the franchises. "The night before the ceremony, I had trouble sleeping," he told me. "I lay on my bed wondering whether I was doing the right thing. Suddenly, I heard a voice talking to me."

"What was it saying?" I asked him, half expecting a humorous punch line.

"It said, 'Joey, you're not getting enough money.' The next morning, I went down and asked for another half million dollars, and got it."

Joey was describing a classic case of escalation—raising demands after both sides reached agreement. Of course it's outrageous and unethical, but just as Joey thought he heard voices telling him to do it rather than accept responsibility for his actions, the perpetrators don't see any harm in cutting the best deal by any means possible.

Why is anyone ever allowed to get away with such outrageous behavior? Too often, the other side swallows its pride and concedes just as easily as that corporation conceded the extra half million. In that case, the corporation paid rather than face the humiliation of having to call off the press conference. In other cases, the other side has simply become too emotionally involved in the purchase to back out.

The history of big business is full of stories of people who extorted a little more out of a deal simply because they had enough leverage to do so. Frankly, I have mixed emotions about how to respond. My heart tells me that if people do that, you should call their bluff and walk away from the deal on principle. However, I also believe in keeping emotions out of a negotiation. If that New York corporation was able to pay the extra half million and still have it be a good deal (and it was still a very good deal), then they were right to swallow their pride and pay the money.

Integrity at Any Price

Fortunately, the history of big business is also full of stories of people who would not sell their integrity at any price, such as the rancher who shook hands on a deal to sell his land in Orlando. Later that day, the *Orlando Sentinel* broke the news that Walt Disney was secretly buying up all the land to create Walt Disney World. The rancher could have held out and made millions more, but his sense of integrity stopped him from doing it.

When Henry Hollis sold the Palmer House hotel in Chicago to Conrad Hilton, he shook hands on Hilton's first offer of $19,385,000. Within a week, he received offers of more than a million dollars above that, but he never wavered on his word. As Hilton said in his autobiography, "I have done business with a great many men in my time. I do not think I have ever had a greater experience than dealing with this perfect gentleman. I felt throughout that I was watching a master in the greatest traditions of American business."

There are some responses to escalation other than swallowing your pride or walking away. You might try these:

- Protect yourself with Higher Authority (see Chapter 7). Tell them that their suggestion does not offend you, but that your board of directors will never renegotiate a deal once it has been made, and they will force you to walk away. Then

Position for Easy Acceptance (see Chapter 18) by telling them that, although you cannot budge on the price, you might be able to offer them something of value in another area.

- Escalate your demands in return. Tell them that you are glad that they want to reopen the negotiations because your side has been having second thoughts also. Of course, you would never renege on a deal, but, because they have chosen to negate the original proposal, your price has now gone up also.

It is better to avoid Escalation than to have to deal with it. Avoid it by using these techniques: Tie up all the details up front. Don't leave anything to "we can work that out later." Unresolved issues invite Escalation. Build personal relationships with the other parties that make it harder for them to be ruthless. Get large deposits so that it's harder for them to back out. Build win-win negotiations so that they don't want to back out.

Chapter 25

Planted Information

Returning from a speaking engagement, I was discussing the presidential press conference with my seatmate. "I don't believe he's telling the truth," he told me. "I met a man who knew someone who works at the White House, and he told me the president did know all about it all along. He's covering something up." What amazed me about this was I found myself believing what this man was telling me, rather than believing what I had earlier heard the president of the United States say at the press conference. Why? Because we tend to believe information we have obtained surreptitiously.

Planted Information can be an astoundingly powerful influencer. A salesman is making an impressive presentation to a board of directors. Flip charts and audio visual aids surround him. He is fervently making a plea that they go with his company because it offers the best value in the marketplace. He believes that no competitor can undercut his prices, and feels confident that he can close the sale at his asking price of $820,000—until he sees one of the directors pass a note to another director who nods and lays the note on the table in front of him.

Curiosity gets the better of the salesman. He has to see what's on that note. He finishes his presentation, then approaches the table and dramatically leans toward them. "Gentlemen, do you have any questions?" Out of the corner of his eye, he can now see the note. Even reading upside down, he can see that it says, "Universal's price is $762,000. Let's go with them."

The chairman of the board says, "I do have one question. Your price seems high. We're obligated to go with the lowest price that meets our specifications. Is $820,000 the best you can do?" Within minutes, the salesman has lowered his price by $58,000.

Was the note real or was it Planted Information? Although it was just an unsubstantiated note scrawled on a piece of paper, the salesperson believed it because he obtained the information surreptitiously. Even if they had planted it, could the salesperson cry foul later? No, because they didn't tell him that the competition's bid was $762,000. He obtained the information surreptitiously, and he must accept responsibility for his assumptions.

Simply knowing about planted information will help you to diffuse this unethical tactic. Any time that you are negotiating only based on information that the other side has chosen to tell you, you are extremely vulnerable to manipulation. When the other side may have planted the information for you to discover, you should be even more vigilant.

Negotiating Principles

Chapter 26

Get the Other Side to Commit First

Power Negotiators know you're usually better off if you can get the other side to commit to a position first. Several reasons are obvious:

- Their first offer may be much better than you expected.
- It gives you information about them before you have to tell them anything.
- It enables you to bracket their proposal (see Chapter 1). If they state a price first, you can bracket them, so if you end up splitting the difference, you'll get what you want. If they can get you to commit first, they can then bracket your proposal. Then if you end up splitting the difference, they get what they wanted.

To a neophyte negotiator, this may sound all wrong. Let's say that you have a neighbor who has a motorboat parked in his driveway. He's lived there for five years, and you can't recall him ever taking it out on the lake. If you can get it for a good price, you'd consider buying it. Asking him how much he wants for his boat may seem like a bad idea. What if he gets the impression he has a live one on his hands and deliberately inflates the price? Let's say a fair price is $10,000, but you're hoping to steal it for $5,000.

When you approach him, he gets greedy and says, "That boat is in brand-new condition. I haven't even taken the cover off it in five years. I wouldn't take a penny less than $15,000." You could argue that, in letting him state his price first, you have expanded the negotiating range and made it harder for you to reach your goal. You can't even bracket that range. If he wants $15,000 and you're willing to pay only $5,000, you'd have to ask him to pay you $5,000 to take it off your hands to accurately bracket. If it seems that getting him to go first was a mistake, you're forgetting that you can do several things to get him to modify that opening offer without having to state your offer first. You can use these approaches:

- Plead poor. "Mike, I don't think for a moment that I can afford to buy your boat from you, but I did notice that you never use it, and I thought you might just want to sell it to me at a giveaway price."
- Apply the pressure of Higher Authority. "Mike, my wife is going to kill me for even asking you this, but…."
- Use the power of competition. "Mike, I've been looking at a boat similar to yours that seems like a real bargain, but before I go ahead I thought I'd see what you would want for yours." By using these approaches, you modify Mike's aspirations without having to commit to a position. The less you know about the other side or the proposition that you're negotiating, the more important the principle of not going first becomes.

How the Beatles Went First and Lost Millions

If the Beatles' manager Brian Epstein had understood this principle, he could have made the Fab Four millions more on their first movie. United Artists wanted to cash in on the popularity of the singing group, but was reluctant to go out on a limb because the studio didn't know how long the Beatles would be popular. They could have been a fleeting success that fizzled out before their movie hit the screens. They planned it as an inexpensively made exploitation movie, and budgeted only $300,000 to make it. This was clearly not enough to pay the Beatles a high salary, so United Artists planned to offer the Beatles as much as 25 percent of the profits. The Beatles were such a worldwide sensation in 1963 that the producer was very reluctant to ask them to name their price first, but he had the courage to stay with the rule. He offered Epstein $25,000 up front and asked him what percentage of the profits he thought would be fair.

Brian Epstein didn't know the movie business and should have been smart enough to play Reluctant Buyer (see Chapter 5) and use Good Guy/Bad Guy (see Chapter 14). He should have said, "I don't think they'd be interested in taking the time to make a movie, but if you'll give me your very best offer, I'll take it to them and see what I can do for you with them." Instead, his ego wouldn't let him play dumb (see Chapter 27), so he assertively stated that they would have to get 7.5 percent of the profits or they wouldn't do it. This slight tactical error cost the group millions when director Richard Lester, to every one's surprise, created *A Hard Day's Night,* a brilliantly humorous portrait of a day in the group's life, became a worldwide success.

If both sides have learned that they shouldn't go first, you can't sit there forever with both sides refusing to put a number on the table, but as a rule, you should always find out what the other side wants to do first.

Apart from price, you're always better off to have the other person bring a proposal to you than you are to take one to them. Some crafty negotiators go to incredible lengths to make it look as though the other side approached them when the reverse was true. Movie producer Sam Goldwyn once wanted to borrow a contract actor from Darryl Zanuck, but couldn't reach Zanuck because he was in a meeting. After many tries to reach Zanuck, an exasperated Goldwyn finally insisted that the call be put through. When Darryl Zanuck finally picked up the phone, Sam Goldwyn, who had initiated the call, blithely said, "Darryl, what can I do for you today?"

Lewis Kravitz, an Atlanta executive coach and former outplacement counselor, counsels patience and knowing when not to speak. He tells of a young man he coached who had just been sacked and said he was willing to take a $2,000 pay cut to $28,000 on his next job. But Kravitz coached him to let the prospective employer make the first move. In this case, the interviewer offered $32,000, stunning the overjoyed job-seeker into momentary silence, which the interviewer interpreted as dissatisfaction. He upped the offer to $34,000. "In negotiating, he who speaks first generally comes out on the short end of the stick," he says.

Key Points to Remember

1. You are at a disadvantage if you have to state your price first.
2. Don't let that stop you from trying to modify their opening negotiating position. ("It would have to be a giveaway price but we might be interested," or "We've already turned down an offer for $10,000.")

Chapter 27

Acting Dumb Is Smart

To Power Negotiators, smart is dumb and dumb is smart. When you are negotiating, you're better off acting as if you know less than everybody else does, not more. The dumber you act, the better off you are, unless your I.Q. sinks to a point where you lack any credibility.

There is a good reason for this. With a few rare exceptions, human beings tend to help people that they see as less intelligent or informed, rather than taking advantage of them. Of course, there are a few ruthless people out there who will try to take advantage of weak people, but most people want to compete with people they see as brighter, and help people they see as less bright. The reason for acting dumb is that it diffuses the competitive spirit of the other side. How can you fight with someone who is asking you to help them negotiate with you? How can you carry on any type of competitive banter with a person who says, "I don't know. What do you think?" Most people, when faced with this situation, feel sorry for the other person, and go out of their way to help him or her.

Do you remember the TV show *Columbo*? Peter Falk played a detective who walked around in an old raincoat and a mental fog, chewing on an old cigar butt. He constantly wore an expression that suggested he had just misplaced something and couldn't remember what it was, let alone where he had left it. In fact, his success was directly attributable to how smart he was—by acting dumb. His demeanor was so disarming that the murderers came close to wanting him to solve his cases because he appeared to be so helpless. The negotiators who let their egos take control of them and come across as a sophisticated negotiator commit to things that work against them in a negotiation. These include being the following:

- A fast decision-maker who doesn't need time to think things over.

- Someone who would not have to check with anyone else before going ahead.
- Someone who doesn't have to consult with experts before committing.
- Someone who wouldn't stoop to pleading for a concession.
- Someone who would never be overridden by a supervisor.
- Someone who doesn't have to keep notes about the progress of the negotiation and refer to them frequently.

The Power Negotiator who understands the importance of acting dumb retains these options:

- Requesting time to think it over so he or she can thoroughly think through the dangers of accepting, or the opportunities that making additional demands might bring.
- Deferring a decision while he or she checks with a committee or board of directors.
- Asking for time to let legal or technical experts review the proposal.
- Pleading for additional concessions.
- Using Good Guy/Bad Guy to put pressure on the other side without confrontation.
- Taking time to think under the guise of reviewing notes about the negotiation.

I act dumb by asking for the definitions of words. If the other side says to me, "Roger, I can't believe your hubris in proposing this," I respond with, "Hubris…hubris…hmmm. You know, I've heard that word before, but I'm not quite sure what it means. Would you mind explaining it to me?" Or I might say, "Do you mind going over those figures one more time? I know you've done it a couple of times already, but for some reason, I'm not getting it. Do you mind?" This makes them think: "What a klutz I've got on my hands this time." In this way, I lay to rest the competitive spirit that could have made a compromise very difficult for me to accomplish. Now the other side stops fighting me and starts trying to help me.

Be careful you're not acting dumb in your area of expertise. If you're a heart surgeon, don't say, "I'm not sure if you need a triple bypass or if a double will do." If you're an architect, don't say, "I don't know if this building will stand up or not." Win-win negotiating depends on the willingness of each side to be empathetic to the other side's position. That's not going to happen if both sides continue to compete with one another. Negotiators know that acting dumb diffuses that competitive spirit and opens the door to win-win solutions.

☑ Key Points to Remember

1. Acting dumb diffuses the other side's competitive spirit.
2. Acting dumb encourages them to help you.
3. Ask for definitions of words.
4. Ask them to explain something again.
5. Don't act dumb in your area of expertise.

Chapter 28

Don't Let the Other Side Write the Contract

In a typical negotiation, you verbally negotiate the details, then put it into writing later for both parties to review and approve. I've yet to run across a situation where we covered every detail in the verbal part of the negotiation. There are always points that we overlooked when we were verbally negotiating that we must detail in writing.

Then we have to get the other side to approve or negotiate the points when we sit down to sign the written agreement—that's when the side that writes the contract has a tremendous advantage over the side that doesn't. Chances are that the person writing the agreement will think of at least half a dozen things that did not come up during the verbal negotiations. That person can then write the clarification of that point to his or her advantage, leaving the other side to negotiate a change in the agreement when asked to sign it.

Don't let the other side write the contract, because it puts you at a disadvantage. This applies to brief counter-proposals just as much as it does to agreements that are hundreds of pages long. For example, a real estate agent may be presenting an offer to the sellers of a four-unit apartment building. The seller agrees to the general terms of the offer, but wants the price to be $5,000 higher. At that point, either the listing agent who represents the seller or the selling agent who represents the buyer, could pull a counter-proposal form out of his or her briefcase. They could write out a brief counter-offer for the seller to sign that the selling agent will present to the buyer for approval. It doesn't have to be complicated: "Offer accepted, except that price is to be $598,000" will suffice.

If the listing agent writes the counter-offer, however, he or she might think of some things that would benefit her seller. She might write, "Offer accepted except that price to be $598,000. Additional $5,000 to be deposited in escrow upon acceptance. Counter-offer to be accepted upon presentation and within 24 hours."

If the selling agent were to write the counter-offer, he might write, "Offer accepted, except that price is to be $598,000. Additional $5,000 to be added to the note that the seller is carrying back."

These additions are probably not big enough to be challenged by either a seller or a buyer who is eager to complete the transaction; however, they substantially benefit the side who wrote the brief counter-offer. If the person who writes a one-paragraph counter-offer can affect it so much, think how much that person could affect a multi-page contract.

Remember that this may not just be a matter of taking advantage of the other side. Both sides may genuinely think that they had reached agreement on a point, whereas their interpretations may be substantially different when they write it out.

If you are to be the one writing the contract, it's a good idea to keep notes throughout the negotiation and put a check in the margin against any point that will be part of the final agreement. This does the following:

- It reminds you to include all the points that you wanted.
- When you write the contract, you may be reluctant to include a point in the agreement unless you can specifically recall the other side agreeing to it.

Your notes will give you the confidence to include it, even if you don't remember it clearly.

If you have been team negotiating, be sure to have all the other members of your team review the contract before you present it to the other side. You may have overlooked a point that you should have included, or you may have misinterpreted a point. It's common for the lead negotiator to let her enthusiasm overwhelm her to a point that she feels that the other side agreed to something when it was less than clear to more independent observers.

I'm not a big believer in having attorneys conduct a negotiation for you because so few of them are good negotiators. They tend to be confrontational negotiators because they're used to threatening the other side into submission, and they are seldom open to creative solutions because their first obligation is to keep you out of trouble, not make you money. Remember that in law school they are not taught how to make deals, only how to break deals.

In our litigious society, there isn't much point in making an agreement that won't hold up in court, however, so it's a good idea to have the agreement approved by your attorney before you have it signed. In a complicated agreement, what you prepare and have the other side sign may be no more than a letter of intent. Have the attorneys work on it later to make it a legal document. It's better that you devote your energy to reaching an agreement.

If you have prepared an agreement that you think the other side may be reluctant to sign, you may be smart to include the expression *Subject to your attorney's approval*, to encourage them to sign it.

Once the verbal negotiations are over, get a memorandum of agreement signed as quickly as possible. The longer you give them before they see it in writing, the greater the possibility that they'll forget what they agreed to and question what you've prepared.

Also, make sure they understand the agreement. Don't be tempted to have them sign something when you know they're not clear on the implications. If they don't understand and something goes wrong, they will always blame you. They will never accept responsibility.

Also be aware of a legal technicality. The side that writes the contract is responsible for creating a contract free of ambiguities. If you ever end up in court over a contract conflict, the judge will rule against the side that created the contract if the conflict has been caused by ambiguity in the contract.

I find it helpful to write out the agreement I want before I go into the negotiations. I don't show it to the other side, but I find it helpful to compare it to the agreement that we eventually reach, so that I can see how well I did. Sometimes it's easy to get excited because the other side is making concessions that you didn't expect to get. Then your enthusiasm carries you forward, and you agree to what you feel is a fantastic deal. It may be a good deal, but unless you have clearly established your criteria up front, it may not be the deal that you hoped to get.

☑ Key Points to Remember

1. Being the one to write the contract is a big advantage.
2. When you start to write out a verbal agreement, you will think of all kinds of things that you didn't think of when you were verbally negotiating.
3. Keep precise notes during the negotiation so that you can be sure to include everything in the written agreement.
4. Have your other negotiating team members go over your written notes to be sure you didn't leave anything out.
5. Consider preparing the agreement before you start negotiating so that you can compare your objectives to the final agreement.

Chapter 29

Read the Contract Every Time

In this age of computer-generated contracts, it's a sad fact that you have to read over a contract every time it comes across your desk. In the old days, when contracts were typewritten, both sides would go through it and write in any changes, and then each negotiator would initial the change. You could glance through the contract and quickly review any change that you had made or to which you had agreed. Nowadays, with computer-generated contracts, we're more likely to go back to the computer, make the change, and print out a new contract.

Here's the danger. You may have refused to sign a clause in a contract. The other side agrees to change it and says they'll send you a corrected contract for your signature. When it comes across your desk, you're busy, so you quickly review it to see that they made the change you wanted, and then turn to the back page and sign it. Unfortunately, because you didn't take the time to read over the entire contract, you didn't realize that they had also changed something else. Perhaps it was something blatant such as changing "F.O.B. factory" to "F.O.B. job site." Or it may be such a minor change in wording that you don't discover it until years later when something goes wrong, and you need the contract to enforce some action. By then, you may not even remember what you agreed to, and you can only assume that, because you signed it, you must have agreed to it.

I used to think that this would be a rare occurrence—that the other side would victimize you by secretly changing some other part of a contract. Then I started asking the people at my seminars if they had run into it. A surprising 20 percent said that yes, they had been victimized by this unethical conduct.

Some contracts can be dozens of pages long, so here are some tips on how to do this more easily:

- Hold the two contracts up to the light to see if they match.
- Scan the new contract into your computer and use your word-processing software to compare the two.
- Use a word processing program such as Microsoft Word that keeps track of all the changes. You can print out the final version, but you can always look to see the changes that have been made along the way. This is especially valuable if you're in extended negotiations where the contract is going back and forth by disk or e-mail.

Yes, I agree with you: You have a wonderful case for a lawsuit that the other side defrauded you—but why expose yourself to that kind of trouble? In this age of computer-generated contracts, you should read the contract all the way through, before you sign it.

Chapter 30

Funny Money

There are all kinds of ways to describe the price of something. If you went to the Boeing Aircraft Company and asked them what it costs to fly a 747 coast to coast, they wouldn't tell you "$52,000 dollars." They would tell you 11 cents per passenger mile. Salespeople call that breaking it down to the ridiculous. Haven't we all had a real estate salesperson say to us, "Do you realize you're talking 35 cents a day here? You're not going to let 35 cents a day stand between you and your dream home are you?" It probably didn't occur to you that 35 cents a day, over the 30-year life of a real estate mortgage, is more than $7,000. To protect themselves, Power Negotiators always think in real money terms.

When that supplier tells you about a five-cent increase on an item, it may not seem important enough to spend much time on—until you start thinking of how many of those items you buy during a year. Then you find that there's enough money sitting on the table to make it well worth your while to do some Power Negotiating.

Breaking it Down to the Ridiculous in Bed

I once dated a woman who had expensive tastes. She took me to a linen store in Newport Beach to buy a set of sheets. They were beautiful sheets, but when I found out that they were $1,400, I was astonished and told the sales clerk that it was the kind of opulence that caused the peasants to storm the palace gates.

She calmly looked at me and said, "Sir, I don't think you understand. A fine set of sheets like this will last you at least five years, so you're really talking about only $280 a year." Then she whipped out a pocket calculator and frantically started punching in numbers.

"That's only $5.38 a week. That's not much for what is probably the finest set of sheets in the world."

I said, "That's ridiculous."

Without cracking a smile, she said, "I'm not through. With a fine set of sheets like this, you obviously would never sleep alone, so we're really talking only 38 cents per day, per person." Now that's really breaking it down to the ridiculous.

Here are some other examples of Funny Money:

- Interest rates expressed as a percentage rather than a dollar amount.
- Emphasizing the amount of the monthly payments rather than the true cost of the item.
- Cost per brick, tile, or square foot rather than the total cost.
- An hourly increase in pay per person rather than the annual cost of the increase to the company.
- Insurance premiums as a monthly amount rather than an annual cost.
- The price of land expressed as the monthly payment.

Businesses know that if you're not required to pull real money out of your purse or pocket, you're inclined to spend more. It's why casinos the world over have you convert your real money to gaming chips. It's why restaurants are happy to let you use a credit card although they have to pay a percentage to the credit card company. When I worked for a department store chain, we were constantly pushing our clerks to sign up customers for one of our credit cards, because we knew that credit card customers will spend more and they will also buy better-quality merchandise than a cash customer. Our motivation wasn't entirely financial in pushing credit cards. We also knew that because credit card customers would buy better-quality merchandise, it would satisfy them more, and they would be more pleased with their purchases.

When you're negotiating, break the investment down to the ridiculous because it does sound like less money, but learn to think in real money terms when someone is offering you a price. Don't let people use the Funny Money Gambit on you.

Chapter 31

People Believe What They See in Writing

The printed word has great power over people. Most people believe what they see in writing; even if they won't believe it when they just hear about it. The *Candid Camera* people did a stunt to prove that a number of years back; you may remember seeing it on television. They posted a sign on a road next to a golf course in Delaware that said "Delaware Closed." Allen Funt stood by the sign in a rented trooper's uniform. He wasn't even allowed to speak to the people as they came up, only point up at the sign. What happened amazed me. People were coming to a screeching halt and saying things like "How long is it going to be closed for? My wife and kids are inside." And "Is Jersey still open?"

People believe what they see in writing. That's why I'm such a big believer in presentation binders. When you sit down with someone and you open the presentation binder and it says, "My company is the greatest widget manufacturer in the world." Then you turn another page, and it says, "Our workers are the greatest craftsmen in the business." You turn another page and start showing them reference letters from all your previous jobs. They find it believable even when they know you just came from the print shop with it.

This is how hotels are able to get people to check out of the rooms on time. Holiday Inns used to have a terrible time getting people to check out of their rooms at noon, until they learned the art of the printed word and posted those little signs on the back of the door. Now, 97 percent of guests check out of their rooms on time, without any question at all, because the written word is so believable.

Every chance you get, put things in writing. For example, if you have salespeople selling for you, and you have to put a price change into effect, be sure that they have it in writing. Because there's a world of difference between them sitting with a potential customer and saying, "We're having a price increase at the start of next month, so you should make a commitment now," and them saying, "Look at this letter I just got from my boss. It indicates that we're having a price increase on July 1st." Always show it to people in writing whenever you can. If you're negotiating by telephone, back up what you're saying by also faxing or e-mailing them the information.

If you sell big-ticket items and don't have the software to create proposals, I'd suggest that you stop everything and order the software right now. It'll pay for itself on the first job. Many years ago, I was in Australia on a lecture tour, and a fire broke out on the second floor of my home in California. When I returned I had three contractors bid on repairing the damage. Two of them scrawled out bids by hand. They both bid around $24,000. The third contractor prepared a very comprehensive bid by computer. Every little item was spelled out in detail. But his bid was $49,000, more than twice as much. I accepted the higher bid because the power of the printed word was so great that I just didn't trust the handwritten bids.

What's the bottom line? Because people don't question what they see in writing, you should always present written backup evidence to support your proposal. If the negotiation includes expectations that the other side will meet certain requirements, it also helps to confirm those requirements in writing.

Chapter 32

Concentrate on the Issues

Power Negotiators know that they should always concentrate on the issues and not be distracted by the actions of the other negotiators. Have you ever watched tennis on television and seen a highly emotional star like Serena Williams screaming at a line umpire? You wonder to yourself, "How on Earth can anybody play tennis against somebody like that? It's such a game of concentration; it doesn't seem fair."

The answer is that good tennis players understand that only one thing affects the outcome of the game of tennis. That's the movement of the ball across the net. What the other player is doing doesn't affect the outcome of the game at all, as long as you know what the ball is doing. In that way, tennis players learn to concentrate on the ball, not on the other person.

When you're negotiating, the ball is the movement of the concessions across the negotiating table. It's the only thing that affects the outcome of the game; but it's so easy to get thrown off by what the other people are doing, isn't it?

Losing Perspective in a Large Transaction

I remember once wanting to buy a large real estate project in Signal Hill, California, that comprised 18 four-unit buildings. I knew that I had to get the price far less than the $1.8 million that the sellers were asking for the property, which was owned free and clear by a large group of real estate investors. A real estate agent had brought it to my attention, so I felt obligated to let him present the first offer, reserving the right to go back and negotiate directly with the sellers if he wasn't able to get my $1.2 million offer accepted.

The last thing in the world the agent wanted to do was present an offer at $1.2 million—$600,000 below the asking price—but finally I convinced him to try it, and off he went to present the offer. By doing that, he made a tactical error. He shouldn't have gone to them; he should have had them come to him. You always have more control when you're negotiating in your power base than if you go to their power base. (More about that in Chapter 48 on body language.)

He came back a few hours later, and I asked him, "How did it go?"

"It was awful, just awful. I'm so embarrassed." He told me. "I got into this large conference room, and all of the principals had come in for the reading of the offer. They brought with them their attorney, their CPA, and their real estate broker. I was planning to do the silent close on them. *[That means to read the offer and then be quiet. The next person who talks loses in the negotiations.]* The problem was, there wasn't any silence. I got down to the $1.2 million and they said: 'Wait a minute. You're coming in $600,000 low? We're insulted.' Then they all got up and stormed out of the room."

I said, "Nothing else happened?"

He said, "Well, a couple of the principals stopped in the doorway on their way out, and they said, 'We're not going to come down to a penny less than $1.5 million.' It was just awful. Please don't ever ask me to present an offer that low again."

I said, "Wait a minute. You mean to tell me that, in five minutes, you got them to come down $300,000, and you feel bad about the way the negotiations went?"

See how easy it is to be thrown off by what the other people are doing, rather than concentrating on the issues in a negotiation? It's inconceivable that a full-time professional negotiator—say, an international negotiator—would walk out of negotiations because he doesn't think the other people are fair. He may walk out, but it's a specific negotiating tactic, not because he's upset.

Can you imagine a top arms negotiator showing up in the White House and the president saying, "What are you doing here? I thought you were in Geneva negotiating with the Russians."

"Well, yes, I was, Mr. President, but those guys are so unfair. You can't trust them and they never keep their commitments. I got so upset, that I just walked out." Power Negotiators don't do that. They concentrate on the issues, not on the personalities. You should always be thinking, "Where are we now, compared to where we were an hour ago or yesterday or last week?"

Former Secretary of State Warren Christopher said, "It's okay to get upset when you're negotiating, as long as you're in control, and you're doing it as a specific negotiating tactic." It's when you're upset and out of control that you always lose.

That's why salespeople will have this happen to them. They lose an account. They take it in to their sales manager, and they say, "Well, we lost this one. Don't waste any time trying to save it. I did everything I could. If anybody could have saved it, I would have saved it."

The sales manager says, "Well, just as a public relations gesture, let me give the other side a call anyway." The sales manager can hold it together, not necessarily because he's any brighter or sharper than the salesperson, but because he hasn't become emotionally involved with the people the way the salesperson has. Don't do that. Learn to concentrate on the issues.

Chapter 33

Always Congratulate the Other Side

However poorly you think the other person may have done in the negotiations, you should always congratulate the other side when you're through negotiating, Say, "Wow—did you do a fantastic job negotiating that. I realize that I didn't get as good a deal as I could have, but frankly, it was worth it because I learned so much about negotiating. You were brilliant." You want the other person to feel that he or she won in the negotiations.

When I published an earlier book on negotiating, a newspaper reviewed it and took exception to my saying that you should always congratulate, saying that it was clearly manipulative to congratulate the other side when you didn't really think that they had won. I disagree. I look upon it as the ultimate in courtesy for the conqueror to congratulate the vanquished.

When the British sent a task force down the Atlantic to recapture the Falkland Islands from the Argentineans, it was quite a rout. Within a few days, the Argentine navy lost most of its ships, and the victory for the English was absolute. The evening after the Argentinean admiral surrendered, the English admiral invited him on board to dine with his officers and congratulated him on a splendid campaign.

Power Negotiators always want the other parties thinking that they won in the negotiations. It starts by asking for more than you expect to get. It continues through all of the other Gambits that are designed to service the perception that they're winning. It ends with congratulating the other side.

Section Two

Resolving Tough Negotiating Problems

This section will show you what to do when the going gets rough. In earlier chapters, you learned how to:

- Handle impasses—by setting aside the major issue and creating momentum on minor issues first. (See Chapter 10.)
- Handle stalemates—by changing the dynamics of the negotiation. (See Chapter 11.)
- Handle deadlocks—by bringing in a mediator or an arbitrator. (See Chapter 12.)

In this section you'll learn the difference between mediation and arbitration. You'll learn how to set up and conduct a mediation or an arbitration. Finally, you will learn the fine art of conflict resolution. How do those hostage negotiators resolve those life-threatening conflicts?

Chapter 34

The Art of Mediation

As I explained in Chapter 12, there is only one way to resolve a deadlock, and that's to bring in a third party as a mediator or an arbitrator. A deadlock is "when both sides are so frustrated with the lack of progress, they see no point in talking to each other any more." The UPS strike in the late 1990s got to that stage. Neither side would schedule another meeting because it wasn't getting them anywhere. Secretary of Labor Alexis Herman became a mediator, and was able to get them to compromise and resolve their differences. (Maybe I went too far there, but she did get them to sign a new labor contract, at least.)

There are major differences between mediation and arbitration, and it's important not to confuse the two. Mediators do not have the power to make a judgment or ruling as to who is right and who is wrong. They are there to use their skills to facilitate a solution. Arbitration is when both sides agree up front that they will go along with what the arbitrator thinks is fair. Each party gives him or her the power to make a judgment and impose a solution. I am talking here of binding arbitration; see the following chapter for the differences between binding and nonbinding arbitration.

In mediation, both sides come to the meeting expecting to compromise. They are eager to reach an agreement acceptable to both parties. An agreement is not always reached because both sides have to agree. In arbitration, both sides want to win. They are hoping the arbitrator will see they were right and the other side was wrong. They will present their case as forcefully as they can in the hope of an "award" from the arbitrator. A settlement is always reached, because the arbitrator has the power to force acceptance of the "award."

You can have both mediation and arbitration in the same dispute. For example, when General Motors' employees went on strike in 1997, they and the company mediated a solution. However, they arbitrated just one part of the conflict. Was this a legal strike or not?

The Importance of Mediation

The process of mediation is growing in popularity. It's become less effective for parties to resolve their issues by going to court. By agreeing to mediate a conflict, the parties are freeing up the court system for more important matters. There are many advantages to mediation over litigation. It's less expensive. It's expensive to litigate issues. Unless you can get an attorney to take your case on a contingency basis, meaning the attorney gets nothing if you lose, but a large chunk of your settlement if he wins, expect to spend thousands of dollars before you get to trial. Your attorney will bill you for extensive pretrial discovery that will include taking depositions from everyone even remotely involved, and a great deal of other preparation work.

In addition to being cheaper, it's faster to mediate. It will take months and possibly years before a civil suit comes to trial, and before it does, the judge will insist that you first try to mediate a settlement. It is conceivable to mediate an issue within hours of the parties agreeing to do so. The mediator does not need much time to prepare because to do so may compromise neutrality. His or her preparation is limited to understanding both sides' positions. It is difficult to get a civil suit heard in court. Because of the expense, the long delay, and judges' reluctance to clutter up the court calendar with matters that could be settled by mediation or arbitration, very few civil disputes ever reach a courtroom.

A mediated settlement is not subject to appeal. You can win a settlement in a lawsuit, only to find the award is delayed or even reversed on appeal. The defendant may file bankruptcy to escape paying the settlement. In mediation, both sides agree to the settlement and are more likely to comply with the settlement. It enhances the working relationship of the parties. If both sides have agreed in advance that they will mediate any disputes, they can proceed with confidence that they will never be involved in an ugly lawsuit.

A mediator understands the problem better than a judge. It's common practice to select a mediator who's an expert in the field of the dispute. A real estate specialist would mediate over a building matter. An employment specialist would mediate a labor dispute. The mediator who is a specialist will understand the issues better than a judge. Mediation is less damaging to the relationship of the parties. You can only reach agreement in mediation when both parties agree to the settlement. That's not so in arbitration or civil suits. The parties in mediation can continue their relationship without rancor. All details are confidential. Mediators understand that they may never reveal the details of the mediation, not even years later. All notes taken by the mediator are destroyed. Only the final agreement remains. Lawsuits become matters of public record. Secrecy may be a big advantage to people and companies who do not want it known that they made a mistake, or don't want to reveal that they offered a settlement.

Why Mediation Works

Don't be reluctant to use mediation to resolve a dispute. Don't think, "I don't want to bring my boss into this, because then I'd be admitting that I'm not a good enough negotiator to handle this." It's not that you're bringing in a better negotiator. It's just that there are reasons why mediation works when the original parties cannot agree.

A mediator can go to both sides separately and suggest to each that they take a more reasonable position. (An arbitrator can even force this by telling both sides to bring in a final solution within 24 hours, telling them that he will pick the more reasonable of the two proposals. This forces each side to be more reasonable because they each fear that the other will present a more attractive plan. It becomes, in effect, a closed-bid auction of ideas.)

A mediator listens better to each side because he does not have to filter the information through a prejudiced position. Because he has less at stake, he may well hear something to which an opponent would be deaf. He can persuade better, because both sides perceive him as having less to gain. As I pointed out in my book *Secrets of Power Persuasion,* you lose much of your ability to persuade if the listener sees you as having something to gain. For example, a buyer will believe a salesperson much more readily if he knows that the salesperson is not on commission.

When negotiating directly, you tend to assume that, if the other side floats a trial balloon, that they would be willing to agree to what they're suggesting. A mediator can go to each side and propose a solution without implying that the other side is willing to comply. A mediator can often get both sides back to the negotiating table without having to promise concessions. He or she is often an expert in the field who can bring a fresh perspective to both parties, and will have experience in resolving similar disputes. Apart from the skills that this experience provides, it enables the mediator to bring perspective about what would be a fair and reasonable settlement.

The Mediator Perceived as Neutral Is Important

As I mentioned in Chapter 12, the mediator or arbitrator must be perceived as neutral by both sides. Unless perceived as neutral, he or she can't be effective. For that reason, mediators go to great lengths to service that perception of neutrality. A professional mediator would turn down an assignment if he had done business with one side, but not the other. He would not accept an assignment where one side was a close social acquaintance and not the other. It's not the friendship or the business relationship that is the problem; it's the perception of neutrality. If he were equally friendly with both parties, or had had similar business experiences with both parties, he could still be effective.

Sometimes a mediator starts the process in good faith and then realizes that he knows one of the people involved. He should then explain the situation to both parties and offer to withdraw. If nobody objects, he may continue, but the problem must be addressed. A group of psychologists once did a study to determine the effects of a neutral mediator on the mediation process. One of the things that they investigated was what could be done if the mediator was not perceived as neutral. The answer they came up with was simple common sense when you think about it. A mediator can overcome the perception of favoring one side, by quickly making a concession to the other side. The following story will illustrate how that works in practice.

I once took part in a negotiation of the sale of one company to another. We had two teams of attorneys working, trying to resolve the differences. After weeks of negotiating, we appeared to reach an absolute deadlock. One of the attorneys resolved the deadlock when he was smart enough to say, "This is obviously going to take more time than I thought. I have to be in court this afternoon, but I'll tell you what: My partner, Joe, will be in after lunch to take my place."

While the first attorney was in court that afternoon, Joe came in to take his place. He was completely new to the situation. Each side had to explain where we were in the negotiations. Joe took great pains to position himself as neutral. He did this by saying to his side, "Are we being fair to them in pushing that point? Maybe we could give a little there." That caused the other person to think, "Well, he seems much more reasonable than the last person. Maybe we can find a way past this after all." Having positioned himself as neutral, Joe was able to find common ground in the negotiations that got us past the deadlock. Any time you reach a deadlock in the negotiations, try bringing in a third-party who is perceived as reasonably neutral by the other parties.

Positioning Yourself as Neutral Can Take Years

President Carter was successful in mediating between Israel and Egypt at Camp David in the late 1970s because he was perceived as neutral by both sides. It took years for the United States to position itself as neutral with Egypt. The Egyptian leaders always saw us as the enemy, and the Soviet Union as their friends. Henry Kissinger saw a remarkable opportunity to change that, and he jumped at it. He was in Anwar el Sadat's office at a time when Sadat was trying to get the Soviets to clear the Suez Canal, which was shut down by shipwrecks sunk during the war. He needed the fees he could collect from shipping passing through the canal, which was the lifeblood of Egypt's economy. He needed to get the canal back in to operation quickly.

The Soviets were probably willing to do the work, but their bureaucracy was so great, they couldn't move fast enough. Kissinger said, "Would you like us to help you?" Sadat said, "You would do that?" Kissinger picked up the telephone in Sadat's office and called President Nixon in the White House. Within days, the sixth fleet was on its way to the Suez. Kissinger and Nixon started the process of positioning the United States as reasonably neutral between the Israelis and the Egyptians—an act that eventually led to President Carter's success as a mediator at Camp David.

Today, the conflict between the Palestinians and the Israelis continues, and I see little chance that the United States can effectively mediate a solution because the other countries in the Middle East do not perceive us as neutral. We are seen as a friend of Israel. I don't see much chance of a resolution until an Arab country (such as Saudi Arabia or the UAE) steps forward to mediate the problem.

The Process of Mediation

Neil Berman, my psychotherapist friend, told me once that for psychotherapy to work, the therapist must convince the patient that he knows what he is doing, and he is using a process on the patient that will work. It's not necessary for the patient to understand the process; it is only necessary for the patient to believe that there is a process. When you get down to it, there doesn't even have to be a process. All that matters is that the patient believes there is one. Similarly, the participants in a mediation have to believe the mediator has special skills, and that he or she is using a proven system that works for the benefit of both parties involved in the negotiation. Mediators must demonstrate that they:

- Are neutral.
- Understand the topic of the negotiation, which might be construction, retailing, marital strife, or whatever else the conflict is about.
- Have positive experience in mediating similar problems.
- Will be using a process that is proven successful.

Initial Contact With the Parties

The mediator does this by setting up a conference call. Although the mediator could contact the parties before joint meetings, it is seldom a good idea. If one party feels that the mediator has been too cozy with the other party before the start of the mediation, it could sabotage the aura of neutrality. During the conference call, the mediator will reaffirm that mediation implies the willingness to compromise. He tells them the process will not work if either side insists on maintaining their initial position, and is only interested in trying to prove the other side wrong. He emphasizes the need to be flexible, to prevent deadlocks later. It is critical to the success of the process.

Then, the mediator explains the process to each side (for example, when they will meet and how they will communicate). He emphasizes again that the process is proven and, if followed, will result in a high probability of success. Next, the mediator needs to remove each side's resort to Higher Authority (see Chapter 7). He should insist that the people attending the mediation have the authority to make a settlement. He may not prevail at this because, for example, a large company may not be willing to give carte blanche to the people in the field, but he should try. At least it will remove "fictitious" higher authorities, and prevent unpleasant surprises later in the process.

The mediator then asks each side to send him a written statement of their positions, and to include copies of any supporting documents that are essential to understanding their position. He asks them to keep the statement brief—no more than four or five pages. Each party should also send the same information to the other party. Knowing that any information sent to the mediator also has to be sent to the other side prevents each party from unduly trying to influence the mediator. He will discourage the parties from sending large amounts of backup documentation. Both sides' statements should include the following:

- How the dispute came about.
- The issues that the party wants resolved.
- How they've been damaged by the dispute.
- The settlement that each side is requesting.

The mediator tells each side that, during the first joint meeting, they will be expected to make an opening statement to present their positions. The mediator should then schedule the first joint meeting for as soon as possible. If the parties are eager to get started, and have high hopes that an agreement will be reached, it is better to act as quickly as possible. The mediator will typically set aside a complete day for the mediation, so the initial meeting will be held in the morning. It should be held at the mediator's office or, failing that, in a neutral location. The mediator will start with an opening statement, in which he or she will emphasize the following:

- His or her background in the area of the dispute and success record as a mediator.
- That he is not an arbitrator or a judge, and the parties have not given him the power to impose a settlement.
- That they are not here to convince the mediator or the other party that they are right or wrong.
- They are in mediation to discuss their positions in the hope that they can reach a mutually satisfactory compromise.

The parties should present their positions to each other, rather than appeal to the mediator. The mediator asks permission to take notes, but assures them the notes will be destroyed, and everything said will be held in confidence. Nothing said would be admissible in court. Each party starts by making an opening statement. This is a critical point in the mediation. The parties may have been in conflict for months. Chances are, they have not been communicating with each other. Now, they finally have a chance to present their case directly to the other side. It is enormously therapeutic for the parties to do this. They both feel relieved that they had their say. They're also relieved that the trauma of having to make the presentation is over. This puts them in a good frame of mind to accept a compromise.

If either side presents an argument without being able to prove it, the mediator will gently remind them that they should deal only in facts and be able to prove them. The mediator reads the personalities of the parties while this is going on. If they are dealing in facts and are respectful of each other, there is a good chance that a settlement can be quickly reached. If the parties are focused on attacking each other, the mediator will have his work cut out for him. Here's a recap of what the first joint meeting will accomplish:

- Everybody understands the issues that led to the dispute.
- Each side knows what the other side is asking for.
- The mediator has emphasized the importance of concentrating on facts, not emotions.
- The mediator has empathized equally with both sides. He has "felt their pain."
- Both parties are encouraged that a process is under way, and they are hopeful that a settlement will be reached.

First Private Meeting

Next, the mediator meets separately with each side, while the other side waits in another room. He separately asks each side to rank their issues in order of importance. He probes to determine the validity of each issue. He discusses the strength of their position on these issues, should the dispute eventually end up in court. By questioning the strength of each party's arguments, the mediator nudges each of them to a more moderate position, where they are more willing to compromise in order to reach a settlement.

The mediator knows that each side has weaknesses in their arguments. Perhaps they didn't thoroughly read the contract before they signed it. Perhaps they knew there were ambiguities in the contract, but chose not to point them out. Perhaps they colored their earlier statements. For example, earlier they may have said, "We had no idea that this would happen." During this phase of the mediation, they are willing to modify that position. Now it has become "We were aware that this could happen." Being able to reveal the weaknesses of their argument in a confidential setting is very therapeutic. The parties feel better once they have gotten it out in the open.

Second Private Meeting

During the second round of meetings, the mediator will try to get each side to suggest a settlement, while promising not to reveal the suggested settlement to the other side. He lets them make the suggestion rather than making suggestions himself, because he knows that first settlement offers can be surprisingly good.

Next, the mediator might let each other know in vague terms how far apart the two sides are, and suggest that they let him reveal each offer to the other side. With the offers out on the table, the mediation has moved to a significant new stage, the negotiating stage. All of the negotiating Gambits that I taught you earlier could come into play.

Resolution Stage

After the parties have reached agreement, they should write out a settlement agreement and sign it. They will probably want to have their attorneys draft a final agreement so that it would stand up in court. The mediator does not prepare the agreement, even if he or she is an attorney. It is not proper to represent both parties, and it would make the mediator vulnerable to charges of conflict of interest. This overview of the mediation process may seem vague to you, but look at what the mediator has accomplished. He started with people who were so deadlocked in conflict that they wouldn't even talk to each other. From that hopeless position, the mediator did the following:

- Got them talking to each other.
- Got them to agree to make compromises.
- Allowed them to vent hostilities in a controlled environment.
- Got them focused on the issues, rather than the personalities and emotions.
- Got them to trust the mediator's ability to bring them to a settlement.
- Convinced them that the process of mediation has value and would work.
- Got them focused on their mutual interests rather than their conflicting positions.
- Got them to make an initial settlement offer.
- Got the parties to trust that the other side would live by the agreement reached.

Key Points to Remember

1. There is a big difference between mediation and arbitration.
2. A mediator doesn't have much power. He is there to facilitate a solution.
3. An arbitrator has a lot of power. With binding arbitration, there will be a winner and a loser.
4. Mediation is rapidly growing in popularity because it's so much faster and cheaper that going to trial.
5. There is no appeal process in mediation because both sides have reached agreement.
6. Mediators can be more effective than judges because they often specialize in a narrow field of expertise.
7. The evidence given during mediation can be kept secret, unlike a public trial.
8. A mediator cannot be effective unless he is perceived as neutral by both sides.

Chapter 35

The Art of Arbitration

In the previous chapter, I told you how the mediation process works. Arbitration is similar to mediation in some respects, but very different in others. The similarities are that they are both much faster and less expensive than litigation. The big difference is that with arbitration, there will be a winner and there will be a loser. The parties don't expect to go through arbitration and have the arbitrator suggest that they split their differences and settle. The arbitrator may work to have one or both sides modify their positions, but eventually he or she must pick one side's position over the other. Let me walk you through an arbitration so that you can see how it differs from mediation, which is simpler, and litigation, which is more complex.

Setting Up the Arbitration

Each side tries to agree on an arbitrator whom they both trust and respect. I recommend that you select a member of the American Arbitration Association to assure that he adheres to the highest ethical standards. The association has strict rules for the way their members can arbitrate and produce an award that will stand up in court. The arbitrator should have experience in the area of the dispute.

You may need three arbitrators if:

- Both parties cannot agree on an arbitrator whom they would both trust and respect. When that happens, each side would select an arbitrator and those arbitrators would select a third.
- It is a complicated dispute where arbitrators in several areas of expertise are required.
- When you have more than one arbitrator, there should be an odd number, to avoid deadlocks. Three is usual. They will select one to be the chairperson. This person will administer

the process and run the hearing. With the concurrence of the other arbitrators, he will have the authority to handle procedural matters for the panel, such as the scheduling of meetings and the issuance of subpoenas.

Neutrality of the Arbitrators

The arbitrators must be neutral, be seen as neutral, and be accepted as neutral by the claimant, the respondent, and everyone else involved. This is even more important in arbitration than it is in mediation because of the combative nature of the arbitration process. At the end, one of the parties is going to be unhappy, because the arbitrator chose to make an award to the other side. There is no point in going through this whole process only to have the award overturned on appeal because the losing side claimed that the arbitrator was not neutral.

The arbitrator must reveal any past contact with the parties. He must reveal any information that might even suggest bias. He must avoid any contact with one side when the other is not present (called ex parte contact). To avoid ex parte contact, an administrative assistant should handle any administrative details, such as questions about the location and the timing of the meeting.

Preliminary Meeting

The claimant, who is the person filing the arbitration demand and seeking relief, and the respondent are called to a preliminary meeting. This serves several purposes. It allows the parties to vent their feelings. It explores the possibility of mediating the dispute, rather than arbitrating it, which is a much more hostile process.

After the parties have vented, they may both see the advantage of seeking a win-win solution through mediation, rather than exposing themselves to an award that is basically winner-take-all. If they seek mediation at this point, the arbitrator must point out that, although he could act as their mediator, it would preclude him from arbitrating the case later if they cannot agree through mediation. The information that he would gather at the mediation, such as suggested settlements by either side, would compromise his ability to arbitrate effectively. If the parties now want to attempt to settle the issue themselves, the arbitrator must excuse himself.

The amount of the claim and any counterclaims made so far is made clear to all sides. (The arbitrator will ask the respondent if he plans to counterclaim. This avoids a last-minute counter-claim being used as a delaying tactic.) By now, they may both have come to realize how much time, effort, and expense will go into arbitration, and will be more amenable to mediation.

Both sides agree on the amount of discovery that each side will require. The arbitrator does not have the power to order discovery the way that a judge does. This may be one of the reasons why the parties chose arbitration over litigation. Hopefully, both sides will agree to turn over all relevant documentation. If they won't agree to that, the preliminary meeting is a good place to agree on ground rules for discovery and put a time limit on it, so this issue cannot be used later to delay the procedure.

The parties agree to a time schedule for the exchange of expert reports, depositions, and responses to interrogatories. The parties agree to a hearing date. The preliminary meeting serves many purposes, not the least of which is that the parties may then decide to mediate rather than arbitrate.

Exchange of Information Prior to the First Hearing

Each side should be encouraged to prepare and submit, to the other side and to the arbitrator, an Exhibit Book containing all of the relevant documentation. Each side should submit a list of expert witnesses they plan to call, and a list of documents and witnesses that they want the arbitrator to subpoena. They should also decide whether they want to have the hearing transcribed, which is an optional procedure that would be at the party's expense.

The Arbitration Hearing

The hearing is similar to the trials that you see on television except that there is no audience and no jury. There may be only three people in the room: the arbitrator, the claimant, and the respondent. They may have an attorney present and the attorney may speak for them if they wish.

Each side makes an opening statement. Then witnesses are called and sworn in. Witnesses are cross-examined. Rebuttal witnesses may be called. The closing arguments are given. Each side may object to a question if it is leading, irrelevant, or opinion without foundation.

Conduct of the Arbitrator

The arbitrator will ask clarifying questions of the witnesses or parties. He will ask any questions that he feels are important, even if the subject of his inquiry has not been introduced in evidence. He will listen carefully to the evidence, but be careful not to react to the evidence. He should not nod his head, for example, because this might imply bias. He is constantly examining the evidence for its relevance to the arbitration and the credibility of the speaker.

An Important Difference Between Arbitration and Litigation

The most significant difference between arbitration and litigation is that, with arbitration, there is no jury. The arbitrator plays the role of both judge and jury. The arbitrator cannot ask the jury to leave the courtroom while he listens to the arguments of the parties, as a judge can. He cannot call a sidebar to hear the issue beyond the jury's hearing, as a judge can.

An arbitrator will often hear information that a jury would not be permitted to hear, simply because he or she has to rule on its relevance. It is better for the arbitrator to admit the evidence, and consider its relevance later when he or she makes his award, than refuse to admit the evidence, and have his award vacated on appeal. Hearsay, for example, which is inadmissible in court, is admissible in arbitration. The arbitrator simply decides if he should consider it when rendering an award.

Rendering an Award

Within 30 days of the final hearing, the arbitrator will render a decision in writing to both parties. In a brief document, he states the amount that the parties will recover on their claims and counterclaims, or he can deny the claims. He may disallow part of the claim for a particular reason. For example, he may find that the respondent owes the claimant $200,000 for the cost of a new sailboat. He does not owe the claimant the $20,000 he spent traveling around the Caribbean looking for a new sailboat. What the arbitrator should not do is make a partial award with the hope that it will appease both parties; that could have been handled by mediation.

Most arbitration is binding arbitration. Both sides agree up front that they will go along with what the arbitrator decides. In binding arbitration, the prevailing party can take the arbitrator's award into court and have it recorded, as though it were a judgment.

There is the possibility that the parties will not agree to binding arbitration. It happens when the next step would be a lawsuit, unless they agree to nonbinding arbitration. When both sides agree to non-binding arbitration, they are saying, "I agree to go through the process and get the opinion of the arbitrator. When he sides with me against you, perhaps you'll see the weakness of your case. But if he sides against me, I still reserve the right to sue you." Oh boy! I would hope that they would have been good enough negotiators to avoid that kind of deadlock, but it happens.

Typically, both sides bear their own legal expenses, regardless of who wins, unless there was an agreement in advance that stated that the loser would pay the winner's expenses. The arbitrator will ignore requests that one side pays the other side's legal expenses. He or she does not give a reason for his award. Juries don't have to give a reason for their decisions, and arbitrators don't either.

After the Award

If the arbitrator makes an award, the prevailing party can present the award to a court and have it certified. The arbitrator does not get involved in how the award is decided or how it is paid. He is through once he has rendered his award or denied an award. He sits back and hopes that it won't be overturned.

In most states, the court cannot overturn an award simply because the court would not have made the award if it had heard the case. It can only overturn the award if it questions the actions of the arbitrator. Was there fraud or corruption involved? Did the arbitrator act in a biased way? Hopefully, we can exclude fraud or corruption, which means that the only viable way to overturn an award is to prove that the arbitrator was biased. Do you see why it's so important that the arbitrator do everything he can to prove to the parties that he's neutral?

After the arbitrator has rendered his award, he will destroy any notes that he has taken. He will return all pieces of evidence to the parties after verifying that he has not made any notes on them, or even left a paper clip. There should be nothing to indicate his thinking while examining the evidence.

In the previous two chapters, we have examined two methods of resolving disputes other than going to court. As you can see, there is a huge difference between the two. With mediation, both sides come together in the hope that they can find a compromise that is acceptable to both sides. With arbitration, there will be little, if any, compromise. There will be a winner and there will be a loser.

In the next chapter, I'll teach you how to handle conflict situations that are so far out of control that they have gone beyond mediation or arbitration. You'll learn the art of conflict resolution.

☑ Key Points to Remember

1. With arbitration, unlike mediation, there will be a winner and there will be a loser.
2. Arbitration is faster and less expensive than litigation.
3. Each side must carefully choose an arbitrator that they both trust and respect.
4. If both sides cannot approve of an arbitrator, each side should choose one and collectively pick a third.
5. Members of the American Arbitration Association adhere to the highest ethical standards. The association has strict rules for the way their members can arbitrate and produce an award that will stand up to a court challenge.
6. Arbitrators must be neutral, be seen as neutral, and be accepted as neutral by the claimant, the respondent, and everyone else involved.
7. A preliminary meeting explores the possibility of mediating the dispute, rather than arbitrating it, which is a much more hostile process.
8. Both sides agree on the amount of discovery that each side will require. The arbitrator cannot order discovery as a judge can, which is a major advantage over litigation if the parties want privacy.
9. Hearsay is inadmissible in court, but admissible in arbitration. The arbitrator simply decides if he should consider it when rendering an award.
10. Juries don't have to give a reason for their decisions, and arbitrators don't either.
11. After the award, the arbitrator will destroy all notes, and return all evidence to the parties.

Chapter 36

The Art of Conflict Resolution

It seems like an everyday occurrence these days—at least it does in Los Angeles where I live. Somebody has a gun and they've taken a hostage. SWAT (Special Weapons and Tactics) teams are called in, barricades are set up, and news helicopters circle overhead, transmitting the live drama, as police negotiators try to resolve the conflict.

Sometimes it's a botched robbery; sometimes it's an angry employee or ex-employee who wants to settle a grievance with a boss. Sometimes the issue seems ludicrously minor. In Orange County we recently had an angry parent take a school board member hostage over a dispute about his child's education. How do these hostage negotiators handle these conflict situations? And what can we learn from them that would be helpful in our day-to-day disagreements with others?

In this country, we had given very little thought to hostage negotiations until two major incidents galvanized public attention: the Attica State Prison siege in September 1971 and the hostage-taking at the Munich Olympic Games a year later.

The Attica Prison riot stills stands as one of the most disastrous resolutions of a crisis in history. During the four-day prisoner rebellion at the prison located 30 miles east of Buffalo, New York, the inmates killed a guard and three inmates. After only four days, Governor Nelson Rockefeller ordered the state police to take back the prison by force. Police gunfire killed 29 inmates and 10 hostages. To compound the error, the police initially announced that the prisoners had slit the hostages' throats. The autopsy revealed the truth: that they had been killed by police fire. The prisoners or their families filed 1,280 lawsuits against the prison, the first of which was settled 26 years later for $4 million.

The brutal hostage taking at the 1972 Munich Olympic Games the following year, and a disastrously handled rescue attempt, killed 11 Israeli athletes, five Palestinian terrorists, and a German police officer. The German police now admit that they were woefully unprepared for what happened. They were more concerned that the world would be reminded of Hitler's heavy-handed use of the 1936 Olympic games for propaganda purposes, and were trying to keep a low profile.

Because of this, Palestinian supporters had little trouble getting into the training compound and taking nine athletes hostage, in addition to killing two athletes who had resisted them. From then on, the negotiators made mistake after mistake. Following Israeli Prime Minister Golda Meir's urging not to make any concessions to the terrorists, no telephone lines were set up and there was almost no communication with the terrorists. The police allowed the terrorists to move their hostages to the airport, something that would never be allowed by today's more enlightened hostage negotiators.

The Germans promised the terrorists safe passage to Cairo, although they did not intend to let them leave. Such deception, we know now, usually leads to an enraged response when it is revealed. Finally, when force was used to overcome the terrorists as they tried to board the getaway plane, it was woefully inadequate. Only five poorly trained sharpshooters were used, and they had no night-vision devices, and lacked radio contact.

And just as at Attica, the police tried to cover up their errors. When families of the Israeli victims sued the German government, they denied that any records, "ballistic, forensic, or otherwise," existed. Twenty years after the event the wife of one of the slain athletes appeared on German television and received a call from an anonymous German who gave her 80 pages of stolen autopsy and ballistic reports. Because of this, the German authorities were forced to reveal a storeroom full of more than 3,000 files and 900 photographs.

It was a terrible year for hostage negotiators. More than 1,000 hostages lost their lives, and 760 of those deaths occurred as police stormed the hostage locations. Clearly, the existing strategy of refusing to negotiate with hostage-takers and trying to overwhelm them with force was not working. The cure was worse than the disease.

The New York Police Department developed a program to come up with better responses to crises such as hostage taking and suicide threats. They put Lieutenant Frank Bolz in charge of the program, assisted by clinical psychologist Harvey Schlossberg. The program that they developed, and then tested in the streets of New York, became the model for police departments around the country. Because of this, it is unlikely that any hostage will lose his life once negotiators have arrived at the scene and made contact with the hostage-taker.

In an extensive study by the University of Vermont of child hostage-takings, it was found that 98 percent of child hostages were released without physical injury. Also, far fewer of the perpetrators are being killed, which is particularly significant when you factor in the current trend of "Police Assisted Suicides." This is a term that police apply to hostage-takers who are, in reality, committing suicide. They are inviting the police to kill them. In California now, 25 percent of all police killings of hostage-takers are officially classified as Police Assisted Suicides.

During the NYPD study, Frank Bolz decided that there were five possible responses to a hostage situation. They are as follows:

1. Attack with little or no attempt at negotiation. (This was the approach taken at Attica and Munich, with disastrous results.)
2. Wait out the situation to see what would happen. (This is a good approach if you determine that nothing bad will happen. As I explain in my book *The Confident Decision Maker*, this should be your first consideration when faced with a "do we or don't we" type of decision. What will happen if you do nothing? The people surrounding the compound in Waco, Texas, should have known this. Nothing bad was happening inside the compound, and we should have waited to see what would have developed.)
3. Negotiate without making any concessions. (This was the popular rallying cry of the Reagan years. We will not negotiate with terrorists!) It sounds good to the public, but it is foolishly inflexible. We should be negotiating with terrorists, and the willingness to make minor concessions should be a part of the negotiation. What must not happen is for the terrorists to succeed in their major demands. That would obviously encourage others to emulate their actions.
4. Negotiate and lie about concessions. This approach usually appeals to the public. A gunman once took a class of children hostage at a school in Tuscaloosa, Alabama. Governor Guy Hunt videotaped a pardon of the hostage-taker and sent it to him. He released the children, but was immediately arrested. The governor rescinded the pardon on technical grounds,

saying that 1) you can only pardon a convicted person and 2) that the pardon was given under duress. The hostage-taker was given a life sentence. At first glance, it seems to be an effective technique. Why should we be concerned about lying to violent criminals? However, the tactic of lying to hostage-takers is a classic example of a short-term gain and a long-term loss. It affects the outcome of all subsequent negotiations, because it limits the negotiator's ability to build trust with the hostage-taker. If there is one thing with which hostage negotiators all agree it is this: Don't lie (on major issues) to terrorists.

5. Negotiate and be willing to make concessions.

The program they developed was a variation of the last approach. The model they developed calls for the negotiator to be calm, take a humane approach to the problem, earn the hostage-taker's trust, and offer partial satisfaction by making minor concessions to the hostage-taker.

Let's take a look at the procedure used at a typical crisis scene, and as we do so, let's think of how much of this would apply to the type of crisis situation in which we might be involved, such as an angry customer wanting to cancel an order. There are three types of crises to consider: suicide threats, barricaded suspects, and hostage-taking. The rules for each of these situations are similar.

The first officers to arrive on the scene must assess the seriousness of the situation; secure the area from potential accomplices, the press, and the curious public; judge the threat to hostages and bystanders, and call for the appropriate backup units. Securing the area is a critical component, particularly in hostage situations. In almost every case, the suspect must be denied mobility. To let him leave the area will usually exacerbate the situation.

In a bank robbery in Houghton, a small town in Michigan, a 24-year-old man walked into a bank in the middle of winter, took a teller hostage, and strapped a bomb to her. He then demanded a getaway car from an employee, seriously injuring the bank manager in the process. Police, who quickly stopped him, only found out about the bomb when they opened the car door and told him to get out. He threatened to explode the bomb and they backed off, but as they did, they calmly shot out all four tires. This stopped him from going more than a few yards, because his deflated tires stuck in the snow.

Police surrounded the car and started to negotiate. Unfortunately for the perpetrator, the negotiation did not go well. Seventeen hours later, the standoff ended when police sharpshooters shot the robber as he wearily put down the bomb detonator. The hostage escaped unhurt. Shooting out the tires may seem like a risky thing to do, but securing the area and not giving the hostage-taker mobility is almost always the right thing to do.

The next step is to bring in reinforcements. A team of negotiators, who will make contact with the suspect, identify their demands, and try to resolve the conflict without loss of life or injury to anyone, is set up. This team consists of a primary negotiator, who will communicate with the suspect, and a backup negotiator, who will take notes and offer advice to the primary negotiator. The third member is the intelligence negotiator who gathers information by interviewing anyone who knows the suspect. Particularly critical information includes the suspect's criminal record and mental health record.

Then a SWAT (Special Weapons and Tactics) team is brought in. Hopefully, they won't be needed, but they are there to neutralize the suspect if negotiations fail. The police appoint a field commander to supervise the entire operation. The field commander is very aware that if the situation is not resolved successfully, he will be the subject of very vocal and public criticism. Everyone from the mayor to the newspaper editors will be second-guessing his judgment. To protect himself and the reputation of his department, he wants to complete the operation by the book. He will insist that established procedures be followed. The smart ones use a checklist similar to the one that pilots use in their pre-flight routine. This ensures that they don't overlook a critical step in the height of the trauma.

The first step of the negotiation process is for the primary negotiator to establish communication with the suspect, and cut off his or her ability to communicate with anyone else. The primary negotiator should not have to compete for the suspect's attention. In this way, the suspect becomes dependent upon communication with the primary negotiator, and a process of trust-building begins. If the suspect has access to a telephone, his ability to call out will be cut off. The police do not want the suspect able to communicate with the media or anyone else. They also want to deny access to information about police maneuvers or tactics. Communication is usually by telephone. It is too dangerous to allow the suspect and the negotiator to meet face-to-face.

In Hollywood dramas, you will frequently see a situation where a friend or relative of the suspect is allowed to talk face-to-face with the suspect. Tense moments ensue as the friend, relative, or lover risks his or her life because he or she loves the suspect so much. After a tearful embrace, the suspect surrenders. This would never happen in real life. For one thing, the friend or relative may be the cause of the suspect's rage and exacerbate the situation. The primary reason, though, is that all contact should be through the primary negotiator during the first few days, so that he can gain control of the suspect's world.

If all else fails, a trusted and trained person might be brought in to change the dynamics of the crisis. In 1993, the local sheriff was brought in at Waco, Texas, but only because David Koresh knew and trusted him. When Cuban prisoners rioted at Oakdale, Louisiana, prison in 1987, negotiators brought in a Cuban-born priest. Bringing in a third person, perceived as neutral, is akin to bringing in a mediator to resolve a deadlock, as I told you in Chapter 34. It is not done lightly.

Often, water, heat, and power are turned off also, for several different reasons. It prevents the suspect from gathering information from television. It prevents the suspect from disposing of drugs or other incriminating evidence. It gives a tactical advantage to the SWAT team who can use infrared vision to monitor the scene. It eliminates comforts, such as heat and toilet facilities. This can then be used later as a trade-off.

Turning off the utilities also causes the suspect to bond with the hostages, making it much less likely that the suspect will harm them. People who suffer deprivations together will bond. This was used very effectively in December 1996 by negotiators at the hostage crisis at the official residence of Japan's ambassador to Peru, in celebration of Emperor Akihito's birthday in Lima, Peru. MRTA (Tupac Amaru Revolutionary Movement) terrorists took more than 500 guests hostage. The situation was critical because the Japanese had gone to great lengths to turn the ambassador's residence into a fortress that could easily be defended from attack. The MRTA blew a huge hole in the wall of the compound. Once in, it was an easy building to defend from the inside. The police quickly turned off all the utilities to the building. They wanted the terrorists to be suffering the same deprivations as the hostages, knowing that this would cause them to bond. But after a few days, they turned the utilities back on. If they bonded too much, the hostages would actually thwart a rescue attempt when it was launched. The siege lasted for 126 days before the Peruvian Armed Forces stormed the building. Even though the hostages were held at gunpoint, the terrorists hesitated long enough that none of the hostages were killed (one died of a heart attack). Getting the perpetrators to bond with the victims can help save lives.

Time is the friend of the primary negotiator. Every moment that passes without a bad thing happening is bringing the situation closer to a peaceful resolution (unlike in Hollywood dramas, where the passage of time is used to build tension). A missed deadline can be a breakthrough for a negotiator.

The hostage-taker might say, "Unless the governor of the state is on the phone by twelve noon, I'm going to kill a hostage!" Although this might cause an inexperienced negotiator to panic, it pleases the primary negotiator because now he has a suspect who is willing to negotiate. Also, he knows that if he can get past noon without losing a hostage, the suspect has lost credibility, and has greatly weakened his bargaining power. That is not as callous as it may sound to you, because very few hostages have ever been lost under such a specific threat. Hostages get lost in passionate moments, either very early in the hostage-taking, when passions are running high, or if the suspect feels betrayed by the primary negotiator.

The relationship that the primary negotiator builds with the suspect is the key to peaceful resolution of the crisis. For one thing, the primary negotiator will have spent weeks in classes learning about the personality of hostage-takers and people who publicly threaten to commit suicide. They are experts on neurotic behavior and personality disorders. They thoroughly understand the suspect's state of mind, and know how to manipulate the suspect through the crisis. This is one reason why it is better that only the negotiating team, which consists of the primary negotiator, the backup negotiator, and the intelligence negotiator, are privy to the actual negotiation.

Even the field commander, who may be very experienced in crises, will not understand the nuances of the conversation between the primary negotiator and the suspect. He will be inclined to overreact. When he hears, for example, that the suspect is demanding $10 million, or a press conference with the governor, he might see that as an impossible demand that will lead to violence. The primary negotiator hears it only as an opening negotiating position, and is glad to have some specifics on the table. Nothing is more dangerous than a suspect who won't talk.

The primary negotiator monitors the suspect's state of mind. If he appears volatile, the negotiator will try to draw him into reasoned negotiations by offering small concessions in return for minor reciprocal concession. In this way, the negotiator moves the suspect from thinking with his right brain, which is erratic and volatile, to thinking with his left brain, which is logical and much more controllable. If the suspect is too quiet, it may be a sign of depression. To counter that the negotiator reassures the suspect that there is a way out of the situation, that nobody has to get hurt, and that he still has options. He or she also works to build trust with the suspect. He is careful not to say anything that could later be construed as deception by the suspect. He must comply with every promise or commitment that he makes.

Above all, the primary negotiator works to get the suspect off the positions that he has taken, and focused back on their mutual interests. Positions can be 180 degrees apart, and focusing on them obscures the huge mutual interests that exist between the negotiator and the suspect. This is not to say that the primary negotiator is afraid to be tough with the suspect. The threat of physical force is always present. This is particularly true if the suspect harms anybody. "If you harm a suspect, I can't protect you," the negotiator insists. "It will be out of my hands."

Time passes. The suspect vents his emotions. Deadlines are missed. Demands are modified. No concessions are made without something in return. ("You release a hostage, and we'll send in a sandwich.") A forum for bargaining is established. Time wears down resolve. Acceptance time (see Chapter 37) causes the suspect to modify his demands and accept the reality of the situation. The suspect learns to trust the primary negotiator and, if all goes well, surrenders to his will.

What can we learn from these trained hostage negotiators that we can apply in our daily lives? Whether it is an angry spouse, an employee threatening to quit, or a customer threatening to cancel an order, here are some of my rules for handling conflict in any situation.

- **Contain the situation so that it won't get worse.** That may mean getting a suitcase out of a spouse's hand when he or she is threatening to walk out the door. It may mean getting the car keys out of an angry teenager's hands, or getting that angry customer to agree to a conference call or a meeting.
- **Allow the angry person to vent.** Hostage negotiators will tell you that you must deal with the other person as he perceives the situation, not as you perceive it. He may insist that Abraham Lincoln is talking to him. You don't have to tell him that you hear it also, but you must acknowledge his perception—that

he is hearing Abe's voice. Translated to a day-to-day situation, this means that the other person's anger may be unjustified, but you must acknowledge that anger as real.

➡ **When the other person is angry, look for the hurt.** Anger always follows hurt. What was said or done that caused this person to feel hurt or threatened? Acknowledging the hurt goes a long way toward reducing the anger.

As quickly as you can, get him to tell you what it is he wants. Get him committed to a position. What would it take to resolve the problem? You do this even if you're not prepared to make any concessions to the other side at all. For example, you may have an employee who is threatening to quit unless you give him a raise in pay. You may have a firm rule against giving someone an increase in pay if he's threatening to quit. That's up to you. Even so, you should get him to tell you how much of an increase in pay he would need to stay. Quantifying the problem goes a long way to solving it.

Gather all the information that you can. Think of the primary negotiator using his information negotiator to interview everyone who knows the suspect. Focus on the person more than the problem. The solution is always with the person, not the situation. The more you know about the person, the closer you are to resolution. In this stage, another problem may be revealed. Money may not be the real reason why that person is quitting. He may be upset because a rival was promoted before he was. He may have become romantically involved with another employee and needs to create some distance between himself and the other person. He may be acting on a false rumor.

Work to get the person off the position that he or she has taken. Get him focused on your mutual interests. Positions can be 180 degrees apart. "You lied to me!" "No, I didn't!" "You cheated me!" "No, I didn't!" These are strong positions that are totally opposed, but it doesn't mean that you don't still have strong mutual interests. You may both have a strong mutual interest in that employee staying with your company. Both you and that angry customer may both have a great deal to gain from continuing your relationship.

The problem is that, when you focus too strongly on positions, you can no longer see your mutual interests. The classic example of that was the Cold War. We took very strong positions. We were calling them an evil empire. They were pounding their shoe on the United Nations table, screaming that they were going to bury us. Those are very strong positions. We both still had huge mutual interests. We had a huge mutual interest in reducing military expenditure. We both had a huge mutual interest in doing business together. They had all that titanium. We needed it for our golf clubs! But we couldn't see that while we stayed so focused on our positions!

Take a look at the long-standing conflict between the Taiwanese and Beijing government. For more than half a century, they have stood toe-to-toe with each other, threatening a catastrophic war. The United States has promised to defend the island if the mainland attacks. What is the conflict all about? Each side's position is very clear: The government in Beijing says that Taiwan is a province of mainland China. Taiwan claims to be an independent nation. Those two positions are 180 degrees apart. If you focus instead on mutual interests you see a totally different picture. The Taiwanese economy has been in the doldrums for more than a decade. Improved relations and business dealings with China would cause its economy to boom. Mainland China, on the other hand, desperately needs the business skills that the Taiwanese can teach them. Both sides would benefit enormously from a resolution of the crisis.

The art of conflict resolution is to get people off of their positions and focused back on their mutual interests.

Only when you both have expressed what it would take to resolve the problem, and you have gathered the information and worked to get people focused on their mutual interests, do you move to what most people think of as negotiating—the reach-for-compromise part of it. Here's where the most important thought that a negotiator can have comes into play. I call it the Power Negotiator's Creed. The most important thought you can have when you are negotiating is not "What can I get them to give me?" It is "What can I give them that would not take away from my position, but may be of value to them?"

Key Points to Remember

1. After the disastrous handling of the Attica State Prison riot and the Munich Olympic hostage-taking, the NYPD studied ways of handling hostage situations with a view to protecting both the hostages and the perpetrator.

2. We should be negotiating with terrorists, but we should not make major concessions.
3. All hostage experts agree that you should not lie to hostage-takers, because it undermines the ability of law enforcement to negotiate future crisis situations.
4. The first step of the negotiation process is for the primary negotiator to establish communication with the suspect and cut off his or her ability to communicate with anyone else.
5. The perpetrator must be physically and psychologically isolated.
6. Bringing in family members to talk with the hostage-taker is rarely productive because it may evoke emotional trauma and exacerbate the situation.
7. Negotiators test any deadlines set up by the perpetrator.
8. The art of mediation is to get the parties off the positions that they have taken, and focused back on their mutual interests.
9. When dealing with an angry person, first contain the situation so that it won't get worse. Then allow the angry person to vent. Look for the hurt. Anger always follows hurt.
10. Get the angry person committed to a position, and then gather all the information you can.
11. Remember the Power Negotiator's Creed. The most important thought you can have when you are negotiating is not "What can I get them to give me?" It is "What can I give them that would not take away from my position, but may be of value to them?"

Section Three

Negotiating Pressure Points

Louis (Satchmo) Armstrong used to tell this story about his early days as a musician: "One night this big, bad-ass hood crashes my dressing room in Chicago and instructs me that I will open in such-and-such a club in New York the next night. I tell him I got this Chicago engagement and don't plan no traveling, and I turn my back on him to show I'm so cool. Then I hear this sound: SNAP! CLICK! I turn around, and he has pulled this vast revolver on me and cocked it. Jesus, it looks like a cannon and sounds like death! So I look down at that steel and say, 'Well, maybe I do open in New York tomorrow.'"

As Al Capone once said, "You can get much further with a kind word and a gun than you can with a kind word alone."

Pulling a gun on someone during a negotiation is the crudest pressure point of them all. I imagine that it's remarkably effective, but there's never a need for you to do it. In this section, I'll teach you some pressure points that you can use that are just as effective and far more acceptable. Many of them you could use with the brutality of pulling a gun on someone, but usually you're better off being more subtle. If you have the power, you don't have to flaunt it.

Chapter 37

Time Pressure

Vilfredo Pareto presumably never studied the time element in a negotiation, yet the Pareto principle reveals the incredible pressure that time can put on a negotiation. Pareto was an economist in the 19th century. Born in Paris, he spent most of his life in Italy, where he studied the balance of wealth as it was distributed among the populace. In his book, *Cours d'Economie Politique*, he pointed out that 80 percent of the wealth was concentrated in the hands of 20 percent of the people.

The interesting thing about the 80/20 rule is that it surfaces repeatedly in apparently unrelated fields. Sales managers tell me that 80 percent of their business is done by 20 percent of the salespeople. Eventually, it occurs to them that they should fire the 80 percent and just keep the 20 percent. The problem with that is that the 80/20 then reapplies itself to the remainder, and you're back with the same problem, only with a smaller sales force. Schoolteachers tell me 20 percent of the children cause 80 percent of trouble. In seminars, 20 percent of the students ask 80 percent of the questions.

The rule in negotiating is that 80 percent of the concessions occur in the last 20 percent of time available. If demands are presented early in a negotiation, neither side may want to make concessions, and the entire transaction may fall apart. On the other hand, more problems surface in the last 20 percent of the time available to negotiate, both sides are more willing to make concessions. Think of the last time that you bought a piece of real estate. It probably took about 10 weeks from the time you signed the initial contract to the time you actually became the owner of the property. Now think of the concessions that were made. Isn't it true that during the last two weeks, when things came up to be renegotiated, both sides became more flexible?

Some people are unethical enough to use this against you. They hold out on elements of the negotiation that could have been brought up earlier and resolved simply. Then when you're getting ready to finalize the arrangements, these problems come up because they know you'll be more flexible under time pressure.

Tie Up All the Details Up Front

One thing this tells you is that you should always tie up all the details up front. Don't leave anything to, "Oh well, we can work that out later." A matter that appears to be of little importance up front can become a very big problem under time pressure.

Problems in Big Sky Country

I was in Kalispell, Montana, to do a seminar for the Montana graduates of the Realtors' Institute. These are the highest-trained residential real estate people in the state. We were doing an all-day seminar on Power Negotiating, and during the break, an agent came up to me and said, "Perhaps you can help me. I have a big problem. It looks as though I'm going to lose a big part of my commission on a very large transaction."

I asked her to tell me more, and she said, "Months ago, a man came into my office wanting me to list his $600,000 home. I'd never listed anything so large, and I guess I didn't express much confidence because when he asked me how much commission I charge, he flinched, and I fell for it. I told him six percent. He said, 'That's $36,000! That's a lot of money.' I said, 'Look, if you have to come down much on the price of the property, we'll work with you on the commission.' That's all I said, and I never gave it a second thought.

"As luck would have it, I ended up not only getting the listing, but I found the buyer as well. He didn't have to come down much on the price, so now I have almost the full $36,000 commission coming into my office, and the property is due to close next week. Yesterday, he came into my office and said: 'I've been thinking about the amount of work that you had to do on that sale...."' Remember, the value of services always appears to diminish rapidly after those services have been performed (see Chapter 8). 'You remember you told me that you'd work with me on the commission?'

"'Well, I've been thinking about the amount of work you had to do, and I've decided that $5,000 would be a fair commission for you."' He was only offering $5,000 when she was due $36,000. She was almost panic-stricken. This illustrates that you shouldn't leave anything to "We can work that out later" because a little detail up front can become a big problem later when you're under time pressure.

That story also illustrates how we always think we have the weaker hand in negotiations—whichever side we're on. In fact, the real estate agent in Montana was in a very strong position, wasn't she? As I explained to her, she had a written contact for the six percent. If anything, she had verbally modified it with a vague comment that wouldn't hold up in court anyway. She had all the power, but didn't think she had any.

However, why expose yourself to that kind of problem? Tie up all the details up front. When the other side says to you, "We can work that out later, it's not going to be a big problem," bells should start to ring and lights should start to flash. Don't let people do that to you.

People Become Flexible Under Time Pressure

The next thing Power Negotiators have learned about time is that people become flexible under time pressure. When do your children ask you for something? When my daughter, Julia, was attending the University of Southern California, she lived in a sorority house and would sometimes come home for the weekends and need money for books. When would she ask me? Seven o'clock on a Monday morning, just as she was racing out the door she'd say, "Dad, I'm sorry, I forgot; I need $60 for books."

I'd say, "Julia, don't do this to me. I teach this stuff. How come you've been home all weekend, and we didn't have a chance to talk about it before?"

"Oh sorry, Dad, I didn't think about it until I got ready to go, but I'm late now. I've got to get on the freeway, or I'll be late for class. If I can't get my books today, I won't be able to get my assignment in on time. Please, can I have the money now, and we'll talk next weekend?" Not that children are manipulative, but instinctively, over all those years of dealing with adults, they understand that under time pressure, people become more flexible.

Was the Shape of the Table That Important?

It's interesting to look at international negotiations and how time pressure has affected the outcome. Remember the Vietnam peace talks that were held in Paris? You'll recall that in the spring of 1968, Lyndon Johnson had announced he wouldn't run for reelection and would devote his time to the peace talks. He was eager to reach a peace agreement before November, when his vice president, Hubert

Humphrey, would be running for election. He sent our negotiator, Averell Harriman, to Paris with clear instructions: Get something done, fast, and right now. Texas-style.

Averell Harriman rented a suite at the Ritz Hotel in Paris on a week-to-week basis. The Vietnamese negotiator, Xuan Thuy, rented a villa in the countryside for two and half years. Then the Vietnamese proceeded to spend week after week after week talking to us about the shape of the table.

Did they really care about the shape of the table? Of course not. They were doing two things. Number one, they were projecting, very successfully, that they were not under any time pressure. They'd been in the war for 30 years or so, and another year or two here and there wouldn't bother them one way or the other. Second, they were trying to push us up against our November deadline, which they did very successfully. On November 1st, only five days before the election, Johnson stopped the bombing of Vietnam. Under that kind of time pressure, it was a wonder that he didn't give everything away.

When you're negotiating with people, never reveal that you have a deadline. Let's say, for example, that you have flown to Dallas to resolve a negotiation with a hotel developer and you have a return flight at 6 p.m. Sure, you're eager to catch that flight—but don't let the other people know. If they do know you have a 6 p.m. flight, be sure to let them know you also have a 9 p.m. backup flight or, for that matter, that you can stay for as long as it takes to work out a mutually satisfactory arrangement.

If they know you're under time pressure, they could delay the bulk of the negotiations until the last possible minute. Then there's a real danger that you'll give things away under that kind of time pressure. In my Power Negotiating seminars, I set up exercises so the students can practice negotiating. They may have 15 minutes to complete a negotiation, and I impress on them the importance of reaching agreement within that time limit. As I slowly walk around the room eavesdropping on the progress of the negotiations, I can tell that during the first 12 minutes, they have trouble making any progress. Both sides are stonewalling the issues and there is very little give and take. At 12 minutes, with 80 percent of the time used up, I take the microphone and tell them they have only three minutes left. Then I continue periodic announcements to keep the time pressure on them and end with a countdown of the seconds from five to zero. It's very clear to see that they make 80 percent of the concessions in the last 20 percent of the time available to negotiate.

What to do when both sides are approaching the same time deadline? An interesting question is raised when both sides are approaching the same time deadline. This would be true if you lease your office space, for example. Let's say that your five-year lease is up in six months, and you must negotiate a renewal with your landlord. You might think to yourself, "I'll use time pressure on the landlord to get the best deal. I'll wait until the last moment to negotiate with him. That will put him under a great deal of time pressure. He'll know that if I move out, the place will be vacant for several months until he can find a new tenant." That seems like a great strategy until you realize that there's no difference between that and the landlord refusing to negotiate until the last minute to put time pressure on you.

There you have a situation where both sides are approaching the same time deadline. Which side should use time pressure and which side should avoid it? The answer is that the side that has the most power could use time pressure, but the side with the least power should avoid time pressure and negotiate well ahead of the deadline. Fair enough, but who has the most power? The side with the most options has the most power. If you can't reach a negotiated renewal of the lease, who has the best alternatives available to them?

To determine this, you might take a sheet of paper and draw a line down the middle. On the left side, list your options if you are unable to renew the lease. What other locations are available to you? Would they cost more or less? How much would it cost you to move the telephones and print new stationery? Would your customers be able to find you if you move? On the right-hand side of the page, list the landlord's options. How specialized is this building? How hard would it be for him to find a new tenant? Would they pay more or would he have to rent it for less? How much would he have to spend on improvements or remodeling to satisfy a new tenant? You must compensate for the fact that, whichever side of the negotiating table you're on, you always think you have the weaker hand. After all, you know all about the pressure that's on you, but you don't know about the pressure that's on the landlord. One thing that makes you a more powerful negotiator is understanding that you always think you have the weaker hand and learning to compensate for that. When you list each side's alternatives in this way, you'll probably end up with the conclusion that the landlord has more alternatives than you do.

Compensate for that, but if you do so and clearly the landlord still has more alternatives than you do, he's the one who has the power. You should avoid time pressure and negotiate the lease renewal with plenty of time to spare. However, if clearly you have more alternatives available to you than the landlord does, put him under time pressure by negotiating at the last moment.

Putting Time Pressure on the Wrong Side

In September 1994, former President Jimmy Carter, along with Senator Sam Nunn and former Chief of Staff Colin Powell, flew to Haiti to see if they could get General Cedras to give up power without our having to invade the country to force him out. At the end of the second day of negotiations, President Clinton called President Carter to tell him that he had already started the invasion, and Carter had 30 minutes to leave the country. Isn't that an ultimate example of applying time pressure to a negotiation? The only problem was that Clinton was putting time pressure on the wrong side. We had all the power in that negotiation because we had all the options. It should have been Carter putting time pressure on Cedras, not Clinton putting time pressure on Carter.

As Negotiations Drag on, People Become More Flexible

The longer you can keep the other side involved in the negotiation, the more likely the other side is to move around to your point of view. The next time you're in a situation where you're beginning to think that you'll never budge the other side, think of the tugboats in the Hudson River off Manhattan. A tiny tugboat can move that huge ocean liner around if it does it a little bit at a time. However, if the tugboat captain were to back off, rev up its engines, and try to force the ocean liner around, it wouldn't do any good. Some people negotiate like that. They reach an impasse in the negotiations that frustrates them, so they get impatient and try to force the other side to change their mind. Think of that tugboat instead. A little bit at a time, it can move the liner around. If you have enough patience, you can change anybody's mind a little bit at a time.

Unfortunately, this works both ways. The longer you spend in a negotiation, the more likely you are to make concessions. You may have flown to San Francisco to negotiate a large business deal. At 8 a.m., you're in their office feeling bright, fresh, and determined to hang in and accomplish all of your goals. Unfortunately, it doesn't go as well as you hoped. The morning drags on without any progress, so you break for lunch. Then the afternoon passes, and you've reached agreement on only a few minor points. You call the airline and reschedule for the midnight red-eye flight.

You break for supper and come back determined to get something done. Look out. Unless you're very careful, by 10 p.m., you'll start making concessions that you never intended to make when you started that morning.

Why does it work that way? Because your subconscious mind is now screaming at you, "You can't walk away from this empty handed after the time and effort you've spent on it. You have to be able to put something together." Any time you pass the point where you're prepared to walk away, you have set yourself up to lose in the negotiations (more about this in Chapter 39). A Power Negotiator knows that you should disregard any time or money that you have invested in a project up to any given point. Time and money are gone, whether you strike a deal or not. Always look at the terms of a negotiation as they exist at that moment and think, "Disregarding all the time and money we've poured into this deal up to now, should we go ahead?"

Never be reluctant to pull the plug if it doesn't make sense any more. It's much cheaper to write off your investment than it is to plow ahead with a deal that isn't right for you just because you have so much invested in it. That's one of the things that makes Donald Trump such a powerful negotiator: He's not afraid to pull the plug on a deal that no longer makes sense. For example, he spent $100 million to acquire the site for Television City on the West Side of Manhattan. He spent millions more designing plans for the project that would include a 150-story tower, the world's tallest, and a magnificent television studio to which he hoped to attract NBC. However, when he couldn't negotiate the right tax concessions from the city, he shelved the entire project. You have to look at a negotiation in the same way. Forget what you've already invested, and examine whether it stills looks good the way things stand now.

Acceptance Time

Another way of using time to your advantage is what negotiators call "acceptance time." Your initial proposal may be abhorrent to the other side. Absolutely no way will they even consider it. But if you can be patient and leave the proposal on the table long enough, the other side may eventually find it acceptable. The time it takes a person to accept this unacceptable suggestion as the best they can do is acceptance time. Here are some examples:

- **Death.** This may take a few decades, but we all learn to accept it eventually.
- **Hijacking.** The hijacker wants $10 million and a ticket to freedom. He settles for the chance to surrender with dignity.

- **Selling real estate.** We thought we'd get a million dollars for the home we've come to love. After putting it on the market for six months, we reluctantly accept that buyers are not going to love it as much as we do.
- **Corporate promotions.** We hoped that we'd get the vice presidency in New York. After an anguished weekend, we accept that the district manager's job in El Paso may have to come first.
- **College acceptance.** We had our heart set on sending our son to Stanford. We reluctantly accept that, with his grades, he is lucky to get into community college.

Be aware of the acceptance time phenomena and be patient. It may take the other side a while to consider your proposal seriously. Time is comparable to money. They are both invested, spent, saved, and wasted. Do invest the time to go through every step of the negotiation, do use time pressure to gain the advantage, and don't yield to the temptation to rush to a conclusion. Power Negotiators know that time is money.

☑ Key Points to Remember

1. Eighty percent of the concessions occur in the last 20 percent of time available.
2. Tie up all the details up front. Don't leave anything to "We can work that out later."
3. People become flexible under time pressure.
4. Never reveal that you have a deadline.
5. Try to establish that the other side has a deadline.
6. In a situation where both sides are approaching the same time deadline, the side that has the most power could use time pressure, but the side with the least power should avoid time pressure, and negotiate well ahead of the deadline.
7. Power is directly related to the options that each side has in the event that they cannot reach agreement.
8. Acceptance time means that you should give the other side time to accept that they will not get as much as they expected.

Chapter 38

Information Power

Why do countries send spies into other countries? Why do professional football teams study the replays of their opponents' games? Because knowledge is power, and the more knowledge one side is able to accumulate about the other, the better chance that side has for victory. If two countries go to war, the country that has the most intelligence about the other has the advantage. That was certainly true in the Persian Gulf War: The CIA spies had photographed every building in Baghdad, and we were able to completely take out their communication systems in the first few bombing runs.

Know What the Other Side Will Propose

Governments spend billions of dollars finding out about the other side before they'll go into an arms-control talk. It was interesting to see Henry Kissinger being interviewed before a summit meeting. "Mr. Kissinger," the interviewer said, "do you think it's possible our negotiators know what the other side will propose at the talks, before they actually propose it?" He said, "Oh, absolutely—no question about it. It would be absolutely disastrous for us to go into a negotiation not knowing in advance what the other side was going to propose."

Can you imagine the cost of getting that kind of information? The CIA is very secretive about what it spends, but at an intelligence gathering conference in San Antonio, Mary Graham, the deputy director of intelligence and a 27-year veteran at the CIA, let slip that it spends $44 billion a year. If our government thinks it's that important, shouldn't we at least take some time gathering information before we go into a negotiation?

When Bill Richardson, our former United Nations ambassador, was asked by *Fortune* magazine what it took to be a good negotiator, the first thing he said was, "You have to be a good listener. You have to respect the other side's point of view. You have to know what makes your adversary tick." When asked how he prepared for a negotiation, he again immediately went to information gathering: "I talk to people who know the guy I'll be negotiating with. I talk to scholars, State Department experts, and journalists. Before meeting with Saddam Hussein, I relied a lot on Iraq's ambassador to the United Nations. He told me to be very honest with Saddam—not to pull any punches. With Castro, I learned that he was always hungry for information about America. Sure enough, he was fascinated by Steve Forbes, and fascinated with the congressional budget impasse. He fancies himself an expert on U.S. politics. With Cedras of Haiti, I learned that he played good guy, bad guy frequently."

If two companies are planning to merge, the company that knows the most will usually end up with the better deal. If two salespeople are vying for an account, the salesperson who knows more about the company and its representatives stands a better chance of being selected for the account.

Despite the obviousness of the important role that information plays in a negotiation, few people spend much time analyzing the other side before starting a negotiation. Even people who wouldn't dream of skiing or scuba diving without taking lessons will jump into a negotiation that could cost them thousands of dollars without spending adequate time gathering the information they should have.

Rule 1: Don't Be Afraid to Admit That You Don't Know

If you're a homeowner, think back to when you bought your present home. How much did you know about the sellers before you made an offer? Did you know why they were selling and how long they had been trying to sell? Did you find out how they had arrived at their asking price? How much did you know about their real needs and their real intentions in the negotiation? Very often even the listing agent doesn't know, does he? He's been in direct contact with the sellers when they listed the property. However, when asked about the objectives of the sellers, he will very often reply, "Well, I don't know. I know they want cash out, so they're not willing to carry back paper, but I don't know what they're going to do with the cash. I didn't think it was my place to ask."

In my all-day and two-day seminars I have the students break into teams of negotiators, with some assigned as buyers and others as sellers. I give them enough information to complete a successful negotiation. In fact, I purposely give each side discoverable strengths and weaknesses.

I tell each side that if the other side asks them a question to which they have been given an answer, they may not lie. If one side unearthed only half of these carefully planted tidbits of information, that side would be in a powerful position to complete a successful negotiation.

Unfortunately, no matter how many times I drill students on the importance of gathering information—even to the point of assigning 10 minutes of the negotiation for only that—they are still reluctant to do a thorough job.

Why are people reluctant to gather information? Because to find things out, you have to admit that you don't know, and most of us are extraordinarily reluctant to admit that we don't know. Let me give you a quick exercise to prove this point. I'm going to ask you six questions, all of which you can answer with a number, but instead of having you try to guess the right number, I'll make it easier for you by asking you to answer with a range.

If I asked you how many states there are, instead of saying 50, you'd say, "Between 49 and 51." If I asked you for the distance from Los Angeles to New York, you might be less sure so you'd say, "Between 2,000 and 4,000 miles." You could say from one to a million and be 100 percent sure of course, but I want you to be 90 percent sure that the right answer falls within the range you give. Do you have the idea?

Here are the questions:

Q: How many provinces are there in Canada?

Between __________ and __________.

Q: How many wives did Brigham Young have?

Between __________ and __________.

Q: How much did we pay Spain for Florida in 1819?

Between __________ and __________.

Q: How many Perry Mason novels did Erle Stanley Gardner write?

Between __________ and __________.

Q: How many eggs do chickens lay each year in the United States?

Between __________ and __________.

Q: What is the length of Noah's Ark in feet, according to Genesis?

Between __________ and __________.

Answers

A: There are 10 provinces in Canada (and two territories).

A: Brigham Young, the Mormon leader, had 27 wives.

A: We paid $5 million for Florida.

A: Erle Stanley Gardner wrote 75 Perry Mason novels.

A: About 67 billion eggs are laid in the United States each year.

A: Noah's Ark was 450 feet long. According to Genesis 6:15, the ark was 300 x 50 x 30 cubits, and a cubit equals 18 inches.

How did you do? Did you get them all right? Probably not, but think how easy it would have been to get them all right. All you would have had to do is to admit that you didn't know, and make the range of your answer huge. You probably didn't do that because just like everyone else, you don't like to admit that you don't know. The first rule for gathering information is: Don't be over-confident. Admit that you don't know and admit that anything you do know may be wrong.

Rule 2: Don't Be Afraid to Ask the Question

I used to be afraid to ask questions for fear that the question would upset the other person. I was one of those people who say, "Would you mind if I asked you?" or "Would it embarrass you to tell me?" I don't do that anymore. I ask them, "How much money did you make last year?" If they don't want to tell you, they won't. Even if they don't answer the question, you'll still be gathering information.

Good reporters ask all kinds of questions that they know the other person will not answer, but they ask them anyway. It might put pressure on the other person or annoy him so that he blurts out something he didn't intend to. Just judging the other person's reaction to the question might tell you a great deal.

You Can Solve a Tough Problem Just by Asking

Sometimes people are involved in a conflict negotiation, and they're afraid to ask the other side what they want. Many years ago, I was the assistant manager of the Montgomery Ward store in Auburn, California. Our company's policy stopped me, or any other employee, from saying no to a customer. If we didn't feel that a customer's complaint was justified, they would transfer the complaint up the customer-service ladder. This meant that if a customer kept complaining without getting satisfaction for his or her complaint, the problem would eventually work its way to the chairman of the board at the head office in Chicago.

An elderly couple had bought a Franklin stove from the company's catalog. They had installed it themselves and, according to their complaint letter, the stove had malfunctioned, blackening the walls of their home, and burning a hole in their carpet.

Everyone who tried to deal with this complaint assumed that it would be very expensive to satisfy this couple, so everyone was reluctant to admit blame and offer a settlement. The letter made its way from desk to desk until it came to rest on the desk of the regional vice president. The last thing he wanted to do was let the complaint reach the head office in Chicago, so he wrote to me, requesting that I visit the couple and take some pictures so that they could estimate the cost of a settlement.

I drove out to their small cottage in the countryside and met the people who were complaining. They were a sweet, trusting old couple who had bought a stove out of the catalog and were genuinely disappointed at the results. The husband calmly showed me how soot from the chimney had blackened the outside of his home. Then he took me inside to show me the hole in their carpet caused by hot coals falling from the stove. He quickly convinced me that the stove had malfunctioned, and the problem wasn't in the way they had installed it.

Fearing that we would be talking about a settlement of several thousand dollars, I starting with a question that I assumed many of our people had asked them before: "Exactly what do you think our company should do for you? How can we compensate you for this?"

To my surprise, the husband answered, "You know, we're retired and have a lot of time on our hands. The wall is a mess, but we can certainly clean it up. It's no problem at all. However, we are concerned about the hole in our carpet. It's quite large, but we really don't expect you to replace the entire carpet. If we had a scatter rug that we could put over the hole, that would take care of it."

He was asking for so little that it stunned me. Then I recovered enough to say, "Do you mean to tell me that if we gave you a scatter rug, that would solve the problem?"

"Oh, yes," he answered. "We'd be very happy with that."

We all got into my car and drove straight to the store, where I helped them choose a beautiful rug to put over the hole in their carpet. I got them to sign a complete release form confirming that the settlement satisfied them and sent it off to the regional vice president. Several days later, I got a letter from the vice president congratulating me on "what was obviously a masterful job of negotiating." That was nonsense, of course; I had solved the problem merely by asking what nobody had the courage to ask before: "What exactly is it you want?"

This lesson served me well in the coming years as I worked my way up the corporate ladder. I was able to easily solve customer complaint problems simply because I bothered to get adequate information, starting with "What do you want?"

When I later became president of a large real estate company, I started using the lesson to solve the problem of buyers who were not happy with the home they'd bought. The sellers of the home had usually moved out of the area, leaving the company—and me—to solve the problem.

I would sit my visitors down in my office, and, with a large piece of paper in front of me, ask, "Please, I would like to know exactly what your complaints are, and exactly what you think we should do for you in each instance."

"Well," they would say, "the light switch in the living room doesn't work." I would write on the paper "Light switch in living room." I would continue to ask them if there was anything else until they had aired all of their grievances, and carefully write them down on my paper.

When they ran out of complaints, I would draw a line across the sheet under the last item and show the paper to them. Then I'd negotiate what we would or wouldn't do for them. Most people are willing to compromise, and if I offered to send out a plumber to fix the leaking faucet, they would be willing to replace the light switch in the living room. With this method, what they wanted was clear from the beginning; they had laid all of their cards out, face up, and I was in the controlling position, because I could decide what my response would be.

Doing it the other way is foolish, but it's the way most people who handle complaints do it. They ask what the problem is and then handle it item by item. The homeowners complain that the light switch doesn't work and because that's not an expensive item, the person handling the complaint says, "No problem. We'll take care of it." The homeowners would immediately think that it would be easy to get more concessions and keep thinking of other things that were wrong. In negotiating terms, that's called escalating the demands. By asking them to commit first to a list of demands, you put parameters on the demands.

If you want to learn about another person, nothing will work better than the direct question. In my own experience—now that I'm no longer afraid to ask—I've met only a few people who were seriously averse to answering even the most personal questions. For example, how many people get offended when you ask them "Why were you in hospital?" Not very many.

It's a strange fact of human nature that we're very willing to talk about ourselves, yet we're reticent when it comes to asking others about themselves. We fear the nasty look and the rebuff to a personal question. We refrain from asking because we expect the response "That's none of your business." Yet how often do we respond that way to others?

As president of a real estate company in California, I wanted to encourage our agents to knock on doors searching for leads. Real estate people call it farming. I found our agents very reluctant to do it. I eventually formulated a plan where I would take each one of our 28 office managers out separately knocking on doors, and we would play the information game. I would say, "Okay. I'm going to knock on the first door, and I'm going to see how much information I can get from these people. You knock on the second door—see if you can get more information than I did."

It was amazing to see the amount of information the people would volunteer to a stranger on the doorstep. I could get them to tell me where they worked, where their wives worked, sometimes how much money they made, how long they'd been in the property, how much they paid for it, how much their loan payments were, and so on. People are often eager to volunteer information, if we'll only ask.

Asking for more information in your dealings with others will not only help you to be a better negotiator; it will also be a major factor in helping you get what you want out of life. Asking questions is a good habit for you to adopt. Just ask. Sounds easy, doesn't it? Yet, most of us are squeamish about asking someone a question.

When you get over your inhibitions about asking people, the number of people willing to help you will surprise you. When I wanted to become a professional speaker, I called up Danny Cox, who is a speaker I greatly admire, and asked him if I could buy him lunch. Over lunch, he willingly gave me a $5,000 seminar on how to be successful as a speaker. Whenever I see him today, I remind him of how easy it would have been for him to talk me out of the idea. Instead, though, he was very encouraging. It still astounds me how people who have spent a lifetime accumulating knowledge in a particular area are more than willing to share that information with me without any thought of compensation.

It seems even more incredible that these experts are very rarely asked to share their expertise. Most people find experts intimidating, so the deep knowledge that they have to offer is never fully used. What a senseless waste of a valuable resource—all because of an irrational fear.

Rule 3: Ask Open-Ended Questions

Power Negotiators understand the importance of asking and of taking the time to do it properly. What's the best way to ask? Rudyard Kipling talked about his six honest serving men. He said:

> *I keep six honest serving-men.*
> *(They taught me all I knew);*
> *Their names are What and Why and When*
> *and How and Where and Who.*

Of Kipling's six honest serving men, I like Why the least. Why can easily be seen as accusatory. "Why did you do that?" implies criticism. "What did you do next?" doesn't imply any criticism. If you really need to know why, soften it by rephrasing the question using what instead: "You probably had a good reason for doing that. What was it?" Learn to use Kipling's six honest serving men to find out what you need to know.

You'll get even more information if you learn how to ask open-ended questions. Closed-ended questions can be answered with a yes, no, or a specific answer. For example, "How old are you?" is a closed-end question. You'll get a number and that's it. "How do you feel about being your age?" is an open-ended question. It invites more than just a specific answer response. "When must the work be finished by?" is a closed-ended question. "Tell me about the time limitations on the job" is an open-ended request for information.

Here are four open-ended Gambits you can use to get information. First, try repeating the question. They say, "You charge too much." However, they don't explain why they feel that way, and you want to know why. You repeat the question: "You feel we charge too much?" Very often, they'll come back with a complete explanation of why they said that. Or if they can't substantiate what they said because they were just throwing it out to see what your response would be, maybe they'll back down.

The second Gambit is to ask for feelings. Not what happened, but how did they feel about what happened? You're a contractor, and your foreman says, "Did they ever cuss me out when I showed up on the job. The air was turning blue." Instead of saying, "What caused that?" try saying, "How did you feel about that?" Maybe the response you get will be, "I probably deserved it. I was an hour late and they did have three truckloads of concrete sitting there, waiting for me."

The third Gambit is to ask for reactions. The banker says, "The loan committee usually requires a personal guarantee from small business owners." Instead of assuming it's the only way to get the loan, try saying, "And what's your reaction to that?" She may come back with, "I don't think it's necessary, as long as you'll guarantee to maintain adequate net worth in your corporation. Let me see what I can do for you with them."

The fourth Gambit is to ask for restatement. They say, "Your price is way too high." You respond, "I don't understand why you say that." Chances are that instead of repeating the same words, they'll come back with a more detailed explanation of the problem.

Let's recap the four open-ended Gambits for gathering information.

1. Repeat the question. "You don't think we can meet the specifications?"
2. Ask for feelings. "And how do you feel about that policy?"
3. Ask for reactions. "What was your response to that?"
4. Ask for restatement. "You don't think we'll get it done on time?"

Rule 4: Where You Ask the Question Makes a Big Difference

Power Negotiators also know that the location where you do the asking can make a big difference. If you meet with people at their corporate headquarters, surrounded by their trappings of power and authority, and their formality of doing business, it's the least likely place for you to get information.

People in their work environment are always surrounded by invisible chains of protocol—what they feel they should be talking about and what they feel they shouldn't. That applies to an executive in her office, it applies to a salesperson on a sales call, and it applies to a plumber fixing a pipe in your basement. When people are in their work environments, they're cautious about sharing information. Get them away from their work environments, and information flows much more freely. And it doesn't take much. Sometimes all that it takes is to get that vice president down the hall to his company lunchroom for a cup of coffee. Often, that's all it takes to relax the tensions of the negotiation and get information flowing. And if you meet for lunch at your country club, surrounded by your trappings of power and authority, where he's psychologically obligated to you because you're buying the lunch, then that's even better.

Rule 5: Ask Other People—Not With Whom You'll Negotiate

If you go into a negotiation knowing only what the other side has chosen to tell you, you are very vulnerable. Others will tell you things that the other side won't, and they will be able to verify what the other side has told you.

Start by asking people who've done business with the other side already. I think it will amaze you—even if you thought of them as competition—how much they're willing to share with you. Be prepared to horse trade information. Don't reveal anything that you don't want them to know, but the easiest way to get people to open up is to offer information in return.

People who have done business with the other side can be especially helpful in revealing the character of the people with whom you've been negotiating. Can you trust them? Do they bluff a great deal in negotiations, or are they straightforward in their dealings? Will they stand behind their verbal agreements, or do you need an attorney to read the fine print in the contracts?

Next, ask people further down the corporate ladder than the person with whom you plan to deal. Let's say you're going to be negotiating with someone at the main office of a nationwide retail chain. You might call up one of the branch offices and get an appointment to stop by and see the local manager.

Do some preliminary negotiating with that person. He will tell you a lot (even though he can't negotiate the deal) about how the company makes a decision, why one supplier is accepted over another, the specification factors considered, the profit margins expected, the way the company normally pays, and so on. Be sure that you're "reading between the lines" in that kind of conversation.

Without you knowing it, the negotiations may have already begun. For example, the branch manager may tell you, "They never work with less than a 40 percent markup," when that may not be the case at all. And never tell the branch manager anything you wouldn't say to the people at his head office. Take the precaution of assuming that anything you say will get back to them.

Next, take advantage of peer-group sharing. This refers to the fact that people have a natural tendency to share information with their peers. At a cocktail party, you'll find attorneys talking about their cases to other attorneys, when they wouldn't consider it ethical to share that information with anyone outside their industry. Doctors will talk about their patients to other doctors, but not outside their profession.

Power Negotiators know how to use this phenomenon because it applies to all occupations, not just in the professions. Engineers, controllers, foremen, and truck drivers all have allegiances to their occupations, as well as their employers. Put them together with each other and information that you couldn't get any other way will flow.

If you're thinking of buying a used piece of equipment, have your driver or equipment supervisor meet with his counterpart at the seller's company. If you're thinking of buying another company, have your controller take their bookkeeper out to lunch. You can take an engineer from your company with you to visit another company and let your engineer mix with their engineers. You'll find out that, unlike top management—the level at which you may be negotiating—engineers have a common bond that spreads throughout their profession, rather than just a vertical loyalty to the company for which they currently work. All kinds of information will pass between these two.

Naturally, you have to watch out that your person doesn't give away information that could be damaging to you, so be sure you pick the right person. Caution her carefully about what you're willing to tell the other side and what you're not willing to tell—the difference between the open agenda and your hidden agenda. Then let her go to it, challenging her to see how much she can find out. Peer-group information gathering is very effective.

Rule 6: Ask Questions for Reasons, Not Gathering Information

Though the primary reason for asking questions is to gather information, the following shows there are many other purposes for asking questions:

- To criticize the other side. Have you resolved the delivery problems you were having? How did that consumer lawsuit work out? Why did you close your Atlanta office after only six months of operation? Why did Universal pull their business from you? Is the FTC investigation going forward? You may already know the answers to these questions or the answer may be unimportant to you.
- To make the other side think. Are you sure that expanding into Puerto Rico is the right thing to do? How comfortable are you with your new advertising agency? How would your people react to your doing business with us? Doesn't giving all of your business to that vendor make you nervous?
- To educate them. Were you at the association meeting where we got the packaging award of the year? Did you see the review of our product in *Newsweek*? Were you aware that we have a new plant in Bangkok? Were you aware that our vice president used to be president of Universal?
- To declare your position. You're aware that experts regard our delivery system as the best in the industry? Why would we be willing to do that? Do you know anybody else who believes that? Then why do 95 percent of our customers continue to increase the size of their orders?
- To get a commitment. Which model would work best for you? How many should we ship you? Will you want the deluxe packaging or the mail-order packaging? How quickly will you want delivery?
- To pull the two sides closer together. This is a technique used frequently by mediators and arbitrators. They say: Can we both agree on that? What would happen if I could get them to agree to a 5-percent increase? But what would you do if they decide to picket your stores? You don't really expect them to go along with that, do you?

I think of the information-gathering process as similar to the game of Battleship that I used to play when I was a youngster. You can buy electronic versions of it in toy stores today, but when I was growing up in England after World War II, no toys were being manufactured. We had to entertain ourselves with little games that we could create without having to buy anything, and the game of Battleship was great fun.

My cousin Colin and I would sit at the table across from each other and build a barrier between us so that we couldn't see the piece of paper that was in front of the other person. We usually constructed the barrier with a pile of books. Each of us would take a piece of paper and draw a hundred different squares marked with the alphabet down one side and numbers along the bottom. On this graph, we would draw our fleet of battle ships, cruisers, and destroyers. My cousin couldn't see where I had located mine, and I couldn't see where he had located his. Then we would attempt to bomb each other's fleets by calling out the graph number. When we made a successful hit, we would mark the position on our chart, and in doing so, gradually build up a picture of the other person's hidden fleet.

The parallel here is that the hidden piece of paper in negotiations is the other person's hidden agenda. By judicious questioning, you should try to find out as much as you possibly can about that person's hidden agenda and recreate it on your side so that you know exactly where he's coming from and what he's trying to achieve.

Power Negotiators always accept complete responsibility for what happens in the negotiations. Poor negotiators blame the other side for the way they conducted themselves.

Performers Never Have a Bad Audience

I was conducting a negotiating seminar in the San Fernando Valley, and comedian Slappy White was in the audience. During the break, I told him how much I admired comedians. "It must be fun to be successful like you," I told him, "but coming up through those comedy clubs with all their hostile audiences must be sheer hell."

"Roger," he told me, "I've never had a bad audience."

"Oh, come on, Slappy," I replied, "When you were starting out, you must have had some awful audiences."

"I've never had a bad audience," he repeated. "I've only had audiences that I didn't know enough about."

As a professional speaker, I accept that there is no such thing as a bad audience. There are only audiences about which the speaker doesn't know enough. I've built my reputation on the planning and research that I do before I'll get up in front of an audience.

As a negotiator, I accept that there's no such thing as a bad negotiation. There are only negotiations in which we don't know enough about the other side. Information gathering is the most important thing we can do to assure that the negotiations go smoothly.

Key Points to Remember

1. Good information gathering is essential to successful negotiating.
2. Don't be afraid to admit that you don't know.
3. Be a good reporter. Ask the tough questions.
4. Don't assume that you know what the other side wants. Get them to tell you.
5. Ask open-ended questions that cannot be answered with a yes or no. Asking what, why, when, how, where, and who will teach you all you want to know.
6. Be cautious about asking why. Don't imply criticism.
7. Repeat the question. "You don't think we can meet the specifications?"
8. Ask for feelings. "And how do you feel about that policy?"
9. Ask for reactions. "What was your response to that?"
10. Ask for restatement. "You don't think we'll get it done on time?"
11. Don't rely only on information given to you by the other side.
12. People share information more readily when away from their workplace.
13. Use peer group information-gathering techniques. People share information more easily when they relate to the other person better.

Chapter 39

Being Prepared to Walk Away

Of all the negotiating pressure points, this one is the most powerful. It's projecting to the other side that you will walk away from the negotiations if you can't get what you want. If there's one thing that I can impress upon you that would make you a 10-times-more-powerful negotiator, it's this: Learn to develop Walk-Away power. The danger is that there's a mental point that you pass when you will no longer walk away.

- There's a point you reach in the negotiations when you start thinking, "I'm going to buy this car. I'm going to get the best price I possibly can, but I'm not leaving here until I get it."
- Or you are an employer and you're thinking, "I'm going to hire this person. I'm going to get them for the lowest salary and benefits that I can, but I'm not going to let this person slip through my fingers."
- You're looking for work and thinking, "I have to take this job. I'm going to fight for the best pay and benefits I can get, but I have to take this job."
- You fall in love with a new home, and you're thinking, "I'm going to buy this house. I'll get the seller down as low as I can, but this is the one I want."
- Or you're a salesperson thinking, "I have to make this sale. I can't walk out of here without a commitment."

The minute you pass the point when you're willing to say, "I'm prepared to walk away from this," you lose in the negotiations. Be sure you don't pass that point. There's no such thing as a sale you have to make at any price, or the only car or home for you, or a job or employee that you cannot do without. The minute you pass the point when you think there is, you've lost in the negotiations.

At seminars, when people tell me that they made a mistake in negotiations, this is always a part of the problem. They passed the point where they were willing to walk away. Some place in relating the story, they'll say to me, "I made up my mind that I was going to get it," and I know that was the turning point in the negotiation. It was the point at which they lost.

How to Make a Thousand Dollars an Hour

Many years ago, my daughter, Julia, bought her first car. She went down to the dealer and test-drove a fine used car. She fell in love with the car, and they knew it. Then she came back and wanted me to go back down with her, to renegotiate a better price. That's a tough situation, isn't it? On the way down there, I said, "Julia, are you prepared to come home tonight without the car?"

And she said, "No, I'm not. I want it. I want it."

I told her, "Julia, you might as well get your checkbook out and give them what they're asking because you've already set yourself up to lose in the negotiations. We've got to be prepared to walk away."

We walked out of the showroom twice in the two hours that we spent negotiating and bought the car for $2,000 less than she would have paid for it. How much money was she making while she was negotiating, bearing in mind that I waived my normal fee? She was making a thousand dollars an hour. We'd all go to work for a thousand dollars an hour, wouldn't we? You can't make money faster than you can when you're negotiating.

You become a Power Negotiator when you learn to project to the other side that you will walk away from the job if you can't get what you want. If you're the one who's selling something, be sure that you've built enough desire before you threaten to walk away. Obviously, if they don't particularly want your product or service yet and you threaten to walk away, you're going to find yourself standing on the sidewalk saying, "What happened?"

You should consider selling as a four-step process:

1. **Prospecting.** Looking for people who want to do business with you.
2. **Qualifying.** Determining if they can afford to do business with you.

3. **Desire-building.** Making them want your product or service above everybody else's.
4. **Closing.** Getting the commitment. Walking away is a stage-four Gambit. You use it after you've built desire, and you're going for the commitment.

Remember that the objective is to get what you want by threatening to walk away, not to walk away. Don't e-mail me to say, "Roger, you'd be so proud of me. I just walked away from a million-dollar sale." It's like General Patton saying to his troops, "Keep the objective clear. The object of war is not for you to die for your country, but to make the other poor bastard die for his country."

In a heavy situation, when there's a big issue at stake, don't threaten to walk away without the protection of Good Guy/Bad Guy. Don't do it alone. You should have a Good Guy left behind. Then, if you threaten to walk away and they don't say, "Hey, wait a minute, where are you going? Come on back; we can still put this together." If they don't say that, then you still have the Good Guy left behind, who can say, "Look, he's just upset right now. I think we can still put this together, if you can be a little bit more flexible in your pricing."

Developing Walk-Away Power

You develop Walk-Away power by increasing your alternatives. Remember that the side with the most options has the most power. If you've found the home of your dreams and are planning on making an offer on it, here's what you should do: You should find a couple of other homes that you'd like just as well. That way you'll be a tougher negotiator when you're dealing with the seller of the first home. Instead of thinking that this is the only home in which you'd be happy, you're thinking, "No problem. If I don't get a good price on this one, I'd be just as happy with one of the other two that I've picked out." It doesn't mean that you're not going to get the first one. It just means that when you give yourself options, you give yourself power.

If you're trying to buy a boat from an owner, first find two more boats that would make you just as happy. The side with the most options has the most power. If you are the only buyer with whom the seller is dealing, and you have three boats that would make you equally happy, you have enormous power as a negotiator.

How to Project Walk-Away Power

Let me tell you how to project Walk-Away power by telling you how a real estate broker used it on me. I owned a couple of properties in Long Beach, California, about 50 miles from where I live. I wasn't that familiar with the marketplace, and I was having trouble finding a good real estate agent to handle it for me. Finally, I heard about Walter Sanford, a real estate broker who seemed to be very aggressive in the way he went about business. He seemed to be the kind of person that I wanted to have representing me in the sale of this property.

I called him and said, "I've got a couple of properties very close to your real estate office. I'd like you to list them for me." His response was: "I might be prepared to represent you. When can you come to my office so that we can talk about it?" I liked that. He clearly was familiar with Power Negotiating. Number one, he was prepared to walk way from the listing. He didn't take the typical real estate attitude of "Wow, for two listings, I'll drop everything and come right now." He said: "I might be prepared to represent you."

Second, he knew that you should always try to negotiate in your own territory. He was a lot better off if he could talk me into coming to his office than if he came to my home to discuss it.

Third, he was starting the process of getting me to follow instructions. If you can get people to start doing what you ask them to do, even if it's a very small thing, you start to take command of the relationship. A momentum begins to build that ends up with: "Bear down, the fourth copy's yours."

I made an appointment for three or four days later and went to his office to meet with him. Meanwhile, he had checked out the properties and prepared a couple of information folders with his suggested selling prices. These prices were way below what I had hoped the properties were worth.

By this point, however, I had developed a lot of confidence in him and was thinking, "Well, he does know the territory a lot better than I do. Either I trust him or I don't. I'll go along with his proposed listing prices." Then he said to me: "Roger, you do understand that I won't work with anything less than a nine-month listing, don't you?"

I said: "Wait a minute, Walter. Nine months, when we've never worked together before? I don't think I'm prepared to take my property off the market for nine months."

What he did next was very bright. He stood up, closed the folders that he'd been consulting, and reached across the desk with his hand extended, saying, "Mr. Dawson, I'm very sorry, but I guess we won't be doing business together after all."

He was prepared to walk away from the listings if he couldn't get what he wanted. Where did that put me? Now I was in the position of having to negotiate with him to get him to accept the listings.

Of course, he had no idea that he was dealing with such a great negotiator. I was able to get him all the way down to six months on those listings, which is probably what he wanted in the first place!

I admired that. You should always ask for more than you expect to get—so that you set up a climate in which the other person can win in the negotiations. The important issue here is to communicate to the other side that you're prepared to walk away. What will typically happen for you is what happens when you're in the stores in Mexico. When you're prepared to walk out of the store, they will come racing out after you. Power Negotiators know that learning to communicate subtly to the other side that you're prepared to walk away is the most powerful Gambit of them all.

☑ Key Points to Remember

1. Always project that you're prepared to walk away.
2. Once you project that you won't walk away, you're projecting that you have no options, and you have lost all your power.
3. Selling is a four-step process: prospecting, qualifying, desire-building, and closing.
4. The objective is not to walk away. Your objective is to get concessions from the other side because they are convinced that you will walk away.
5. In a serious negotiation, protect yourself with Good Guy/Bad Guy.
6. Develop Walk-Away power by developing options before you start negotiating.
7. Learning to communicate to the other side that you're prepared to walk away is the most powerful Gambit of them all.

Chapter 40

Take It or Leave It

In the last chapter, I told you that projecting that you're prepared to walk away is the most powerful pressure point of them all. If you use it, however, be sure that you're gentle when you tell them that you're prepared to walk away. Remember that the objective is to get what you want by projecting that you're prepared to walk away. The objective is not to walk away—any idiot can do that.

If you're too blunt in the way you project this, you may antagonize them, so be careful. Don't use that obnoxious expression "take it or leave it." Even people of good will who feel that they're willing to meet your demands may recoil if you use that. Instead, use more subtle expressions such as "Sorry, but that has to be my walk-away price," or "We never deviate from our published price list."

What Not to Do in a Negotiation

The "take it or leave it" approach to union negotiations even has a name: Boulwarism. Lemuel Boulware was head of labor relations for General Electric during the 1950s and 1960s. His negotiating method was to make one offer that he thought was fair to the company, the union, and the stockholders, and never deviate from it. This "take it or leave it" attitude obviously creates bad feelings because it doesn't give the union negotiators a chance to have a win for their members. I'm sure it didn't escape Boulware's attention that if the union took the first offer, the members would begin to wonder why they needed a union. In 1964, the National Labor Relations Board found GE guilty of not bargaining in good faith. Even worse, Boulware's intransigence caused 13 unions to join in a walkout against the company in 1969.

A great way to be firm without being offensive is to use the Higher Authority Gambit. Who could take offense when you say, "I'd love to do better, but the people back at head office won't let me"? You can put a lot of pressure on people without confrontation using Higher Authority.

I knew a man who owned a small hotel in Manhattan. One of the problems he faced was friends who wanted to stay free of charge. He solved the problem by establishing a mother-in-law rate. They would call up to see if he had a room free, and he would say, "I tell you what I'll do. I'll give you my mother-in-law rate. This is what she pays when she stays here. Nobody stays for less." In that way, he was firmly telling them "no freebies," but he was doing it in a very diplomatic way.

Responding to Take It or Leave It

When somebody uses the blunt, "take it or leave it" approach on you (and it may be more subtly expressed, such as "That's our price; we don't negotiate"), you have three options:

1. Call his bluff. Tell him that your higher authority insists on concessions, and if that remains their position, there's no way that you can put this together. Perhaps you walk out and hope that they'll call you back.

   Before you consider this drastic response, consider whether the other negotiator has much to lose from your walking away. If it's a sales clerk in a retail store who is not on commission, he'll probably have little, if anything, to lose and will let you walk. I never had any luck negotiating price with communists, for example, because profit was not a motivating factor for them. Even if I bribed them, there was nothing they could spend money on anyway.

Why It's Tough to Negotiate With Communists

I remember checking into a hotel in East Berlin a few weeks after the wall had come down, but while the city was still in communist hands. It was 4 a.m. and I had just driven in from Zermatt, Switzerland—a monstrous drive. Frankly, I was lost and didn't even realize that I was in East Berlin until the desk clerk refused to budge on the room rate. My initial suggestion was that, because it was already 4:00 a.m., he not charge me for the first night, and I would pay for the following night. He refused. I tried for 50 percent off the first night, and finally 25 percent off, all to no avail. Eventually he said, "Maybe they do that in West Berlin, but we don't do it here."

I said, "Wait a minute. I'm in East Berlin? How did I get here? I didn't see any wall."

"The wall is down," he bluntly told me. Well, I had heard that news, but I always thought that the wall was a huge thing, several feet thick.

I could swear that I'd seen pictures of people standing on top of the thing. I didn't realize that it was mainly poured concrete slabs stood up on end that were comparatively easy to remove. Consequently, I had driven past where it used to be without seeing any sign of it. Once I knew that I was dealing with a communist, I gave up trying to get a concession from him. He had no incentive in his system that would make him want to please me.

Before you walk out, consider how much the other person has to lose by letting you do that. If they have nothing to lose, you probably won't get anywhere by walking out.

2. Go over the person's head. That doesn't always mean demanding to see his boss or calling his boss to complain. A gentler way is to ask, "Who is authorized to make an exception to the rule?" A little stronger would be to ask, "Would you mind checking with your supervisor and seeing if you can get her to make an exception to the rule? I'm sure that if anybody could get her to do it, it would be you." Even stronger would be, "Would you mind if we talked to your supervisor about this?"
3. Find a face-saving way for the other person to modify his or her intransigent position. Of course, this is the most desirable way to handle "take it or leave it." It is especially effective if the other negotiator has something to gain by finding a way around the impasse, which would be true if you're dealing with the owner of a business or someone on commission. "I can understand why you feel so strongly," you say, "but surely if I were willing to pay you a bonus, you'd be willing to make an exception to the rule, wouldn't you, Joe?" Or you might try, "Joe, let me ask you something. What would it take for you to change your position on that, just a little bit, and just this one time?"

☑ Key Points to Remember

1. Avoid the obnoxious expression "take it or leave it." It makes people dig in their heels.
2. You can put a lot of pressure on people without confrontation using the Higher Authority Gambit. "I'd love to do that, but I can't sell it to my people."
3. Respond to a "take it or leave it" attitude by a) calling his bluff, b) going over the person's head in a tactful way, or c) finding a face-saving way for the other person to give in to you.

Chapter 41

The Fait Accompli

Fait accompli is a French expression meaning "it is done." For example, by the 16th hole, Tiger Woods's victory was a fait accompli.

As a negotiating Gambit, it takes on a slightly different meaning.

If you have ever sent someone a check for less than they're asking and marked the back of the check "Payment in full is acknowledged," you have used the Fait Accompli Gambit. It's when one negotiator simply assumes the other will accept the assumed settlement rather than go to the trouble of reopening the negotiations. It works on the principle that it's a lot easier to beg forgiveness than it is to get permission.

In California and other states, Fait Accompli became so common in the auto repair industry that we passed laws against it. It was common for service stations to fix your car without getting your approval of the estimate, figuring that there wasn't much you could do about it once they had fixed the car, and they could hold it until you paid for it.

A friend of mine owned an outdoor advertising company in Asheville, North Carolina. He was negotiating with a farmer who had let trees grow on his property until they obscured one of Mike's billboards, reducing its commercial value to zero. Mike tried to negotiate a good faith payment in return for the farmer letting him trim back the trees, but the farmer demanded an outrageous amount of money because he thought Mike had no options. Mike decided to use the Fait Accompli Gambit on him.

One morning he had four of his workers sneak onto the farmer's property and fire up their chain saws in unison. Before the farmer could reach for his shotgun, the trees were down and his workers were back over the fence and driving off. Later in the day, Mike went by to apologize for the misunderstanding and was able to reach a much more reasonable settlement with the farmer.

The Fait Accompli Can Be Dangerous

The Fait Accompli Gambit does not engender warm feelings from one side to another. When *Batman* movie producers Peter Guber and Jon Peters were offered key positions at Sony Studios, when they were already under contract to Warner Brothers, they decided to sign anyway and present the Fait Accompli to Steve Ross, their boss at Warner. Ross went ballistic at the way Guber and Peters had handled this and decided to fight them on it.

It ended up costing Guber and Peters more than $500 million to buy out their contract. It was a bad choice of negotiating tactic because Ross probably would have released them without penalty if they had not antagonized him so much. What does this teach you? Don't use a Fait Accompli unless you don't care how the other side reacts, because it won't endear you to them.

Sometimes Fait Accompli is done so outrageously that you have to smile at the nerve of the person who does it to you. When I was young, I lent an expensive camera to an older man who had been an important mentor to me. He promptly pawned it and sent me the pawn ticket. Attached was a note that said, "Sorry about this, but I had to have the money. This is a very important lesson for you to learn in life—don't trust anybody."

More recently, a speaker's agent booked me to do a speech and collected the speaking fee from the company, but didn't send me my share, which was more than $6,500. He told my business manager that he had spent the money to pay his creditors, who were turning nasty. When pressed for a reason for stealing from me like this, he said, "I just figured that Roger was rich and didn't need the money nearly as much as I did." His audacity stunned and amused us so much that we let him make payments to us.

More subtle forms of Fait Accompli are effective ways of putting pressure on the other side. If you have been overcharged, sending them a check for the correct amount with a "paid in full" endorsement on the back may be simpler than arguing the point. If you are signing a contract and disagree with any of the points, make the changes and send the corrected contract back to them. They may well accept the changes rather than take the trouble to reopen the negotiations.

Key Points to Remember

1. *Fait accompli* is a French expression that means "it is done."
2. As a negotiating Gambit, it takes on a slightly different meaning. It refers to sending the other side an agreement to sign that assumes they will make the concessions you requested.
3. The tactic can infuriate the other side, so don't use it if you're concerned about their reaction.

Chapter 42

The Hot Potato

The next pressure point is the Hot Potato. That's when somebody wants to give you his or her problem and make it your problem. It's like tossing you a hot potato at a barbecue.

What Hot Potatoes are you tossed? Do you ever hear "We just don't have it in the budget"? Whose problem is it that they didn't budget properly for your fine product or service? It's their problem, right? Not yours. But they'd like to toss it to you and make it yours.

How about "I can't authorize that"? Whose problem is it that he hasn't developed the trust of the people to whom he reports? It's his, right? Not yours. But he'd like to toss it to you and make it yours.

If you're a contractor, customers have probably called you to say, "I need you to move my job up. If you're not here first thing in the morning, this entire project comes to a screeching halt." Whose scheduling problem is that? Theirs, right? Not yours. But what they'd like to do is toss you their problem and make it yours.

What you should do is what the international negotiators would tell you to do when the other side tries to give you its problems. I've found out from my study of international negotiations that exactly the same principles apply—the same rules that applied for the negotiators in Geneva during arms-control talks also apply to you when the other side is putting pressure on you. The same things apply, and the same responses are appropriate.

Here's how the international negotiators would tell you to respond to the Hot Potato: First, test it for validity. This is what international negotiators do when the other side tries to give them their problem. You have to find out right away whether it really is a deal killer that they've tossed you, or whether is it simply something they threw onto the negotiating table to judge your response. You must find out right away. Later is too late. If you work on their problem, they soon believe that now it's your problem and it's too late to test it for validity.

I used to be president of a 28-office real estate company in Southern California. In real estate, we used to get tossed the Hot Potato all the time, such as from the buyer, who would come into one of our offices and say, "We have only $10,000 to put down." Even in blue-collar areas, that would be a very low down payment. Our real estate agent could possibly work with it, but it would be tough.

I taught the agents to test it for validity right away—to tell the buyers, "Maybe we can work with $10,000. But let me ask you this: If I find exactly the right property for you, in exactly the right neighborhood, the price and terms are fantastic, your family is going to love it, your kids are going to love having their friends over to play, but it takes $15,000 to get in, is there any point in showing it to you, or should I just show it to my other buyers?"

Once in a great while they would respond, "Don't you speak English? Watch my lips: $10,000 is it and not a penny more. I don't care how good a buy it is." But nine times out of 10 they would say, "Well, we didn't want to touch our certificate of deposit, but if it's a really good buy, we might. Or maybe Uncle Joe would help us with the down payment." Immediately, the agent found out that the problem the buyers tossed her was not the deal killer that it had appeared to be.

If you sell home furnishings, one of your customers might say, "We've got $20 a square yard for carpeting and that's it." If you catch that Hot Potato, instead of tossing it back, you will probably start thinking of cutting prices right away—if you assume that what they told you was final. But instead, you test for validity up front, saying, "If I could show you a carpet that would give you double the wear and still be looking good five years from now, but cost only 10 percent more, you'd want to take a look at it, wouldn't you?"

Nine times out of 10 they'll say, "Sure, we'll look at it." Immediately, you know the price is not the deal buster that it appeared to be. Another way to counter the Hot Potato of "We don't have it in the budget" is to say, "Well, who has the authority to exceed the budget?" Sometimes you'll kick yourself at what happens next. They'll say, "That would take a vice president's authorization." You say, "You want to do it, don't you? Why don't you call the vice president and see if you can get an okay to exceed the budget?" He'll pick up the telephone, call the vice president, and argue for an okay. Sometimes, it's that simple. Test for validity right away.

I remember doing a seminar for the Associated General Contractors of Alaska. They put me up at the Anchorage Hilton, and on my departure day, I needed a late checkout. There were two young women standing right next to each other behind the registration desk, and I said to one of them, "Would you give me a 6 p.m. checkout in my room, please?"

She said, "Mr. Dawson, we could do that for you, but we'd have to charge you for an extra half-day."

Testing for validity, I said, "Who would have the authority to waive that charge?"

She pointed to the woman standing next to her and said, "She would." The woman standing right next to her!

I said to the other woman, "And how would you feel about that?"

She said, "Oh, sure. That would be fine. Go ahead."

Another way to handle the "we don't have it in the budget Hot Potato" is to ask them when their budget year ends. Here's how that paid off for me.

How This Gambit Made Me $6,300

I trained the 80 salespeople at one of the top HMOs in California. A few weeks before the meeting, the training director called me and suggested we have dinner so that she could fill me in on how the company operates. Because I figured that she was going to pay for dinner, I picked the top French restaurant in Orange County, and we had a great dinner.

As dessert was served I said, "You know what you should do? You should invest in a set of my audio CDs for each of your salespeople so that they have the advantage of a continuous learning process." As I said that, I was mentally computing that 80 salespeople at $79 per set of CDs would be another $6,300 income on top of the speaking fee to which they'd already agreed.

She thought about it and said, "Roger, that probably would be a good idea, but we just don't have it in the budget."

I need to make a confession here. I'm very ashamed of what I thought next, but I want to share it with you because it may help you if you've ever had the same thought. I thought, "I wonder if I cut the price whether she would say yes." Isn't that a shameful thought? She hadn't said a thing about the tapes costing too much. She hadn't told me that she might be tempted if I lowered my price. She had simply told me that she didn't have it in the budget.

Fortunately, I caught myself and instead tested for validity. I asked, "When does your budget year end?" This was August, and I thought that she would tell me December 31st.

To my surprise, she said, "At the end of September."

"So you would have it in the budget on October 1st?"

"Yes, I suppose that we would."

"Then, no problem. I'll ship you the tapes and bill you on October 1st. Fair enough?"

"That would be fine," she told me. In less than 30 seconds, I had made a $6,300 sale because I knew that when she tossed me what was essentially her problem, I should test for validity.

I was feeling so good about this that when the waiter brought the bill, I slid my credit card into the leather case. He took it away, and she quietly said, "Roger, we were thinking of paying for dinner." I thought, "Roger, there are days when nothing goes right. You suffer through those. This is a day when nothing can go wrong, so why not relish it?" I called the waiter back and told him that we gave him the wrong credit card.

Look out for people giving you their problems. You have enough of your own, don't you? It's like the businessman who was pacing the floor at night. He couldn't sleep, and his wife was getting frantic. "Darling, what's bothering you? Why don't you come to bed?" He said, "Well, we have this huge loan payment due tomorrow, and the bank manager is a good friend of ours. I just hate to face him and say that we're not going to have the money to pay him."

His wife picked up the telephone, called their friend the bank manager, and said, "That loan payment we have coming due tomorrow, we don't have the money to pay it."

The husband exploded. He said, "What did you do that for? That's what I was afraid of."

His wife said, "Well, dear, now it's his problem, and you can come to bed."

Don't let other people give you their problems.

Key Points to Remember

1. Beware of the other side giving you their problems.
2. Test for validity when they do. Is this really a deal killer?
3. Don't buy into their procedural problems. If they don't have it in the budget, they can change the budget. If it goes against company procedure, they can change the procedure.

Chapter 43

Ultimatums

Ultimatums are very high-profile statements that tend to strike fear into inexperienced negotiators. Terrorists are holding a plane full of hostages and tell negotiators that, unless their demands are met, they will start shooting hostages at noon on the following day. An ultimatum is a powerful pressure point, but it has one major flaw as a gambit: If you say that you are going to shoot the first hostage at noon tomorrow, what had you better be prepared to do at noon tomorrow? That's right. Shoot the first hostage. Because if 12:01 p.m. rolls around and you haven't done that, you have just lost all of your power in the negotiation.

The same weakness applies to an ultimatum in a business negotiation. If you tell a supplier that unless she can deliver by noon tomorrow you will go with her competitor, what had you better be prepared to do at noon tomorrow? That's right: Go with her competitor. Because if the deadline passes and you haven't done that, you have just lost all of your power in the negotiation. You should only use ultimatums as a pressure point if you are willing to follow through. Don't bluff, because all the other side has to do is wait through your deadline to find out that you were only bluffing and your threat had no teeth in it.

When you understand the weakness in using ultimatums as a pressure point, you can easily figure out that the strongest Counter Gambit is to call their bluff and let the deadline pass. There are other less blatant responses, however. If someone gives you an ultimatum, you have four ways to respond, and I list them here in increasing levels of intensity:

1. Test the ultimatum as soon as you can. They tell you that the shipment must be there by noon tomorrow. Test the ultimatum by asking if having a partial shipment there by noon would solve their problem. Could you airfreight enough for them to keep their assembly line going and surface ship the balance?

2. Refuse to accept the ultimatum. Tell them that you have no idea if you can make that deadline or not, but that they can be assured that you're doing everything humanly possible to get it done.
3. Play for time. Time is the coin of the realm when one side is threatening the other with an ultimatum. The longer they go on without carrying out the threat, the less likely they are to follow through with the threat. Terrorist negotiators always play for time. This happens in hostage negotiations where the perpetrators are demanding a getaway helicopter or car. The police negotiator plays for time by saying that he needs to get the governor's approval or that the getaway car is on its way, but it's stuck in traffic. As the time passes, the scales tip upward dramatically in favor of the negotiators.
4. Bluff your way through and let the ultimatum pass. If it works, it's the best alternative because it not only solves this immediate crisis, but it also lets them know that you're not going to let them push you around in the future. Bluffing takes courage, however, and you shouldn't do it capriciously. Get all the information you can about the situation. The essential thing to find out is whether anything has changed. Since you signed the contract with them, has a new supplier appeared who could supply them on time and for less money? If you have a contract or an option to buy, have they had a better offer from someone else? If nothing else has changed, you may be safe in taking the chance. What you're trying to uncover, of course, is if they want to continue the relationship with you, or if the ultimatum is their method of getting you out of the picture.

☑ Key Points to Remember

1. Only use ultimatums when you are prepared to do what you threatened to do.
2. Don't tell people that the price is only good if they buy now unless you mean it.
3. Experienced negotiators always test ultimatums.
4. Respond to an ultimatum by: a) testing it, b) refusing to accept it, c) playing for time, and d) bluffing and letting the deadline pass.

Section Four

Negotiating With Non-Americans

At my Secrets of Power Negotiating seminars, I am usually asked about negotiating with non-Americans and new Americans—the immigrants who bring their customs and values with them. It seems just about everyone has had a frustrating experience dealing either with a non-American, or a person of foreign origin. Although I've been living in the United States since I emigrated from England in 1962 and a have been a proud citizen of this country since 1972, I can relate to the difficulty of dealing with non-Americans. Along with my experience of moving here from England and adapting to the American way of doing things, I have also traveled to 113 other countries around the world.

Because of my background, I know how different America is from any other country on Earth. America is deceptively different to non-Americans because many of them have had a great deal of exposure to American culture from watching our movies and television shows. Movies and television don't reveal what is in the American heart and mind, however, and that's what determines our approach to business.

Conversely, we tend to look at non-Americans and think we understand them. True, they may dress in Western business suits and speak our language, but that doesn't mean that their traditional values and mind-sets have changed. They may prefer American music and movies, but their beliefs in their way of life and the values that they place on their traditions are as strong as ever.

I believe that, underneath all of our apparent similarities, there lie enormous differences in our approaches to business. In this section, I'll try to unravel the mysteries of negotiating with non-Americans and new Americans.

Chapter 44

How Americans Negotiate

The American Art of the Deal

New York real estate investor Donald Trump wrote a best-selling book, *The Art of the Deal*, that detailed many of his early real estate negotiations. The title and the premise of the book illuminate the overriding concern of most American negotiators: the cutting of the deal. We do live in a very deal-conscious environment.

I suppose that sociologists would tell you that we concentrate more on cutting the deal than other nations because we are such a mobile and diverse society that we have little sense of roots. Instead of trusting the people and the way things are done, as is common around the world, we place all of our trust in creating an unbreakable deal. "Will it hold up in court?" we demand, as though anyone who doesn't consider the possibility of having to defend the deal in court is naïve.

Sociologists would also point out that this is a recent change in the fabric of our society. During the first half of the 20th century, we still looked to community pressures to enforce our obligations. To renege on a deal was unthinkable because of the dishonor that it would bring us in our community. We also had our religious community to police any thoughts of reneging on a commitment. It would be unthinkable to let down our priest, minister, or rabbi. Also, before television commandeered our leisure time, we belonged to many community organizations. We did not stray far because the members of our Lions, Kiwanis, or Optimist club—or the members of our PTA or Masonic or Elks lodge—might ostracize us. Sadly, that way of life is lost to us in the 21st century. Now what are left to us are the deal and an all-too-common resort to the courts to enforce the deal at all costs. The deal is finite, the deal is static, and the deal has been made and cannot be changed.

Most non-Americans completely reject our dependence on the deal. Should they choose to sign a contract at all, it is simply an expression of an understanding that existed on a particular date. It is a formal expression of a relationship that now exists between the parties. As with any other relationship, it must mold itself to changing conditions.

Most Americans are astounded to learn that you can sign a contract in Korea and have it mean nothing six months later. "But we signed a contract," the Americans howl.

"Yes," their Korean counterpart patiently explains. "We signed a contract based on the conditions that existed six months ago when we signed it. Those conditions no longer exist, so the contract we signed is meaningless."

"Foul," cries the American. "You are trying to cheat me." Not at all. What seems to us to be disreputable action is not to them, and we should not attempt to paint it as such. It is merely their way of doing things.

Americans are often delighted to find that they had so little trouble getting their Arab trading partners to sign a contract. Then they are horrified to find out that in the Arab world, signing the contract announces the start of the negotiations, not the end. A signed contract means less in their culture than a letter of intent does in ours. I am not putting this down, and you should not either. What we should do is recognize that different nationalities and cultures have different ways of doing things, and it behooves us to learn, understand, and appreciate those ways.

It will come as no surprise to you to learn that Americans resort to legal action more quickly and frequently than any other people on Earth. This would be laughable to a businessman in India, where the civil legal system is close to nonexistent. The country's trial courts currently have a backlog of close to 30 million cases. The chief justice of the Delhi courts estimates that it would take 466 years to clear the backlog. In 2010, the courts finally decided the Union Carbide case that was filed more than 25 years previously.

Clearly, Indians must rely on their faith in the person with whom they are doing business. I remember trying to explain to an Indian the American custom of the bride and groom signing a prenuptial agreement before they marry. He was incredulous. "Why on earth would you marry someone that you did not trust," he wanted to know. What I couldn't make him understand was that wanting to put an agreement in legally acceptable written form does not denote distrust to an American.

In America, legal action is so common that companies continue to do business with a company that is suing them. We see it as a normal way to resolve a dispute and no reason for rancor. In most foreign countries, there is such a loss of face involved in being sued by another company that they will refuse to deal in any way with a company that is suing them. When I lecture in China, businesspeople are incredulous when I tell them that, in America, one company can sue another and still continue to do business with each other. In China, that would never happen.

High-Context vs. Low-Context Negotiations

The word *context* describes the degree of importance attached to the relationship between the parties, as opposed to the details of the contract. When the relationship is paramount, we call it a high-context negotiation. When the deal is the thing, we call it a low-context negotiation. Different nationalities place greater or lesser importance on context—the environment in which the proposal is made. These cultures are listed from high-context to low-context: Asia, Middle East, Russia, Spain, Italy, France, England, United States, Scandinavia, Germany, Switzerland.

Communication is also low-context in the United States. By that, I mean that words and expressions mean the same, regardless of where they are said. "No" means "no," whether it is whispered on a date, or yelled at you by your boss. We take that for granted in this country. I've even seen t-shirts worn by women (who are presumably students of linguistics) that say, "What part of 'No' don't you understand?" That is not so in high-context countries, where, in order to understand what was said, you would have to understand who said it to whom, where the comment was made, and in what context it was made.

To give you an example of this from my experience, let's suppose that Dwight, an American, has been to see a play, and you ask him how he enjoyed it. Dwight might say, "It was quite good." The meaning of that is very clear to an American. It means that Dwight thought the play was very good. Now let's suppose that it was Rodney, an Englishman who went to see the play. When he says, "It was quite good," that could mean a whole range of things. It could mean it was awful, but "I'm a polite enough fellow to not say that to the author in public." If the person who gave him the tickets asked him how he enjoyed the play, "quite good" could mean that the play was average but he appreciated being given the tickets. If Rodney's son wrote the play, "quite good" could mean "outstanding, but I'm not about to give you a swelled head."

When Scottish golfer Colin Montgomerie played in the U.S. Open at the Olympic Club in San Francisco, a reporter from the *Los Angeles Times* asked him how he had managed the impressive feat of playing an entire round without being in a single sand trap. Montgomerie replied, "Well, I am quite good." The reporter took this to be an arrogant response, and wrote it up in a blistering attack on Montgomerie's personality. That was unfair, because I think that what the golfer intended to convey was a wry, self-deprecating response. If he had known that American English is a low-context language, he would probably have said, "Well, I am fairly good." It's a thought that an American would have conveyed by saying, "It's because I played this course once before."

You will need a translator to do business in China. Be aware of the difficulties that he or she will have translating English into Chinese and vice-versa. First, find out if you are dealing with a translator (who will translate what you say) or an interpreter (who will translate what you mean). Interpreters take pride in understanding the intent of your speech, rather than literal translation of your words.

Chinese is a very high-context language. When I first gave seminars in China, I was very careful to talk about their child, not their children. Because of the country's one child-policy, I didn't want to offend anyone (or have the government think that I was disrespectful to their policies). My interpreter, Paul Yeh, explained to me that it didn't matter how I said it, because there is no singular or plural in Chinese. If someone tells you in Chinese that they are building a house, you don't know if they mean one house or a thousand houses. You must listen to the conversation to figure it out.

Chinese doesn't have tenses either. If some tells you in Chinese that they "build a house" you don't know if it means they are building a house, they were going to build a house, they did build a house, or they will build a house. You have to listen to the conversation and figure it out.

Paul, who is based in Taiwan, and is one of Mandarin's top translators, explained to me that it is much easier to translate English into Chinese than the other way around. Because English is a very specific language, it's easy to translate into Chinese. But with Chinese, you might have to listen to a paragraph or two to get the meaning of what is being said before you can translate into English.

The first thing we should learn about negotiating with non-Americans is that the deal is not the major issue to them. They put far more trust in the relationship between the parties. Is there good blood between the parties? If there is only bad blood, no amount of legal maneuvering will make the relationship worthwhile. While you are trying to hammer out the fine points of the deal, they are spending time assessing the fine points of your character.

Getting Down to Business With Non-Americans

Now let's concentrate on the other major mistake that we Americans make in dealing with non-Americans: We want to get down to business too quickly.

Nobody gets down to business faster than Americans do. Typically, we exchange a few pleasantries to ease any tension, and then get right down to hammering out the details of the deal. We socialize afterward. Non-Americans may take days, weeks, or even months before they feel comfortable moving from the getting-to-know-you stage to the point where they feel good about doing business.

When the Shah of Iran fell from power, the real estate company of which I was president in Southern California did a huge amount of business with Iranians (they prefer to be called Persians) who were fleeing the new regime, often with millions in cash to invest. Often, I would watch our people make the mistake of trying to talk business too quickly, which caused the Iranians to distrust them. We learned quickly that they wanted to sit and drink tea for several hours as they sized us up.

If you fly to Japan to conduct business, you may have to socialize for many days before they feel that it's appropriate to talk business. Be careful, however, that they're not just trying to push you up against a time deadline. At my seminars, many people have told me that their joy at being treated so well soon turned to chagrin as they realized how difficult it would be to get down to business at all. They have told me horror stories of not being able to negotiate until they were in the limousine on the way back to the airport. It's a two-hour ride out to Narita Airport, but that is negotiating under excessive time pressure. Terrified at the thought of going home empty-handed, they went straight to their bottom line.

When negotiating with non-Americans, we Americans would do much better if we would slow down. We tend to speak first, then listen to the response, and observe the behavior of the other negotiators. Non-Americans tell us that we should reverse that order. We should observe first, then listen, and finally speak. In fact, reacting slowly to the proposal of the other side is a mark of respect. Your silence does not indicate acceptance of their proposal, merely that you are giving it the consideration it deserves.

Americans fall into two major traps when dealing with non-Americans:

1. We over-emphasize the deal and don't attach enough importance to the relationship of the parties.
2. We get down to business too quickly.

The two are closely related, of course. Building a relationship with the other side to the point where you feel comfortable with them takes time. Enlarging on that relationship to the point where you trust the other person, and don't have to rely on the contract being airtight, takes a great deal of time.

Key Points to Remember

1. Americans focus on getting the contract signed.
2. Other cultures focus on the relationship of the parties.
3. To Americans, the contract is the end of the negotiations.
4. To Koreans, the contract would be void if circumstances change.
5. To Arabs, the contract signing signals the start of the negotiations.
6. Americans can sue each other and still do business. That would be unthinkable in most other countries.
7. High-context negotiation means that the relationship between the parties is paramount.
8. Low-context negotiating focuses on getting the contract signed.
9. American English is a low-context language. What is said is clearly understood. Chinese is a high-context language. You must listen to the conversation to understand the meaning.
10. Americans get down to business very quickly and socialize later. Other cultures want to spend time getting to know the other side before they will start negotiating.

Chapter 45

How to Do Business With Americans: A Guide for Non-Americans

I've been in this country since I emigrated from England in 1962, and I'm still learning about Americans. That makes this chapter a work in progress. I'm going to give you some observations about Americans and the way they do business. This is for non-Americans. If you're an American you might want to skip this chapter, because you won't agree with everything I say, and I don't want to upset you. On the other hand, you might take the enlightened viewpoint that, in order to understand other cultures, you must first understand your own.

Americans Are Very Succinct

This is the first thing that I had to learn when I came to this country. Americans can say in a few words what other nationals, particularly the English, take all day to say. An Englishman might walk out of his front door in the morning and say, "What a wonderful day! I feel positively overwhelmed by the beauty of the morning!" An American would say, "Great day!" and it means exactly the same thing.

I noticed this in the press briefings during the Gulf War. The British information officer would announce to the press, "I'm very pleased to report that we are on our battle plan, and if I may be so bold, slightly ahead of plan. Furthermore, I don't hesitate to say I believe we will stay ahead of plan." The American information officer would get up and with a sly grin on his face say, "We're kicking butt!" It means exactly the same thing! You as a non-American might see this succinctness as being very blunt, but Americans don't mean any offense by it.

Americans Answer Questions With One Word

When Americans ask you how you like your hotel, they don't want to know your reaction to your hotel. They just want reassurance that you're content. You can answer their inquiry with one word, and the word is "Great!" The same goes for any other question that starts with "How did you like..." or "How was the..." or "Did you like...?"

Are you ready to practice? Here we go:

Question: "How did you like America?"
Answer: "Great!"

Question: "How do you like Americans?
Answer: "Great!"

Question: "How are you enjoying your stay?"
Answer: "Great!"

Question: "What do you think of the American habit of answering every question with one word?"
Answer: "Great!"

Americans Talk in Idioms

Americans love idioms! An idiom is an expression that cannot be taken literally. When you hear one, you'll know right away that it cannot mean what it actually says. Most Americans use copious idioms without even realizing it. My Chinese translator warned me that my audience would not understand idioms and I should avoid them. I went through my talk in my mind and was amazed at how many I used without realizing it.

Here are some examples of idioms:

- He was at the party, but I gave him a wide berth.
- It took me all night to wade through the report.
- I finally ran him to earth at the airport in New York.
- It was a piece of cake.
- He only added fuel to the fire.

Americans need to realize that idioms can be very confusing to people from other cultures. Just to give you an idea of how confusing this sounds, this is what we Americans sound like to foreigners:

He really got in my hair when he pulled my leg, so I left him high and dry. This is straight from the horse's mouth—I feel like a million dollars. He let the cat out of the bag, so I took the bull by the horns. The early bird gets the worm, so I stuck my neck out and spilled the beans, which knocked his socks off. We're willing to bend over backward, we don't want to turn you off, and, because we're not out of the woods yet, we'll cough up, because we think you'll scratch our back.

Americans Are Very Patriotic

There is only one way to answer a question such as "How do you like America?" That is with an enthusiastic outpouring of support. "What a great country," you should say. "I just love it here." Americans do not want to hear that you were stuck in unbelievable traffic on the way from the airport, or that the violent level of crime shocks you.

Your opinions about Americans working too hard or being too materialistic are much better left unpacked in your luggage at your hotel. It's not that Americans are unrealistic about the problems. It's just that they are very paternalistic about their country. Think of America as their child, and a favorite one at that. You wouldn't dream of criticizing your friend's child, would you?

I'm a member of the Traveler's Century Club in Los Angeles. To qualify for membership, you must have traveled to more than 100 different countries. When people hear I've traveled so much, they often ask me, "If you could live anywhere in the world, where would it be?" I would never answer that question with a direct response. I would precede my answer with a compliment to America by saying, "If I couldn't live in the United States, I would live on the north shore of Lake Leman in Vevey or Montreux, in the French speaking part of Switzerland."

You may hear Americans criticize their country and sometimes very vocally. That's an American prerogative. Free speech and the right of assembly are guaranteed in writing by the Constitution. Don't take that criticism to mean that the complainer wants to change the way of government.

You may be amazed at the way presidents and members of Congress are quickly criticized for what may appear to you to be minor indiscretions. It is not so much puritanical outrage, although it's true that Americans are much narrower minded in this regard. British actress Emma Thompson, who portrayed a thinly disguised Hillary Clinton in the movie *Primary Colors,* was asked for her opinion on accusations that President Clinton had had sex with an intern. "I don't quite understand it," she said with exaggerated naiveté. "I could understand what the fuss was about if there was a horse involved or something like that." Realize that American outrage over government scandals is vented with full confidence that the government will not fall over exposing salacious behavior.

The American Class System

One of the things that I first loved about America when I came here was the lack of a class system. My father drove a taxicab in London, and would be forever branded as working class. That would severely limit my ability to advance myself in society. (Things have improved in England since I left and hopefully not because I left. More of that when I teach you how to negotiate with the English in Chapter 47.) America has little of this nonsense.

You may run into some "old money" people who inherited great wealth and have little concept of what it's like to work to advance themselves, but they are rare. Most Americans are where they are because they put forth the effort.

My friend Michael Crowe is also an immigrant from England. He told me, "The difference between England and America is simple. In England, if a worker is digging a ditch and looks up to see a Rolls Royce pass by, he thinks, 'I wonder who he's stealing from?' In America, the ditch digger looks up and thinks, 'One day I'm going to have one of those Rolls Royces.'"

In your country, the profile of wealth is probably a pyramid shape. The base of the pyramid is the poor people. Above that, you have a smaller middle class and the apex of the pyramid is the minority of rich people. The profile of wealth in America is more like a kite. A few very poor people, rising to a large middle and upper-middle class, and tapering off to a few very rich people. If you're here for business, almost all of your contact will be with the middle and upper-middle class.

Because of the lack of a class system in America, titles are important. Titles indicate rank and how well we're doing. Titles also indicate earnings in America, which is not so in other countries, where a general manager might supervise many others managers who earn more than he does. Titles are very important to Americans. It's our attempt at a class system. Class in America, if you can call it that, is based strictly on money. If you are financially successful, you will be admired, and your family background or the school that you attended will not impress anyone. In fact, Americans love to brag about their humble beginnings. Why else would I tell you that my father drove a taxicab?

Religion in America

I found it very hard to believe that America is one of the most religious countries in the world. Perhaps because the Constitution guarantees the separation of church and state, you just don't hear much about it. Perhaps it's because there are so many different religions. Perhaps it's because the most religious states are the rural ones that few newcomers visit. The truth is that Americans are very devout churchgoers. According to a Gallop poll, 41 percent go to church regularly (that's down from 58 percent 20 years ago), and 80 percent of those who don't will tell you that they pray regularly. Ninety percent of people polled say that they believe in God. Compare that to England, where only 15 percent of the people attend church, according to Tearfund, one of the largest relief organizations in the U.K.

This is important to you if you're to do business in America. Although the subject of religion will hardly ever come up in business, you are probably dealing with an American who feels strongly about his or her faith in God. Be careful you do not offend, particularly in the Bible Belt states that sweep down through the center of America from Iowa to Texas and east to South Carolina, which is probably the most religious state of all.

Ram Dass is a new age (metaphysical) religious leader and a very entertaining speaker. He tells a story about being invited to speak in Denver. The Baptist church was sponsoring his lecture, and, at the last minute, the church elders got cold feet. Their concern was: Would this man be saying anything that might go against their religion? He assured the church elders that he would not. "Will there be any praying?" they asked. "Not really," he told them. "At one point, we may all hold hands and push a wish for world peace out into the universe." "We wish you wouldn't do that," they told him.

The Frontier Mentality

Understand how close every American is to being an immigrant, and it will go a long way to helping you understand Americans. A remarkably high percentage of Americans are actually immigrants. It's more than 20 percent in California, the most diverse state. Nationwide, it is almost 10 percent. I don't mean immigrants from another state. I mean that they weren't born in the United States. Most Americans' parents or grandparents immigrated to this country.

It makes Americans value their freedom above all things. Americans hate being told what to do, particularly by their government. That attitude leads to several hard-to-understand facets of American life. It leads to a remarkable lack of city planning. Most Europeans, for example, are happy to comply with the design standards of their village, so that the entire community has a conforming look. Not Americans, because it would take away a freedom from government control that they cherish. Let me give you another example.

One of the most controversial issues in America is the right to bear arms. You'll see bumper stickers that say "When guns are banned, only criminals will have them." Nobody wants to stop people from hunting, but many people question why citizens need the right to own automatic weapons whose sole purpose is to kill people. That will be hard for you to understand, too, until you understand how strongly Americans feel the need to be free of government control.

Time Is Money to Americans

Americans tell a joke about the attorney who died and went to heaven. (That's not the punch line!) St. Peter, who in Christian mythology is the person who admits people to heaven, said to him, "Boy, are we thrilled to have you here. We've never had a 125-year-old attorney before."

The attorney protested, "I'm not 125. I'm 39."

St. Peter said, "There must be some confusion—according to the hours that you've billed...."

The joke is funny to Americans because it references the high-pressure world in which business executives live. Time is a commodity to Americans. We talk about saving it, investing it, and spending it. As a non-American, you'll find the pace of business life here startling. A deal can be a good deal, but it's an even better deal if the person who put it together can brag about how quickly he put it together. Michael Eisner, the chairman at Disney Corporation, ran into the president of Capital Cities, the parent of ABC television, at a conference in Sun Valley, Idaho. He broached the idea of Disney buying Capital Cities. In less than two months, he had purchased the company for $20 billion dollars. The speed of that deal would give him bragging rights at any country club in the land. When an American appears to be rushing you into a deal, he is not trying to trick you. He is just doing things his way.

You will find life in America to be very high-pressure. There is a great sense of urgency to seize an opportunity and make the most of it while you can. Some of this comes from Americans being so young. We are a very young society. Part of it comes from the strong sense of individualism. Katherine Hepburn said, "As one goes through life, one learns that if you don't paddle your own canoe, you don't move."

Another part of it comes from the American experience. Unless you're old enough to remember Pearl Harbor, you have never lived through a war. Until terrorists tore down the World Trade Towers in New York, Americans have never had our very existence challenged. That's the kind of life experience that makes people reevaluate their priorities and determine that there may be more important things in life than making money. To a German, it may make perfect sense to spend three weeks at a spa to rejuvenate their mind and body. To an American, a trip to the spa is more likely to mean a massage between business meetings.

The Opinionated American

A line in a Paul McCartney song talked about there being too many people reaching for a piece of cake. I think of that line whenever I hear of a new protest group that has sprung up. There are too many people in America trying to push their point of view on others. There is not a cause, however obscure, that has not organized into a protest group. You will find Americans are frank, outspoken, and opinionated. Don't take this personally. An American businessman may say to you, "That's hogwash, Hans, and you know it!" Don't take this as a personal attack. It's just that Americans are used to being very open and direct in their communications.

The Friendly American

Americans are eager to have you like them and share their admiration for what they and their country have accomplished. There is a superficial level of friendliness that confuses non-Americans. Part of this comes from the mobility of the society. Very few Americans stay put for long. It's unusual to meet someone who was born in the same state as the one in which they now reside. It's hard to build long-term friendships. Don't be confused by Americans who appear to suddenly have become your bosom buddy. When I first moved to America, I found that people whom I had met only superficially at a party or picnic would say to me, "We'll have to have you over to the house." Or "Let's get together soon." I thought this meant that I should pull out my appointment calendar and set a date. It doesn't mean that at all.

Business Cards

Every American businessperson carries a business card, and business card exchanges are common upon first meeting somebody. In your culture, it may be considered polite to carefully study and admire the card. You don't have to do that here. It's okay to stick it in your pocket with just a cursory glance.

Tipping in America

Load up with one-dollar bills because it's going to cost you a bundle in America. Plan to add 15 percent to restaurant bills, bar bills, and taxi fares. Skycaps who check your bags at airports and bellhops who carry your bags to your room expect $1 per bag. Hotel doormen expect a dollar when you arrive for holding the cab door open for you, and again when they call a cab for you when you leave.

Don't be looking through your coins trying to figure out an appropriate tip. Tips fold in America; they don't clink. Just round up to the next dollar. If you come from a country that doesn't believe in tipping, all of this will seem outrageous to you, but it's the way it works here. Don't withhold or reduce tips even for bad service, particularly when you're with businesspeople. It will just make you look cheap.

The Diverse Population of America

America is one of the most populated countries on Earth and one of the most diverse. You will certainly encounter people from all ethnic backgrounds. If you come from a homogenous country, this will confuse you. My friend Jack visited me from England and, as he looked around the restaurant, he said, "I can't believe how many non-Americans there are in this country." I told him, "Those are not non-Americans, Jack. They are Americans. You're the only non-American here."

California, where I live, is the most diverse state. Twenty percent of California's residents were not even born in the United States. If you live in the City of Los Angeles and are a Caucasian, you are the minority. Approximately 20 percent of the population of Los Angeles is of Asian descent, 30 percent is of Mexican descent, and 10 percent is African Americans. As newspaper columnist Calvin Trillin remarked, "I believe in open immigration. It improves the diversity of the restaurants. I'd let anybody in except the English."

Don't assume that you can tell a person's status from the way he or she looks. You may have an appointment with the president of a company that does $100 million a year in sales. That president may be Asian in appearance, or African-American, or of Mexican descent. You just can't tell. And you certainly can't assume that the president will be a man.

The Self-Reliant American

Individual accomplishment is glorified in America. From an early age, children are encouraged to be competitive, discover their strengths, and pursue their own dreams. To Americans, accomplishment is king, even when that takes the individual away to opportunities that are far away from his or her family or community. This may seem very strange to you if you're from Japan, where to stand out from the team seems arrogant, or from Australia, where it would seem like hubris, and the "tall poppy" always gets cut down.

American business executives are well-paid by world standards, but that is justified by boards of directors and stockholders, because a single executive brought in to run a company can dramatically affect the fortunes of the company. This competitiveness extends all the way through the organization. Although in recent years companies have tried to install quality circles and team problem-solving, it goes against the grain. Even down on the assembly line, workers want to out-work and out-produce their fellow employees. The country is successful in large part because America is a very competitive society.

You will encounter this competitiveness in your business dealings. Americans want to win. They do not want to compromise. They will compromise if that is in their company's best interest, but it is not in their heart. This is epitomized in the saying of a legendary American football coach, Vince Lombardi. You may see this slogan proudly displayed on plaques on the walls of executive suites. It says, "Winning isn't everything, but making the effort to win is."

America is also a ruthless society. The rewards are great for the individual who succeeds, but those who fail find little support. There is no such thing as termination pay in America. An office worker who loses her job will be told at 4:30 p.m. on a Friday afternoon and is expected to be out of the building by 5:00. The company owes that employee nothing other than any earned vacation days that have not been taken, and that is a matter of company policy, not government fiat. The employee will have been required to pay into a state unemployment fund and will be able to appeal to the state agency for survival benefits for just 13 weeks.

A Final Word About Americans

"O beautiful for spacious skies, for amber waves of grain

For purple mountain majesties, above the fruited plain

America! America!
God shed His grace on thee, and crown thy good with brotherhood
From sea to shining sea."

That song, "America the Beautiful" by Katharine Lee Bates, is not the national anthem. The American national anthem is a battle hymn. Some pacifists wanted to make "America the Beautiful" the national anthem until they were told that, even for Americans, it's just a little too narcissistic. Americans are very proud of their country. They believe fervently that it's the best country in the world. I'll prove it to you, and they'll tell you: "Even the people who don't like it here won't leave."

Key Points to Remember

1. Americans are succinct. They don't spend all morning saying something that can be said in a word or two.
2. You probably can answer any question an American will ask you with one word: "Great!"
3. Americans talk in idioms. Don't take them literally, or you'll quickly be lost.
4. Americans love their country and they expect you to love it, too.
5. The American class system is based on how much money you've made.
6. America is a very religious nation.
7. Americans love their freedom and hate any form of government control.
8. Life in America proceeds at a hectic pace.
9. America is a very diverse with a high percentage of immigrants from other countries.

Chapter 46

Negotiating Characteristics of Americans

Let's first look at the characteristics of the typical American who negotiates with non-Americans, and then, in the following chapter, we'll look at the characteristics of foreign negotiators.

Americans Tend to Be Very Direct in Our Communications

We use idiomatic expressions such as "What's your bottom line?" or "How much profit would you make at that figure?" Or, we try to shift the emphasis of the negotiations by saying, "Let's lay our cards on the table," or "Let's wrap this one up tonight." We "tell it like it is," "shoot from the hip," and try to "hit the nail on the head." We seldom "beat around the bush." Although I recommend this kind of directness when negotiating with other Americans because it puts pressure on the other side, realize that to non-Americans, it may seem too abrupt, and such bluntness may offend them.

Americans Resist Making Outrageous Initial Demands

This goes back to our hope that we can "cut the deal" and "get out of Dodge." Because we want to blitz the negotiations and wrap them up quickly, we tend to think in much shorter time frames than non-Americans. We're thinking we can conclude the negotiations in hours, while they're thinking it will take many days. Although a non-American may be comfortable making an outrageous initial demand because he knows that the price and terms will change enormously as the days go by, we see that as slowing the negotiations down or drawing us into endless haggling.

Americans Are More Likely to Negotiate Alone

It's not unusual to find a lone American negotiator showing up at an international negotiation, fully empowered to do business. (He may be able to put together a team of three if it includes his interpreter and driver.) Then when he is led into the negotiating room, he finds that he is faced with a team of 10 or 12 from the other side. This is not good for the American, because he will feel psychologically overwhelmed, unless the negotiating teams are roughly the same size. However, the effect of this on the foreign team concerns me more.

Non-Americans may interpret a lone negotiator as "They're not serious about making a deal at this meeting because they've only sent one negotiator. This must be only a preliminary expedition." Or non-Americans get the impression that the American is merely gathering information to take back to his team of negotiators.

Unless the American understands this, and takes pains to explain that he is the entire negotiating team and that he is empowered to negotiate the deal, he may not be taken seriously. This puts him at a serious disadvantage because he has then removed his resort to Higher Authority (see Chapter 7). If forced to emphasize his authority to negotiate, he should point out that he only has authority to negotiate up to a certain price point. Beyond that point, he will need to get authorization. If pressed to reveal that price point, he should explain that he is not empowered to reveal it.

Americans Are Uncomfortable With Emotional Displays

The English are the most uncomfortable of course, but Americans also see displaying emotions in public as a weakness. If an American wife starts to cry, her husband instantly assumes that he has done something devastatingly cruel to her. In Mediterranean countries, the husband simply wonders what ploy his wife had concocted. This fear of an emotional reaction causes Americans to be tentative in their negotiations with non-Americans, and if the other side does explode with anger at one of our proposals, we tend to overreact. Instead, we should merely see it as a negotiating ploy that might be perfectly acceptable in their culture.

Americans Expect Short-Term Profits

Besides wanting to conclude the negotiations before we have built a relationship with the other side, we also expect quick results from the deal that we cut. We look at quarterly dividends while foreign investors are looking at 10-year plans. The CEOs of many of the companies who have hired me to train their people, particularly those in the volatile high-tech industries, seem to spend a large part of their day worrying about Wall Street's reaction to every move they make. To many non-Americans, this emphasis on short-term profit and today's stock price comes across, unfairly I think, as a "fast-buck" mentality. Where they are looking to build a long-term relationship with us, we appear to concentrate only on profits, and this can be offensive to them.

Americans Are Less Likely to Speak a Foreign Language

There's no question that English is becoming the business language of the world. Before she retired, my wife, Gisela, was the co-founder of one of the most successful product placement companies in Hollywood. She represented companies who wanted to market their products by getting them into movies and television. One of her clients was Philips, the huge Dutch electronics company. Since 1983, Philips has used English as their corporate language. I have done seminars in Mexico for international companies such as GE, where all business is conducted in English.

Whenever one European company merges with another company from a different European country, they will probably adopt English as their corporate language because it is the foreign language that they will both have learned. Conferences in Europe are typically conducted in English now because it is the common denominator language. Most European businesspeople can speak two foreign languages, and one of them is always English. Most Asian businesspeople can at least understand English, even if they cannot speak it well. Sadly, hardly any Americans can speak German or Japanese. If we do know a foreign language, it is probably Spanish or French.

According to a European Union study, 60 percent of Europeans speak a second language. That compares to 26 percent in the United States, half of whom are immigrants from another country.

To realize how arrogant this may appear to non-Americans, you have only to think of how frustrated you became when you first dined in a Parisian restaurant. When the waiter didn't appear to speak any English, you probably thought as I did: "This is a tourist restaurant. They must get English-speaking people in here all the time. Why is he being so difficult by refusing to speak English?"

Unfortunately, this attitude is all too prevalent with American businesspeople. Any expectation that "If they want to do business with us they should learn our language" can come across as irritatingly arrogant to a non-American. We should always appear surprised and delighted that they speak even a few words of our language. We should always make an effort to speak a few words of their language, even if it's only to say "good morning" and "thank you."

Being willing to do business in their language is particularly important if this is your first business foray into their country. They will want to know that you're making a commitment to doing business in their country and be reassured that you're not just trying to take advantage of the easy profits. It may be worth the expense of having your printing materials translated into their language just to make the point that you're there to stay. I always start my seminars in China with a few sentences in Mandarin, which delights the audience.

Americans Are Not World Travelers

America is one of the richest countries the world has ever known, but Americans do not travel nearly as much as other affluent nations. In the security crackdown that followed the terrorist attack on the World Trade Towers in New York, Americans were suddenly required to get passports to return from trips to Canada and Mexico. Some 18 million people applied for passports for the first time, which pushed the percentage of Americans holding passports to 21 percent. Before that, it was only 16 percent.

Part of that makes sense. The United States is a huge country with diverse climates and geography. If you want world-class skiing, mountain climbing, or surfing you can do it in America. Part of it is location. Other than Canada and Mexico, it's a long way to anywhere else. Part of it is fear. Americans are told a lot these days about the scary world in which we live. What America lacks is history. What you can learn from a visit to London, Rome, and Paris is priceless in its ability to give you a perspective on the world.

Don't expect Americans to understand the intricacies of your culture.

Americans Are Uncomfortable With Silence

Fifteen seconds of silence to us seems like an eternity. Do you remember the last time the sound went out on your television? You were probably thumping the top of the set within 15 seconds. Particularly to Asians, who are comfortable with periods of meditation, this impatience appears to be a weakness, and a weakness they can take advantage of. When dealing with non-Americans, don't be intimidated by periods of silence. See it as a challenge to not be the next one to talk. After an extended period of silence, the next person to talk loses. The next person to open his or her mouth will make a concession.

One of my students, a mortgage banker, told me of negotiating in Shanghai, China. "There were 20 of us around a conference table," he told me. "Tens of millions of dollars in mortgages were at stake. Suddenly, the other side went completely quiet. Fortunately, I had learned about this tactic and was prepared for it. I glanced at my watch. Thirty-three minutes went by without a word being spoken. Finally, one of their lawyers spoke up and made a concession that enabled us to put the transaction together."

Americans Hate to Admit That We Don't Know

As I discussed in Chapter 38 on the importance of gathering information, Americans hate to admit that they don't know. This is something that non-Americans know and can use to their advantage. You don't have to answer every question. You are perfectly entitled to say, "That's privileged information at this stage." Or simply tell them that you don't know, or are not permitted to release the information they seek. Not every question deserves an answer.

Please permit me to do a little flag-waving here. People around the world still admire and respect Americans and particularly American businesspeople. They trust us and see us as straightforward in our business dealings. This I believe. In this chapter, I have not been pointing out the shortcomings of Americans dealing with non-Americans. I have been teaching you only how foreign negotiators misperceive Americans. Fair enough?

Key Points to Remember

1. Americans tend to be very direct in our communications.
2. Americans resist making outrageous initial demands.
3. Americans are more likely to negotiate alone.
4. Americans are uncomfortable with emotional displays.
5. Americans expect short-term profits.
6. Americans are less likely to speak a foreign language.
7. Americans are not world travelers. Only 21 percent hold passports.
8. Americans are uncomfortable with silence.
9. Americans hate to admit that we don't know.

Chapter 47

Negotiating Characteristics of Non-Americans

There's an old joke that the restaurants in heaven have a German manager, a French maitre d', English waiters, and an Italian cook. On the other hand, the restaurants in hell have an Italian manager, a German maitre d', French waiters, and an English cook. Comedian George Carlin used to say, "If there's a heaven, there are German mechanics, Swiss hotels, French chefs, Italian lovers, and British police. If there's a hell, there are Italian mechanics, French hotels, British chefs, Swiss lovers, and German police." These are stereotypes, sure, but it would also be wrong to ignore national business characteristics in the name of avoiding any stereotyping.

Let's look at the negotiating characteristics of non-Americans. I would be guilty of massive stereotyping if I implied that all people from these countries or of these national backgrounds had these tendencies. However, it's realistic enough to assume that a large percentage of people from these countries behave this way. It's well worth being aware of the propensities and observing the non-Americans with whom you're negotiating to see if they do fit the mold.

English People

Be sensitive to national origin. Great Britain includes England, Wales, and Scotland. The United Kingdom also includes Northern Ireland. Of the four countries that compose the U.K., 82 percent are English, so unless they have a brogue, you can assume they are English. English people prefer to be called English, not British. Part of this sensitivity comes from massive immigration problems. Until the 1960s, anyone who was born in one of the colonies (which included 60 percent of the land surface of the Earth at one time) carried a British passport and was free to immigrate to England. A refrain you will frequently hear is "I don't wish to be called British. If you are British, you might be from just about anywhere. I am English."

Make appointments well in advance, because the English live by their calendars. Be punctual, but never early. Ten minutes late is better than one minute early for social engagements. The English are excessively polite. Remember that there are more than 60 million Britons jammed into a country half the size of Oregon, and most of them live in the counties surrounding London. In such a crowded country, it is important to have boundaries on one's behavior. Understanding this is the key to understanding the English. If someone on a crowded train started to play a saxophone off-key, it is unlikely that anyone would protest. In America, that person would be yelled down.

This is why you will see such outrageous styles of dress and hairstyles on young people in England. It appears to an outsider that a youth with spiky orange hair wearing a leather outfit with chrome studs can exist in harmony with a bowler-hatted banker who carries an umbrella year-round and has a handkerchief stuffed up his sleeve. This is deceptive. They don't approve of each other's behavior—they are just too polite to protest.

You will find it rare for an English person to ask you a personal question. Although it's acceptable in America to open a conversation with "What do you do?" or "Where do you live?" that would be a hopeless invasion of privacy to an English person. Because they are excessively polite, they would answer the question if you asked them, but would never reciprocate by asking you what you do.

England is still a very class-conscious society, although that is changing rapidly. Indicative of the change is that Margaret Thatcher, John Major, Tony Blair, and Gordon Brown were the first four prime ministers who did not come from the upper classes. And Scotsman Gordon Brown was the first prime minister not English-born. You will still run into a great deal of class-consciousness, especially with older people. If they are evasive about where they live, for example, don't press them because they may feel self-conscious about living in a working-class suburb.

The English do not feel at all comfortable talking to strangers in the same way that Americans do. The proper way to initiate a conversation with a stranger in England is to mention the weather with an innocuous comment such as "Nice day today," or "Might get some rain." If the response is one unintelligible syllable that sounds like "Harrumph," they are not being impolite; they simply don't feel comfortable talking to you at that time. If they want to pursue a conversation, they will respond with an equally innocuous response such as, "My roses need some rain," or

"Wouldn't be surprised to see rain at this time of year. Wouldn't be surprised at all." You may then start a conversation, but remember to not ask them any personal questions.

It's okay to politely decline the offer of tea or coffee, whereas in many parts of the world it's an insult. Be aware that the English view Americans with suspicion. We are seen as too slick for English tastes. They are somewhat wary of getting involved with Americans for fear of being bamboozled by a fast talker.

The English business executive does not move at the frantic pace of the American. I remember having lunch with my nephew when he worked for Lloyds of London. He took me to an old tavern in the city that had been serving lunches in that location for more than 700 years. We sat at a long bench-type table with a group of three English businessmen. They had several gin and tonics before lunch, and then launched into a huge roast beef and Yorkshire pudding lunch, washed down with two bottles of red wine.

After a large dessert, they ordered brandy. I put on my best American accent and said to one of them, "Excuse me, buddy, could I ask you something? Do you go back to work after a big lunch like that?" His reply told a great deal about the English attitude toward work and success. He politely said, "Here in England, we have a different approach to success than do you chaps in the States. Here we consider that success in business entitles us to work less hard. You chaps think that success requires you to work even harder."

French People

I have never had the trouble with French people that most Americans seem to have. I think that much of that comes from Americans being exposed to only Parisians. Paris is to the French what New York is to Americans. It's a pressure cooker of frantic business activity—a very competitive environment—so they come across as less courteous than we would prefer. Remember that France is very centralized. The government, the banking and industrial powers, and the entertainment and fashion industry all emanate from Paris.

Apart from those living in Paris, French people are warm and friendly. Even in Paris, I find people treat you as you treat them. If you have a chip on your shoulder and are expecting to find them hostile, that's exactly what you will get. If you are excited and eager to meet them and explore their culture, you'll find people who are eager to share with you.

The French take pride in Paris being a world center for high fashion. They appreciate elegance, so dress more formally than you would at home. Add some extra touches, such as a pocket-handkerchief or a silk scarf. Remember that the French pride themselves on their language skills. This love of language means that even those who speak a few words of English may be reluctant to do so because they don't want to speak it poorly. It's not because they have the attitude of "If you want to speak to me, you must learn my language." French businesspeople probably understand English well, even if they don't feel comfortable speaking it. (It's true that there is a strong movement to prevent English words from becoming a part of the French language, but that's another matter.)

The French take pride in being eloquent, and love to argue and converse. Nothing is more enjoyable than an abstract argument over their morning croissant and coffee. The point over which they are arguing is less important than the logic they use to win their argument. The French are logical thinkers, and sell with logic and reason rather than an appeal to emotion. In negotiations when the French say yes, they mean maybe. When they say no, it means, "Let's negotiate."

Just as everything in France is centered in Paris, so are French businesses centralized. In large corporations, offices are arranged by rank and spread out from the president's suite. Similarly, authority is organized to emanate from the top down. As with the English, the French value principle over result. Making a fast buck is not reason enough to violate their traditional way of doing business. Be punctual, because to be late is an insult to the French. Shake hands briefly when you meet them. Kissing cheeks is for only close friends. Call all adult women Madame, even if they're single.

Above all, don't ruin a meal by trying to talk business. A French lunch can last two hours, and can be an exquisite experience. Unless your host starts talking business, avoid it. You'll be doing yourself far more good by showing them how much you appreciate their cuisine. Be prepared to pick up a huge bill for the meal. I remember hosting a dinner party at a French restaurant where a guest selected a duck salad as an appetizer. I should have known that I was in trouble when they carved the duck tableside. This appetizer alone was $80!

German People

Germany (and the German-speaking part of Switzerland) is a low-context country; Germans put their emphasis on the deal rather than the relationship of the parties, or the environment in which they signed the contract. Germans are one of the few nationalities to expect more detailed contracts than Americans. They really are masters of the deal that, once they have hammered it out, they will never change. Shake hands firmly when you arrive and leave. Do be punctual because it's very important to them. Don't put your hands in your pockets when you're talking business, as it seems too casual to them. Don't tell jokes in the workplace. Germans consider it totally inappropriate.

Germans appear formal and aloof at first. It takes them a long time to get relaxed with you. In business, they are much more formal than Americans, both in attitude and style. They have a formal and informal distinction in their language. To use the informal (Du) style with a superior, rather than the formal (Sie) style, would be a major mistake. Don't call people by their first name, unless invited to do so.

Germans place great emphasis on titles. Use yours if you have one and respect theirs. Address people as Herr, Frau, or Fräulein, followed by their professional designation (for example, Herr Dokter Schmitt, or Frau Professor Schmitt). German workers who have worked together for decades will still call each other by title and last name.

Germans drive very fast. Posted speed limits are universally ignored. Remember that the fast lane is for overtaking only, however fast you're going. You can be doing 100 mph in the fast lane and still have a car come zooming up behind you and flashing its lights for you to get out of the way.

Asian People

Asians are very relationship-based. They far prefer to trust the person with whom they negotiate than they do the contract they signed. In Thailand and other Asian countries, you may be greeted with a slight bow and both hands pointed toward you with palms together. You should respond with the same greeting but hold your hands level with or slightly higher than theirs. The height of the hands indicates the respect that the person has for the person they are meeting. Someone meeting a servant may hold his or her hands well below their waist. Someone meeting a holy person, or a great leader, might touch his hands to his forehead. Don't get carried away, but indicate respect by holding your hands a little higher than theirs.

Asians often consider promises made during the negotiation as being made to the individuals who negotiated, not to the organization. Americans call the signing of an agreement "the closing." Asians consider it an opening of the relationship. With Asians, it is very important to convey that you consider the signing of the contract a beginning, not an ending. Do not expect eye contact, because they think it's impolite. It's not a sign of shiftiness. Many a Vietcong soldier suffered at the hands of American troops because they couldn't look the American in the eye. The American assumed that this meant the Vietcong was lying.

Korean People

Koreans also look at the agreement as a starting point, not the final solution. They don't understand how any agreement can be expected to anticipate every possible eventuality, so they see a contract as an expression of an understanding on the day that the contract was signed. If conditions change, they don't feel bound by the contract they signed. Your response to this should not be to place less emphasis on the contract, but to draft a contract that is flexible enough to move with changing conditions. If you can predict a shift in conditions, rather than resisting it, you should accept that it could happen, and provide penalties and rewards for the way each side responds to the changing conditions.

Koreans don't believe in fault. They consider that, if they fail to stick with agreement, it is an act of God. Unfortunately, they may have planned to take advantage of you with this.

Chinese People

The Chinese have a saying: "He ging, he li, he fa." It means first examine the relationship between the parties, then look at what is right, and only then worry about what the law says. Many Chinese now shake hands when they meet Americans, but first wait to see if they offer their hands. The traditional greeting is a slight bow from the shoulders that is almost an exaggerated nod and is much less pronounced than the Japanese bow, which is from the waist.

Appear to be low-key in your approach, because loud behavior easily offends the Chinese. The Chinese do business based on building a relationship with you, but they are not above using this as a pressure point and accusing you of breaking a friendship if you hesitate to go ahead with the project.

A strong tendency in Chinese culture is to put the group's needs ahead of personal needs. Remember that for thousands of years, Chinese focus was on the family unit and beyond that the needs of the village. Confucianism also emphasizes the importance of the family, the extended family, and the community.

Chinese negotiators work in teams and arrive at group decisions. The communists eliminated religions from the culture, but Confucianism and Taoism are philosophies, not organized religions. Confucianism puts emphasis on the organization of family, village, and social life. Taoism stresses the importance of being in balance and harmony with nature. Incidentally, Taoism is pronounced as though it starts with a D not a T, as in **dou**-iz-uhm.

A part of this emphasis on the group dynamics is the Chinese concept of Guanxi. This refers to the time-honored concept of reciprocal concessions. It is subtle in its application but it is the underpinning of Chinese society. When one person does a favor for the other, he expects something in return. He doesn't specify what he expects or when he expects it, but the obligation incurred has now become part of the fabric of their relationship. You will encounter Guanxi relationships everywhere you go: in your dealings with business people and government officials, and in every other aspect of Chinese life.

Another strong part of Chinese culture is respect for a person's position. Try to understand the rank of the people with whom you deal. Infants are raised with that kind of concern for position and it stays with them throughout their lives. In the workplace, age rather than ability usually makes promotions. Everyone is expected to defer to his or her elders.

You know, of course, that the Chinese attach great importance to saving face. In business meetings, do not expect them to speak out in support or opposition to your suggestions. They will be concerned that they may lose face or cause you or others to lose face.

Every Chinese person is an entrepreneur at heart and loves to bargain and haggle. Expect them to start high and be willing to make concessions. You should do the same and not be offended by what appears to you to be grinding you down on price. Have fun and enjoy the bargaining.

Japanese People

In Japan, they are reluctant to say no. "Yes" to them means only that they heard you. Don't ask questions that they can answer with a yes or no; instead ask open-ended questions. "When can you do that?" is better than "Can you do that?"

It is impolite for a Japanese person to say no to an elder. However Westernized they may have become they still have trouble with this. I know a man who owns a large fencing company. He sold out to a Japanese company and now reports to a business executive who is younger than he. "Roger," he told me, "I've been dealing with him for years now, and I have never known him to turn down a proposal that I made to him. The problem is that I can never tell whether he likes the proposal or is so uncomfortable saying no to an older man that he would rather approve it." When the Japanese say, "It will be difficult," they mean no.

Japan is a very high-context country. In a culture that values tact and courtesy over honesty, words do not always mean what they appear to mean. There is a big difference between what they say (tatemae) and what they think (honne). "We" comes before "I" in Japan. The group is more important than the individual, which is the opposite of American culture, which glorifies and rewards independence. To punish children in America you ground them—keep them in. To punish children in Japan, you send them out of the house.

As with other Asian cultures that have been influenced by Confucius, the emphasis here is on the hierarchy. Observe how Japanese people bow to each other. The person lowest in the hierarchy will bow first and will bow lowest.

The concept of Wa is strong in the culture. We would translate that as meaning harmony. They want to find a harmonious solution to every problem. To this end, they believe that every situation has unique factors that enable them to bend a solution to maintain harmony. Until Western culture reached Japan in the 19th century, they didn't understand the concept of objectivity. From their point of view, everything is subjective.

The Japanese prefer to work in groups. Don't try to identify the lead negotiator, the one who will make or break the negotiation. There probably isn't one. Don't expect much feedback on your proposal, for several reasons:

- There is a hierarchy in Japanese companies. Individuals do not want to embarrass themselves by speaking out.
- The Japanese businessperson wants to save face and allow you to save face.
- They are adverse to risk and therefore unwilling to state their opinion for fear that it will be rejected by the group.

As I told you, the Chinese have a concept of Guanxi, meaning reciprocity. If I do a favor for you, you now owe me a favor. The Japanese call this Kashi, which literally translates as loan. In restaurants, you will see associates pouring sake or beer for their friends. It is accepted as creating a subtle form of obligation that will be reciprocated. At that level, it's charming. It becomes more complicated when you realize that your Japanese business associates are doing favors for you in full expectation that you will return the favor.

The opening position that the Japanese take depends on how well they know you. If they don't know you or your industry well, they will start high, not to take advantage of you, but because they learn about you by judging your reaction. It's called the "banana no tataki uri" approach to negotiating, a term that refers to the way that banana vendors would ask an outrageously high price from people they didn't know and then lower it quickly if the buyer protested. It sounds unethical to us, but it does make sense. You don't know the negotiating style of the stranger. He may be accustomed to hard bargaining. If you start high, you will quickly learn about them and take a different approach the next time you do business with them.

In my book *The Confident Decision Maker* (William Morrow, 1993), I devoted a chapter to explaining how the Japanese make decisions. Here are some key points:

They make decisions in large groups, so we have trouble figuring out who is making the decision. The truth is that no one person is making the decision. They consider defining the problem to be far more important than searching for the right answer. The group is there to absorb information and feels that once they fully understand the situation, the choice will be obvious. Each member of the group will give their input, starting with the lowest-ranking person and moving up to the top.

Japanese executives see their job as requiring them to come up with creative ideas, not to be held accountable for the results. Whereas we prefer to have one person make the final decision so that he or she can be held accountable, the Japanese let the entire group collectively make the decision. When everyone has given all of their input, the choice may be obvious to the group. If is still not obvious, they may retreat, knowing that they need to absorb more information. This makes Americans frustrated because they feel nothing is happening. The good part of all this is that once they do decide to go ahead, everybody is on board and fully committed to the course of action.

Russian People

I spent two weeks in the Soviet Union when Gorbachev was trying to push through reforms. Frankly, I doubted that they would ever make a transition to a free market economy because the Russians are not entrepreneurial at heart. Understand that the communist system removed all incentives from their way of life. Banning religion meant that there was no moral incentive to do good in their society. Banning profitable private enterprise meant that there was no financial incentive to do good. Remember that, for 70 years, they lived under a system where everybody worked for the government; there was no other employer.

Money was almost meaningless to them because even if they had any, there wasn't anything to buy with it. (President Reagan loved to tell the story of the Russian who saved all his life for an automobile and got a permit from the government to buy one. He took the money and the permit down to the car showroom and said, "When do I get my car?" "You will get your car in exactly seven years," they told him. "Seven years?" "Yes, on this day, seven years from now you will get your car." "Will it be in the morning or the afternoon?" "Comrade, we are talking seven years. What difference does it make?" "Because on that day, in the morning, the plumber has promised to come.") Although some Russians have taken to capitalism like a duck to water, for many it is a difficult transition, so don't expect them to be motivated by profit the way that we would be.

Russians are not afraid to make tough initial demands. They expect you to express your respect for them. That might be considered patronizing to an American. Not so with Russians. Learn about the person with whom you will be negotiating and let him know how impressed you are. Russians have a very bureaucratic mind-set, so they are not afraid to say they don't have the authority. This will give you the most frustration. Russians have learned to protect themselves from blame by getting a dozen other people to sign on to every decision. This is a throwback to the old Soviet days, when mistakes could have very serious repercussions.

Another mind-set you'll encounter is that Russians think that, unless they are authorized to do something, it is forbidden. We Americans think just the opposite. We think that if something is not forbidden, it is okay to proceed. They can say no endlessly to test your resolve.

Russians are not afraid to vocalize their concerns, even if it causes you to squirm. Try to appreciate this openness and not let it bother you. As with any angry person, try to move him off of the position that he has taken and get him refocused on your mutual interests. (See Chapter 36 for more on conflict resolution.) They are self-centered. They're not interested in win-win.

Russia is a higher-context country than you would think. You may get the impression that they are hard and cold in their business dealings because they are very direct. However, underlying that tough negotiating style is a need to feel good about the person with whom they are dealing. This is done at a deeper level than the superficial friendliness of American business relationships. Don't think that because you downed a case of vodka with them and engaged in bear hugs all around that you have built a trusting relationship.

If Russians say that something would be inconvenient, they mean that it would be impossible. It took me a while to figure this out, and I'm still not sure why it is, but presumably it's because of a misunderstanding in translation. For example, I asked the desk clerk at our Moscow hotel to move us to a larger room. She told me, "That would be inconvenient." I took that to mean that if I pushed harder, I could get her to accommodate me. That wasn't what happened at all. She was telling me that it was impossible. It took me nearly 15 minutes of hard negotiating to get us upgraded to a suite!

Middle Eastern People

Be sensitive to ethnic differences when you're negotiating in the Middle East. Above all, don't refer to them as Arabs unless they come from the Arabian Peninsula, which includes Saudi Arabia, Iraq, Jordan, and the Gulf States. Egyptians do not appreciate being called Arabs, and Iranians are horrified because they are proud to be Persians. In Iraq, 80 percent of the population is Arab, but they are reluctant to call themselves an Arab nation. It is best stay away from that discussion.

Do expect to spend a great deal of time, perhaps many days, getting to know the person before he feels comfortable negotiating with you. When people from the Middle East sign a contract, they see it as the start of negotiations, not the end. They sign the contract first and then negotiate. Most Americans who do business there understand this and call them "contract collectors." It's important to understand this and not see it as devious; it's simply the way they do things. A contract to them means less than a letter of intent does to us.

In their world, the ground floor is where shopkeepers ply their trade, and shopkeepers are a lower class than businesspeople. Don't insult your Middle East trading partners by asking them to do business in a ground-floor office. The higher the floor you are on, the more they see you as having prestige.

Don't be offended if they show up late for an appointment, or perhaps don't even show up at all. Appointments are not the firm commitments that they are in this country, and time in general is not prized the way that we value it.

You will often be overwhelmed with hospitality and gifts by the non-Americans with whom you'll be negotiating. This is an overt attempt to win your favor, and you must deal with it. Rather than giving offense by refusing their favors, the best plan is to reciprocate, which eliminates the personal obligation that may have been created. And you have twice the fun.

Key Points to Remember

1. Understanding national characteristics will make negotiating with non-Americans easier.
2. The English don't feel comfortable speaking to strangers the way that Americans do. It's a class-conscious society, so beware of asking them where they live or what they do for a living.
3. France is the most centralized large country on Earth, so Parisians are living with more stress than those in rural areas. French businesspeople probably understand English well, even if they don't feel comfortable speaking it.
4. Like America, Germany is a low-context negotiating country. Getting the contract signed is more important that building the relationship. Germans put great emphasis on titles.
5. Asians value the relationship more than the contract. They often think of the contract as an agreement between the people who signed it rather than with the company.
6. Koreans see a contract as an expression of an understanding on the day that the contract was signed. If conditions change, they don't feel bound by the contract they signed.
7. Guanxi, the time-honored concept of reciprocal concessions, is a big part of Chinese business life. You will receive gifts and are expected to return the favor. Translating from Chinese to English is difficult because English is a far more specific language.

8. The concept of Wa is strong in the Japanese culture. We would translate that as meaning harmony. They want to find a harmonious solution to every problem. They make decisions as a group, not as a hierarchy. Don't try to identify the lead negotiator, the one who will make or break the negotiation. There probably isn't one.
9. Russians are not afraid to make tough initial demands. They expect you to express your respect for them. Learn about the person with whom you will be negotiating, and let him know how impressed you are.
10. In the Middle East, don't call people Arabs unless they are from the Arabian Peninsula, which does not include Egypt and Iran. Expect to spend many days building a relationship before Arabs will feel comfortable enough to conduct business.

Section Five

Understanding the Players

In the previous sections, I've concentrated on how to play the negotiating game. Now I want to focus on the importance of understanding the other negotiator and realizing that it is a major key to Power Negotiating. People are different. They throw who they are into the negotiation. It affects the kind of strategy that they develop, it influences which of the Gambits they will use and how they will use them, and it determines their entire style of negotiating.

Remember that you're always dealing with an individual, not an organization, even if you are negotiating with a union boss who heads up a 10,000-member union. I don't blame you for assuming the needs of his members dictate his actions, but I believe that his personal needs guide his actions. A secretary of state may have explicit instructions from the president on how he or she should conduct international negotiations, but personal needs may still dominate his or her actions. Understand the person, and you can often dominate the negotiations.

We'll look at you and see if you have what it takes to be a Power Negotiator as I cover how to read the body language of the other side, and listen for the meanings that are hidden in the way they talk. Then you'll learn the personal characteristics, attitudes, and beliefs of Power Negotiators.

People seem to think that some people are born with the characteristics that make them successful negotiators. "Oh, he's a born negotiator," you'll hear people say. You know that's not true. I challenge you to open any newspaper in the land and show me a birth announcement that says, "A negotiator was born at St. Bartholomew's Hospital today." No, people are not born negotiators. Negotiating is a learnable skill. In this section, I'll teach you how to feel comfortable with any style of negotiator, so you can easily read various negotiators and their approach to getting what they want. Then I'll show you how to adapt your style of negotiating to theirs.

Chapter 48

Body Language: How to Read People

In this chapter, I'm going to teach you how Power Negotiators read body language.

Unfortunately, body language is a subject with which many people get carried away. I think that's true of a lot of other areas, too. I've met people who believe in astrology so much that they won't even leave the house on a particular day, when their sign's not right. Some people believe so strongly in handwriting analysis that they won't hire someone whose handwriting doesn't conform to their system. I've even heard of people who believe they can spot someone who's committed a murder from the way they write. And you may have lost a job opportunity because you didn't interpret a Rorschach inkblot test accurately.

We don't want to go that far with body language. But it's true that a great amount of our communication is non-verbal. Remember we talked about this when we were discussing flinching—the importance of the visual reaction to a negotiating proposal? As much as 80 percent of the reaction that people have to what is going on in the negotiation can be non-verbal.

If you want to illustrate how much we can communicate without speaking, at your next staff meeting, go around the room and ask everybody to tell you something non-verbally. For example, a thumbs-up gesture means good. A thumbs-down gesture means bad. A shrug of the shoulders means indifference, and so on. I've done it with as many as 50 people and haven't come up with a shortage of gestures. I suspect that you could do it with 100 people, and still be going strong. There is an awful lot we can and do communicate non-verbally.

Just to give you an idea of what you can communicate non-verbally, let's see if we can up with 20 things you can say with just one hand:

1. Beckon a person.

2. Bless someone. In the Christian world, a three-finger blessing (the thumb, and the index and middle fingers) represents the Trinity.
3. Tell someone he is talking too much by flapping your thumb against your four fingers.
4. Ask for the check in a restaurant.
5. Give yourself permission to tell a lie by crossing your fingers.
6. Tell someone you think that he's crazy by circling your forefinger next to your head.
7. Acknowledge someone by pointing your forefinger with your fist clenched in the shape of a pistol.
8. High-five someone to share a celebration.
9. Hitch a ride with a clenched fist and pointing thumb.
10. Stave off bad luck by tapping the knuckles of your closed fist against the side of your head in a "knock on wood" symbol.
11. Refer to money by rubbing your thumb against your index and middle finger.
12. Greet someone with a handshake.
13. Pledge allegiance with your hand over your heart.
14. Express approval by patting a child or a dog on the head.
15. Tell someone to "hang loose" by extending your thumb and little finger and shaking your hand.
16. Say "let's leave," by clenching your fist and shaking your thumb toward the door.
17. Ask someone to telephone you by extending your little finger and thumb and shaking your hand next to your ear.
18. Indicate that you're a pacifist (or wish someone victory) with the middle and index finger raised in a V-shape.
19. Indicate that you're a Star Trek fan by raising all your digits, palm out, and separating the ring and middle fingers—the Vulcan salute.
20. Wave hello or goodbye.

And that's just with one hand! Note that I've omitted all kinds of obscene gestures and all sorts of sports gestures such as the Atlanta Braves tomahawk chop and the University of Texas longhorn wave.

However, if we get carried away, we can easily misunderstand gestures. For example, women much more naturally cross their arms than do men. It's just more comfortable position for them. If we interpret that as shutting us off, we can be misreading the situation completely.

If we see somebody tug his ear while he's in conversation with us, and we automatically think that means he's asking for more information—when in actual fact their ear may just be itching—it can be a big mistake.

Particularly, if you're dealing with people of other nationalities, you can make serious mistakes. Do you know that, whereas in this country when you nod your head it means yes and to shake your head means no, to an Eskimo exactly the opposite is true? But let's not get carried away. You probably you won't be negotiating with many Eskimos.

Allow me just tell you the story of probably the biggest non-verbal misunderstanding of all time. Back in 1960, when Neil Armstrong stepped onto the moon and was asked: "What's it like up there?" He replied non-verbally, using an A-OK gesture with his hand.

Now that was fine for millions of Americans that were watching, because the A-OK gesture is traditionally American, and very well understood. But for the other 600 million people watching on television, the gesture was completely misunderstood. Because it's very similar to a gesture that's known around the world, where, when the thumb is touched to the center finger, it's a hostile gesture, bordering on obscene. You may think of it as an Italian gesture, but it's worldwide.

One can easily believe that some Japanese television commentator might have said to the other: "What did he say? What did he say?"

And the other one might have said: "I don't know, but he seems awful mad!"

I can only think of one universal non-verbal communication. I have traveled in 113 different countries, to some of the most remote places on earth, and have always found that a smile means the same thing to all races.

Why It's Better to Negotiate Face-to-Face

The importance of reading body language tells you that it's usually better to negotiate face-to-face rather than over the telephone, or by faxing, e-mailing, or text messaging.

Let's say that you stopped by a developer's office to take him to lunch and go over a shopping center project that he has coming on line soon.

You see through the glass wall of his office that he's on the phone, so you decide to wait outside. He's leaning back in his chair with his feet up on his desk, and the phone tucked under his chin. He's making a steepling motion with his hands, a sure sign of confidence. All of a sudden, his feet come down off the desk, he's sitting upright in his chair, and he starts patting his pockets, looking for a pen.

He looks over to his secretary, touches his thumb to his forefinger and waggles his hand. She knows what this means, so she gives him a pen and he starts to write on his pad furiously. When he gets halfway down the pad and he's finished writing, he draws a big line on the bottom of it and puts a big check mark there.

Then he stands up, goes around the desk, pushes the chair in under his desk, and starts leaning on the back of his chair as he talks.

At that point, he sees you waiting outside, gives you a thumbs-up sign and another sign with the thumb and the forefinger separated slightly, to indicate that he'll only be a couple of minutes, and continues to listen.

Then a worried look comes on his face and, as he responds, he touches the side of his nose. It's a good sign that he's either exaggerating or lying. When he reaches down, making some further adjustments to the figures on his pad, he starts to smile again and reaches for his coat and has it halfway on as he concludes the conversation and hangs up the phone.

The point I'm making here is this: Look at how much more you knew about what was going on in that conversation than the person on the other end of the phone did, even though you couldn't hear a word.

That's why I suggest that you avoid negotiating over the telephone. Always consider meeting the person face-to-face so you can read his body language. You don't always have to go, but here's my rule: If you're wondering whether you need to go or not, you need to go.

Particularly, you can tell much better if he's getting upset, so you can adjust your responses appropriately.

The other bad thing about negotiating over the telephone is that you can't shake hands. And in this country, a handshake to settle a deal is such a powerful negotiating tool that you should never be in a situation where you can't seal the deal by doing it.

Another important thing to remember is that people believe what they see much more readily than they believe what they hear. For example, if I say to you: "Well, I'm not going to let it worry me," but when I say it to you I have my hands in my pockets, my shoulders are slouched, my head is hung low, and I have a worried expression on my face, which would you believe? Am I worried or not? Of course, you'd believe what you saw rather than what you heard.

If you're an analytical, our session on body language will not be nearly detailed enough for you. It'll appear very superficial. But if you're like me, I think you'll learn enough in this chapter to get you started in your study of body language.

I'll give you some basic fundamentals that you can work with that directly apply to the negotiating process. From there, you can continue your own study.

There are two key places where you could continue to study. One is waiting in an airport, and the other is watching television without the sound.

Instead of getting frustrated by the wait at the airport, start getting fascinated by the people around you.

Observe the people who are beyond your hearing range. You can't hear them, but you can see them. Study their posture and their body language. Try to interpret what they're doing, particularly the people that are absorbed with a cell phone conversation. Try to figure out to whom they might be talking. Is it a spouse, a lover, a customer, or an employee? You can probably tell with a little practice, just by reading their body language.

Remember, though, that only a change in body language is a valid signal to read. Don't assume because somebody has his arms folded that he's hostile. The thing to watch for is when something is apparently said that causes him to suddenly fold his arms. That's when body language becomes significant.

I once met with an expert on body language who was frequently hired by attorneys to be present in the courtroom to watch the body language of the witnesses. This is what he told me is the key issue: "Watch for changes in body language. Just because a witness may have a habit of scratching his nose, it doesn't mean that he's necessarily lying. It may just mean that he has an itchy nose. But if, when asked a certain question, all of a sudden his hand involuntarily goes up to the side of his nose, it's a pretty good indication that he's lying."

Incidentally, you can watch that same gesture when you're watching a late-night host start his show. He typically says: "We've got a great show for you tonight." But sometimes you'll see his hand involuntarily go up to the side of his nose, indicating that he really doesn't think it's that great a show.

Back to the witness in the courtroom. He told me: "Just because their finger may go to their collar frequently, it doesn't necessarily mean that they feel a lot of pressure. It may be that they have a brand new shirt on, which hasn't been washed yet, and it's stiff and uncomfortable.

"However, if under the pressure of a particular part of the questioning, then their hand goes to their collar, it definitely means they feel they're under pressure."

This is where my friend would step in, bring it to his attorney's attention, and during cross-examination, the attorney would re-emphasize this point to try and find out what was really going on in the witness's mind.

Now let's consider the actual negotiating session and how body language plays a part.

The Handshake

There are many different ways of shaking hands. Generally, in this country, an acceptable handshake is firm, but not too strong. Several steady shakes. Usually we don't use the other hand, although with a well-known acquaintance we may shake with both hands. In other words, we put our left hand over the back of the other person's hand. Many people consider this a little too forward, particularly when you meet for the first time. It's called the politicians' handshake.

Another variation of this is grasping the other person's forearm with your free hand. That's known as the ministers' handshake.

And yet again, there's putting your hand on the other person's shoulder as you shake his hand. That's a sure signal that he wants you for a committee!

Be careful about any variation from the standard, familiar handshake. Obviously, a damp palm is the sign of nervousness, so look for the person who wipes his hand on their coat as he raises his hand to shake yours.

A few years ago, it was unheard of for a gentleman to offer his hand to a lady before she had indicated that she wanted to shake hands, but now, in today's enlightened society, men should offer a hand to women in a business situation.

I'm still very conscious of this, as I travel around the country giving Power Negotiating seminars. The customs are clearly different in different parts of America. In the South (for example, Alabama, Mississippi, the Florida Panhandle, and so on), I'm still reluctant to offer to shake a lady's hand. It's also true in the Bible Belt states (such as Oklahoma, Kansas, and Nebraska). So be careful, and be sure that you're in accord with the local customs in that area.

Where to Sit at a Conference

Power Negotiators understand that the way you sit around the negotiating table can affect the outcome.

If you're alone and negotiating against two other people, such as the vice president in charge of construction and the president of the development company, be sure you don't seat yourself between them. Because if you do, they can exchange glances and signals between each other, without you being able to catch them. Also, of course, you can't watch the body languages as easily as you could if you had them seated across the table from you. And you're in the uncomfortable position of having to move your head back and forth as if you were at a tennis tournament.

How do you control where they sit? Be sure that you have them sit down first, and then position yourself across the table, not on the same side.

When a large group is negotiating, and there are equal numbers on each side, it's typical for them to sit on opposite sides of the table. If the groups are unevenly numbered, then the larger group will try and maintain that same separation so that their larger numbers, on one side of the table, can dominate the other side.

However, if you're a member of the smaller group, you'll want to attempt to split up the seating arrangement so that your team is dispersed among the other members of their group. It tends to eliminate that feeling of being overpowered.

When two people who are on the same negotiating team sit together, they tend to be perceived as speaking with one voice. If they split up, they appear to be presenting two opinions—which gives them more strength. If you have one other person on your side, but they bring in three people, and you're sitting at a round table, you wouldn't want to sit together.

When to Get Down to Business

Having met everybody and seated yourself at the table, the next thing to consider is this: When should the small talk stop and the serious negotiating begin? Power Negotiators know that it's always good to relieve tensions with some inconsequential banter to get everybody feeling comfortable and ready to go. But when do you get down to business?

Power Negotiators watch for the coat button phenomenon. Men will normally keep their coat jacket buttoned until they feel more comfortable with you. If you have members of the group who still have their coats buttoned, keep on with the small talk until they reach down and relax by opening their jacket. There was a survey done once at a wedding reception, where the person doing the survey didn't know whether the people who were there were members of the family, or just invited guests. They were able to tell with 80-percent accuracy who was there as a member of the family, because their coats were unbuttoned. The people who were strangers to the group kept their coats buttoned much longer.

Here are some other signs that they are relaxed enough for you to start talking business:

- Shoulders are hanging loose.
- Hands are relaxed and are just used to emphasize a point.
- Voice is easy-going with consistent pitch, timbre, and speed.
- Eyes are not blinking rapidly.
- Hands are separated, not clutched together.
- Slight smile on their face.

Eye Blink Rate

As you look around the negotiating table, try to study how frequently people's eyes blink. If you haven't done this before, you'll probably be surprised at how frequently we blink our eyes; up to 60 times a minute is not unusual (although some people are much slower: around 15 to 20 blinks per minute). You'll need this information later because when a person's eye blink rate changes dramatically, you'll know that he's either very alert to what you're saying, or under a high degree of tension—and may not be telling the truth.

Watching television is another fascinating way to study body language. Try watching news commentators with the sound turned off. Watch for the blinking of the eyes. You'll be amazed at how much you can tell about the kind of story that they're relating. In England, they have an expression that says "he's a blinking liar." Probably without realizing that he was reading body language, he's noticed that the other person's eyes are blinking at a very rapid rate. This is a very sure indication that the person is exaggerating, is lying, or feels very uncomfortable with what he's having to say.

If you watch news commentators with the sound off, so you can concentrate better, you'll be amazed to see the different frequency of eye blinks. When they're uncomfortable with a news story they're having to read, you'll see their eye blink rate go up maybe four or five times.

Watch for the Head Tilt

The tilt of the head tells you whether people are paying attention to you or not. People whose heads are completely upright as they look at you are probably not paying attention. A slight tilt to the head, particularly if their hand goes up to their chin, is a very good indication that they're paying attention.

We speakers learn to study this. We can spot the members of the audience who are paying close attention by the tilt of the head. And if we have a large segment of the audience who is sitting with perfectly straight heads, even if they have a smile on their face and appear to be paying attention, we know that they're not. When that happens, we'll direct a question to that segment of the audience for which a response is required. Or we'll change pace, or in some way make that section of the audience more alert.

Of course, if a speaker notices that the people are leaning toward the door, it's a good body language sign that they're losing interest!

When the Hand Goes to the Head

Watch carefully anytime the hand goes to the head. A stroking of the chin with the thumb and forefinger indicates they're very interested in what you're saying. Knuckles folded, and under the chin, reveal the same type of interest. But when the chin goes into the heel of the hand and the head leans on the hand, it's a clear sign of boredom.

When a person strokes the side of his nose, it's almost a clear indication that he is exaggerating or lying to you, unless it's a normal nervous mannerism of his.

When a person tugs at his ear, he is saying to you, "I want to hear more about what you have to say."

When a person scratches the top of his head, he is embarrassed or uncomfortable with what's going on. You might want to back off and change direction.

Keep Your Eyes on the Hands

What can we learn from the hands? We know that fingers drumming on the tabletop indicates impatience. We know that under severe strain, people may wring their hands. Watch for steepling, too. Steepling means two hands with just the tips of the fingers touching, without the heels of the hands meeting. It's an indication of supreme confidence. It's very difficult to do that when you're extremely nervous. If you see somebody doing that, you know he feels himself to be in a superior position.

When a man brings one or more hands to his chest, it's a sign of openness and sincerity. Although when a woman does it, it tends to be one of shock or protectiveness.

Squeezing the bridge of the nose, particularly when he also closes his eyes, means the person is really concentrating on what's going on.

A hand placed at the back of the neck, whether it's a finger inside the collar or a palm rubbing the back of the neck, is almost a sure sign of annoyance. People really do get hot under the collar, and they really do feel that you're a pain in the neck sometimes.

What Eyeglass Wearers Can Tell You

What can you tell from a person who wears glasses? Well, you know what looking over the top of the eyeglasses means. It says: "I don't believe you," or "I disapprove." Someone who repeatedly cleans his glasses, and this can happen three or four times an hour during a negotiation, is telling you the same thing as a pipe smoker who's constantly relighting his pipe: He needs more time to think about it. When we see that, a Power Negotiator will either stop talking, or talk about something inconsequential, while the other side mulls over the more important points.

Anytime somebody puts something in his mouth, whether it's the earpiece of their glasses, or a pen or pencil, think of it as needing more nourishment. He likes what he hears, but he wants to hear more.

Of course, if somebody took off his glasses suddenly and tossed them on the table, you'd know that he was upset with you and was shutting you off. But watch for this when it's a more subtle signal, too, when he's just laying down his glasses. If someone takes off his eyeglasses and lays them down on the table, it means he's no longer listening to you.

Proxemics Is the Study of Personal Space

Another fascinating part of body language is to consider how much space you should give a person when you're communicating with him. This study of how close you should get to another person in the negotiating process has a name all to itself: proxemics.

Researchers have determined that anything less than 18 inches is the intimate zone. You shouldn't intrude upon it without permission. From 1 1/2 to 4 feet is the personal zone. Beyond 4 feet is the public zone, where you can feel comfortable with strangers.

There are a lot of variables here. One is the national background of the person to whom you're talking. People who come from very crowded countries, such as England, where I was raised, or Japan, are more comfortable in a crowded environment than Americans tend to be. At the same time, we can shut ourselves off more easily. We can be alone in a crowd much more comfortably than an American who's more used to wide open spaces. You can get closer to an Englishman or a Japanese person without him feeling pressured.

Of course the same applies to someone who's raised in a city, such as Los Angeles, Chicago, or New York, as opposed to someone who is raised in a wide-open, rural environment.

The other variable is your size in relationship to the person to whom you're talking. If you're talking to someone who's considerably shorter than you, you must stand back considerably further than you would with someone your own height. Otherwise, you'd tend to overpower that person. Another way that you can lessen this overpowering effect is to turn sideways a little bit, as you talk to the person, so you don't project a gigantic wall.

Knowing about body language can give you an important edge in negotiations. And there is one time when it can be invaluable and that's when the person with whom you're dealing is a student of body language. If you know that he is studying your body language, you have a great opportunity to use your body language to influence his thinking.

I like to mirror people's body language for a while. If they cross their legs or arms, I cross mine. If I see that they spot this, I know that they are studying my body language!

Key Points to Remember

1. As much as 80 percent of the reaction that people have to what goes on in the negotiation can be non-verbal.
2. Be aware of culture differences. With the exception of a smile, which is universal, different gestures can mean different things to different cultures.

3. Study people in airports, and on television with the sound turned off, to appreciate how much you can learn non-verbally.
4. Study how people shake your hand. It tells you a lot.
5. At a conference, don't sit between two representatives from the other side because you can't read their body language, and are at a disadvantage, having to turn your head back and forth.
6. If you and your partner are outnumbered, don't sit together. Your arguments have more strength if you separate.
7. Don't start business until they have unbuttoned their jackets and their body language is relaxed.
8. A fast eye blink rates indicates that the other person is not comfortable with what you or he is saying.
9. When people are paying attention, their heads are slightly inclined.
10. Pay attention when a person's hand moves to his head. What he does next tells you a lot.
11. Be aware of proxemics. Know how close you can be to another person without making him feel uncomfortable.
12. Your use of body language is critical when you realize that the other person is studying your body language.

Chapter 49

Hidden Meanings in Conversation

As if I haven't given you enough challenges with learning all the negotiating tactics, learning how to analyze the different personalities you'll be dealing with, and carefully watching language, I now want to add one more dimension to it. That is looking for hidden meanings in conversation.

When the president of the United States makes a speech, he invariably reads it, particularly if it involves foreign affairs. This is because every single word in that speech will be analyzed—will be put under a microscope by the other countries—to determine exactly what he meant to say. And, very often, what is left out of a speech will be just as meaningful as what was put in.

If you knew that someone who's very skilled at analyzing conversation would be analyzing every word that you said in the negotiation, you would have to be very cautious. Not only must you be skillful in analyzing their hidden meanings, but you must also be careful not to give away your own.

I was once involved in a negotiation that would have led to the merger of two companies. One of the skeletons that we had in our closet was that one of our major stockholders was in serious financial straits and was very eager to complete the merger at any price. We didn't want the other side to know this, of course.

At one point in the negotiations, the president of the other company said, "I'm concerned about your relationship with Mr. X. I feel that if we ran a credit check on him, we'd find that he has serious financial problems." The manner in which the statement was made puzzled me. He didn't say, "We ran a credit check on him," which he was perfectly within his rights to do. He didn't start off his sentence with "As you're well aware, so and so has credit problems." He said, "If we were to run a credit check." This alerted me to the fact that he was in contact with someone within our organization who had passed this information on to him.

Later on, in a conversation he had with me, he said, "Roger, you're an outside director of the corporation." (That means that, although I sat on the board of directors, I didn't work for the corporation.) He continued, "I understand that you recently spent an entire day at the corporation, interviewing all of the key employees. That's a strange thing for an outside director to do. Why did you do that?"

I'd done it because I suspected there were some severe conflicts within the ranks of the organization. It hadn't turned out as badly as I feared, but I didn't quite know how to respond to his question. Then I remembered how he had phrased the earlier question, during the negotiations, and my suspicion that there was someone within our company who was feeding him information based on that response. I immediately knew that he already read my confidential report from that day's activities. I responded with a series of questions that caused him to reveal the name of the collaborator.

The lesson here is to listen very, very carefully to the words that people use. If something strikes you as being very strange, then jot it down, word for word, and analyze it later. Very often, people can say one thing and mean exactly the opposite.

Opposites

Let's take a look at a few of those expressions that probably mean exactly the opposite of how they sound. If someone starts off a conversation with "In my humble opinion," he probably means exactly the opposite. He's not humble. In fact, he's egotistical. He's so great that he can profess to be humble.

When you ask an opinion of someone and that person responds, "Well, he's a fine church-going person," this probably means that church attendance is his only attribute. And if someone says to you, "We can work out the details later," that probably means that there's quite a bit of negotiating to be done yet. You're not in as close agreement as this person wants you to believe. The classic, of course is, "Don't worry." If your daughter calls you up at 3 a.m. and says, "Daddy, don't worry," what should you do? Start worrying!

Throwaways

There's another group of expressions that should really alert you because they precede a very important part of the conversation. They're called throwaways, such as "As you are aware," "Incidentally," "Before I forget," "I just remembered," and "By the way." "As you're aware" may be used as follows. "As you're aware, we control 51 percent of the proxy votes in the company." Well, of course you were not aware of that. It's a major point, and they just tried to drop it in at the tail end of a sentence. "Incidentally," "before I forget," and "by the way" are throwaway expressions that usually precede a monumental announcement.

The classic use of a throwaway took place when President Truman was meeting with Churchill and Stalin in Potsdam at the end of World War II. The war in Europe was over, and the war with Japan was still going on. Truman told Churchill that we had successfully tested an atomic bomb just three days before, but he had not told Stalin. He felt obligated to tell him, but didn't want to reveal that it was an atomic bomb for fear that it would help the Soviets to develop one. At the end of the day's meetings, Truman walked over to Stalin and said, "Oh, by the way, Mr. Stalin, we have a new weapon of unusual destructive force." You can tell that Truman was trying to downplay the importance of this announcement by using the throwaway "by the way."

Stalin's response was equally fascinating. He replied, "Oh, yes, we're aware of that." We assumed that he was lying, and that he did not know that the Allies had an atomic bomb. It was nearly 50 years later, after the Cold War was over and the Soviet Union had collapsed, that we found out that he did know. He had placed a spy in Los Alamos that was keeping him informed. That night, he called the Russian scientists, who were frantically trying to develop their own atomic bomb, and told them to hurry up and get it finished.

Frequently, these throwaways, such as "incidentally" and "by the way," precede the most dramatic pronouncements. Perk up when you hear them!

Legitimizers

These are expressions such as "frankly," "honestly," and "to tell the truth." They're usually used to try to legitimize a statement that is not completely true. When somebody says to you, "Honestly, I don't think we could live with a proposal like that," what does he mean by honestly? Has he been dishonest up to now? Or could it be that he's just trying to add a little more convincing power to what he's telling you? Even then, he's not being strictly honest with you.

Another popular legitimizer is "in actual fact." A fact is a fact. Trying to make it sound grander by adding *actual* to it reveals a pretense. Harold Geneen, when he was president of ITT, once exploded over the misuse of the word *fact* and wrote a scathing memo to all his people that said:

"Yesterday, we put in a long hard-driving meeting mostly seeking the facts on which easy management decisions could be then made. I think the most important conclusion to be drawn is simple. There is no word in the English language that more strongly conveys the intent of incontrovertibility, i.e. 'final and reliable reality' than the word 'fact.' However, no word is more honored by its breach in actual usage. For example, there are and we saw yesterday:

'Apparent facts'

'Assumed facts'

'Reported Facts'

'Hoped-for facts'

'Accepted facts' - and many others of similar derivation.
In most cases these were not facts at all."

Another legitimizer that has become popular on evening news shows is the expression "exactly right." Anchor Brian Williams says to Anne Thompson, "That has become a big problem, hasn't it, Anne?" and Anne sycophantically replies, "That's *exactly* right, Brian." It is either right or it isn't! Adding exactly detracts from the statement.

One of the favorite legitimizers in American literature is among the last words of *Gone With the Wind,* by Margaret Mitchell, when Rhett Butler says to Scarlet O'Hara, "Frankly, my dear, I don't give a damn." (In 2005, the American Film Institute voted it the number-one movie line of all time.) Students of language and of hidden meanings in conversation would instantly pounce on that word *frankly.* It's a legitimizer. He's trying to make legitimate what he really doesn't believe. In fact, he did give a damn. And when Alexander Ripley wrote *Scarlett,* the sequel to *Gone With the Wind,* we learned that only Rhett's love for Scarlett could save her from the gallows.

Justifiers

Justifiers are words that lay the foundation for failure, such as "I'll try my best" or "I'll see what I can do. I'll try to keep it under $300." These expressions fall far short of a firm commitment, don't they? And they're preparing you for the fact that they might fail, so, unless you're willing to live with that, at that point, challenge it. Even worse is when a justifier is changed to the plural tense. Instead of saying "I'll give it every effort," all of a sudden it becomes "We'll give it every effort," hiding behind the group. No salesperson worth his or her salt would ever accept the excuse of "Well, I'd like to think it over." But if the "I" changes to "we," then really look out!

If, during the entire negotiation, a person has been saying "Well, I don't think I can afford to pay that much," or, "I wouldn't be willing to do that," or, "I would have to get you to…," and then all of a sudden the person switches to "Well, we'll have to think it over and we'll give you a decision tomorrow," you're in serious trouble. You'd better get back in there and do some more selling, because it's just not going to fly. Switching from "I'll try" to "we'll try" is a clear attempt at evasion.

Erasers

There are many erasers. The two most popular ones are "but" and "however." What you have to learn about these words is that they erase everything that has gone before them. Someone can tell you for ten minutes how much he or she enjoys your product, and the person can look like he or she is certain to buy. But if this 10-minute discourse ends with a "but" or a "however," erase those 10 minutes and know that you'll have to start again. Because the eraser word *but* or *however* literally erases everything that's gone on before.

Deceptions

When the eraser is preceded by a sentence such as "I'm just a country boy, but…" or "I'm no student of law; however,…" or "I never graduated from college, but…" or "I've never fully understood it; however…" or "It's none of my business, but…" these are called deceptions. And that's exactly what they are.

For example, somebody once said, "I'm just a country boy" to Lyndon Johnson when he was in the White House. Lyndon Johnson, who himself was a country boy, exploded and said, "Listen, mister, in this town, when somebody says that to me, I feel like putting my hand on my wallet." If somebody says to you that they're no student of the law, they might not be, but you can rest assured that they know exactly what they're talking about in this particular instance.

Preparers

A group of sentences that are very important to salespeople are called preparers. When a salesperson says to you, "I don't mean to be personal," you can be sure that he or she is about to become very personal. "I don't mean to be personal, but when did you file for bankruptcy?" When he says, "I don't want to intrude," what is he about to do? Intrude!

Exaggerations

Another way to prepare people for a potentially difficult question is to exaggerate it. Let's say that someone wants to ask you what your income was last year, because he's filling out a credit application for you. He may say to you, "This is very embarrassing, but...." In those three seconds, all kinds of things are running through your mind about how embarrassing this could be. And when you find out that the only thing he's asking for is your income, it's much easier to take.

Someone might say to you, "I need a big, big favor." You're thinking she is going to ask for $1000, or at least $500. When she asks you for $50, it seems like such a small amount.

Trial Balloons

In the negotiating process, you will frequently encounter trial balloons.Trial balloons are the sentences that start off with "I haven't given it a lot of thought, but..." or "Just suppose that we..." or "Off the top of my head, I would think that..." or "What would happen if we...?" People who have made up their minds that they'd like to try something, but they're not sure if you'll go along with it, send up these little trial balloons.

This tells you two things. First, it tells you that this person would accept what he is suggesting, however little thought the person claims to have given the matter. In effect then, the person has narrowed his negotiating range. It also tells you that the person is not sure you'll accept it, so you can probably do a lot better if you push a little harder.

Neuro-Linguistic Orientation

Another important part of hidden meaning in conversation is the realization that people tend to be oriented toward one of their senses. By that, I mean that we all interpret everything we experience through our different senses (seeing, hearing, feeling, touching, or tasting), and most of us have an orientation toward one of those senses.

Taste and smell are seldom a predominant sense. The three most popular senses you'll encounter are seeing, hearing, and feeling. You can tell which orientation a person has by the kind of language the person uses.

Let's suppose, for example, that three people get together and attend a symphony concert. The three people are an oil painter, a piano player, and a poet. Now, if they follow their professions, you would expect that the oil painter would be primarily sight-oriented. What he sees will be much more important than what he feels or hears. The piano player will be oriented to hearing. What he hears will be more important than what he sees or feels. The poet will be oriented to his feelings. What he feels will be more important than what he sees or hears. Each one of them will come away with a different interpretation of what happened.

Although the orientations of people you'll meet in a negotiation may not be that pronounced, they still exist, and they can still be important to your strategy. The people may tell you which orientation they have from the way that they express themselves. For example, a person whose orientation is through sound, like a piano player, will say, "That *sounds* good to me" or "I *hear* you." And the person who primarily is a feeling-type person, like the poet, will say things like, "I *feel* good about this" or "I can *warm up* to that suggestion."

If you're dealing with someone who is primarily visual, you'll want to use a presentation binder or go to a chalkboard and draw it out for him or her so the person can actually see it. This won't be so important with someone who has an audio orientation. In fact, you could even turn off somebody like this. The person might even resent you visually explaining what you just said. His inner language may be saying, "You don't have to paint me a picture. I heard you the first time." Be sure you mirror the conversations of people. If people are in the audio mode, they're saying, "That *sounds* good to me."

Don't respond with "That *looks* good to me, too." Among people who study that kind of thing, that's called a crossed response. As with the study of body language, there are people who can get completely carried away with the study of hidden meanings in conversation. What I've given you here, of course, is a very brief overview. As you become more aware of the subject, as you study more closely what people say, and as you learn to interpret with more skill what people say, you'll become more interested in it, and your knowledge will automatically grow.

☑ Key Points to Remember

1. If you recorded and transcribed a negotiation, you would be able to detect all kinds of hidden meanings in the way things were said.

2. Some expressions alert you to things that mean the opposite of what is being said. For example, "in my humble opinion," "he's a fine church-going person," and "don't worry" are what we call opposites.
3. Throwaways such as "as you are aware," "incidentally," "before I forget," and "by the way" precede important pronouncements.
4. Legitimizers are usually used to try to legitimize a statement that is not completely true, such as "frankly," "honestly," and "to tell the truth."
5. Justifiers are used to prepare you for the other side not doing what they offered. Examples include "I'll try my best," "I'll see what I can do," or "I'll try to keep it under $300." Even worse is "We'll try."
6. Erasers are words that erase everything that has gone before them such as "but" and "however."
7. When the eraser is preceded by a sentence, such as "I'm just a country boy, but...," "I'm no student of law; however ...," "I never graduated from college, but...," "I've never fully understood it, however...," or "It's none of my business but...," these are called deceptions.
8. Preparers prepare you for difficult questions. "I don't mean to be personal" and "I don't mean to intrude" pave the way for the speaker to do just that.
9. Exaggerations make it easy for you to get something. Someone might say to you, "I need a big, big favor." You're thinking she is going to ask for $1000, or at least $500. When she asks you for $50, it seems like such a small amount.
10. Trial balloons tell you that the other side will accept what they are proposing.
11. Listen to the way people talk. It will reveal whether they are visuals, auditories, or feeling people. Rephrase your talk to match theirs.

Chapter 50

The Personal Characteristics of a Power Negotiator

To be a Power Negotiator, you need to have or develop these personal characteristics: the courage to probe for more information, the patience to outlast the other negotiator, the courage to ask for more than you expect to get, the integrity to press for win-win solutions, and the willingness to be a good listener. In this chapter, we will take a look at each of these in more detail.

The Courage to Probe for More Information

Poor negotiators are always reluctant to question anything the other says, so they negotiate knowing only what the other side has chosen to tell them. Power Negotiators are constantly challenging what they know about the other side and, what is more important, the assumptions that they have made based on that knowledge. You should adopt many of the approaches of investigative reporters as you gather information.

Ask the tough questions—the ones that you feel sure they won't answer. Even if they don't answer, you will learn by judging their reaction to being asked. Ask the same question of several people to see if you get the same responses. Ask the same question several times during an extended negotiation to see if you get consistent answers. As you know, I devoted Chapter 38 to the importance of gathering information before and during the negotiation.

The Patience to Outlast the Other Negotiator

Patience is a virtue to a good negotiator. I remember going around the country on a press tour to promote an earlier book on negotiating.

A couple of times, I showed up at television stations, and the interviewer said to me, "You don't look like a negotiator." I knew what they meant and it didn't offend me. They meant, "We thought you'd look tougher. We thought you'd look meaner." Perhaps from seeing movies about union negotiators, many people think of negotiators as tough, ruthless people who will pull any ruthless stunt to trick the other side into losing. Nothing could be further from the truth. Good negotiators are very patient people who won't let time pressure bully them into making a deal that is not in everyone's best interests.

Remember the Vietnam peace talks? Averell Harriman rented a suite at the Ritz Hotel in Paris on a week-to-week basis. The Vietnamese negotiator, Xuan Thuy, rented a villa in the countryside for two and half years. With your government, your people, and the world press breathing down your neck for results, it takes courage to show that much patience, but it's very effective.

The Courage to Ask for More

Former Secretary of State Henry Kissinger once said, "Effectiveness at the conference table depends upon overstating one's demands." Apart from projecting the willingness to walk away if you can't get what you want, I don't think that there is anything more important than understanding this principle and having the courage to apply it.

We all lack courage sometimes simply because we fear ridicule. Remember when I taught you about the Bracketing Gambit in Chapter 1? I told you that you should make a super-low offer, which brackets your objective, when buying something. Then again, I told you that when you're selling something, make your initial proposal so high that it brackets your real objective.

You should always advance your maximum plausible position. Sometimes that's hard to do. We simply don't have the courage to make those far-out proposals because we're afraid the other side will laugh at us. The fear of ridicule stops us from accomplishing many things with our lives. To be a Power Negotiator, you must get over that fear. You must be able to comfortably advance your maximum plausible position and not apologize for it. (I'll teach you more about fear in Chapter 55 on Coercive Power.)

The Integrity to Press for a Win-Win Solution

Straight Up, by James Ramsey Ullman, was an excellent biography of young mountain climber John Harlin, who, at 30 years of age, died trying to climb the Eiger Mountain diretissima—straight up. The author, a famous chronicler of mountain-climbing events, wrote about Harlin's life in the preface. He said: "Straight up is a way of serving a drink. It is also a way to climb a mountain and of living a life."

I believe that straight up is the way to negotiate. Often, the opportunity to take quick advantage of a weakened opponent will tempt you. You'll be in a situation in which you know something that, if the other side knew, would make them less eager to settle. Having the integrity to push for a win-win solution, even when you have the other side on the ropes is a rare and precious commodity. I don't mean by this that you make costly concessions to the other side because you're so charitable. I do mean that you continue to look for ways to make concessions to the other side that do not take away from your position.

The Willingness to Be a Good Listener

Only a good listener can be a win-win negotiator. Only a good listener can detect the other side's real needs in a negotiation. Here are some tips for being a good listener in preparing for and conducting the negotiation:

- Increase your concentration by thinking of listening as an interactive process.
- Lean forward.
- Tilt your head a little to show you're paying attention.
- Ask questions.
- Give feedback.
- Mirror what he said.
- Avoid boredom by playing mind games.
- Concentrate on what he is saying, not the style of delivery. You can do this by picking the longest word in a sentence or rephrasing what has just been said. Because you can listen four times faster than the speaker can speak, you need to do something, or your mind will wander.

Increase your comprehension of what's being said by taking notes right from the start of the conversation. Take a large pad of paper with you. Head it with the date and the topic, and start to keep brief notes on what's being said. Paper is cheaper than the time it takes to go back and get the details. This communicates to the other person that you care about what he's saying. An additional bonus is that when people see you're writing things down, they tend to be a lot more accurate in what they're telling you. Next, defer judging of the other person until he's through. If you immediately analyze someone as phony, manipulative, or self-serving, you tend to shut him out and quit listening to him. Just hold off and wait until he's through before you evaluate.

Improve your ability to evaluate what's said by asking the other person to present her conclusions first. Then, if you don't agree with her completely, ask her to support her conclusions. Keep an open mind until she has. Be aware of your personal biases and be conscious of how they're coloring your reactions. If you know that you don't like attorneys, you can evaluate the information much more clearly when you're aware that this is causing you to distrust the person who's talking to you.

Perhaps you're a person who can't stand people trying to hype you. You automatically resist what they have to say, whether it's right or wrong, so be aware of that. It improves your ability to evaluate what they're saying. Learn to take notes with a divided note pad, one with a line down the middle. On the left, you list the facts as they were presented; on the right, you note your evaluation of what was said.

Key Points to Remember

1. Have the courage to ask the tough questions. If you are negotiating based only on what the other side has chosen to tell you, you are very vulnerable.
2. Patience is a tremendous virtue. Don't be so eager to reach an agreement that you overlook opportunities to make the agreement better for both sides.
3. Asking for more than you expect to get takes courage, but it's a vital point. How good a negotiator you are depends on your ability to overstate your initial demands.
4. Have the integrity to press for a solution that is better for the other side. The most important thought you can have is not "What can I get them to give me?" It is "What can I give them that would not take away from my position?" When you give people what they want, they will give you what you want.
5. Listening is a skill, just like talking, but it's more important. Work to improve your listening skills.

Chapter 51

The Attitudes of a Power Negotiator

The Willingness to Live With Ambiguity

A Power Negotiator relishes the idea of going into a negotiation not knowing whether he'll come out a hero, or if he'll come out carrying his head in his hands. This willingness to live with ambiguity requires a particular attitude. People who like people are much more comfortable with ambiguity. People who prefer things to people are not as comfortable. For this reason, engineers, accountants, and architects—members of those professions that depend on accuracy—have a tough time with negotiating. They don't like the push and the shove of it. They would rather have everything laid out in black and white.

Let me give you a little quiz to test your willingness to live with ambiguity:

1. If you're going to a party, do you first like to know who you're likely to meet there?
2. If your spouse is taking you to have dinner with friends at a restaurant, do you like to know exactly which restaurant you are going to?
3. Do you like to plan your vacations to the smallest detail?

If you said "yes" to all three of these, you have a major problem with ambiguity. To become a better negotiator, I suggest that you force yourself to tolerate situations in which you don't know exactly what the outcome will be.

I remember training a large group of architects once. To test their comfort level with ambiguity, I asked them a series of questions that could be answered with a number. I told them that if they didn't know the answer they could give a range, and they could make the range as broad as they wished. One of the questions I asked them was: "How many license plates can you derive from a combination of six letters and six numbers?"

To me, a good answer would have been "between 15 and 20 million." A superbly accurate answer would have been "between 17 and 18 million." Their response to the question fascinated me. They wanted to know if they could use the letter "I" and the number "1." They wanted to know if they could use the letter "O" and the number "0." I said, "What does it matter? Just give me a range." They wouldn't do that and insisted that I tell them if they could use similar-looking numbers and letters.

I noticed that the president of the company was almost falling off his chair because he was laughing so much. Later he told me, "Roger, you don't understand. Architects are trained to be precise. They can't live with ambiguity. They have to know if that building is going to stand up or fall down. They have zero tolerance for ambiguity."

I told them that they could use similar-looking letters and numbers. Only then did they all whip out their calculators and start furiously punching in numbers to give me the answer: exactly 17,576,000. That's enough for every state except California and Texas.

I can vividly remember the moment when I realized that I was uncomfortable with ambiguity. When I was young I was into mountain climbing and had flown to Nepal to trek to the base camp of Mount Everest. On the way, I planned to spend a few days in the capital of India, New Delhi. I didn't have much money, so I arranged a barebones trip to the Taj Mahal in Agra. I found an Indian who spoke good English, and we rode a bus out there, which is a journey of about 150 miles. Agra turned out to be a pretty rundown city—an enormous contrast to the beauty of the monument I had come to see.

I was staring out of the bus window at a couple of backpackers winding their way through a crowded marketplace. They clearly had everything they owned strapped to their backs. I thought, "How scary that must be to be in a strange country and have night come and you don't know where you're going to sleep."

I had never thought about it before, but I suddenly realize that for the thousands of nights that I'd been alive, I had never put myself in a situation in which I didn't know where I was going to sleep that night. I considered myself an adventurous person. I had traveled the world and climbed dangerous mountains, but never once had I trusted myself to find a place to sleep without planning it in advance.

The more I thought about this, the more I realized that I needed to do something about this. I couldn't go on being so scared of ambiguity that I had to thoroughly plan ahead like that.

A few months later, I was scheduled to speak in Australia. Instead of meticulously planning my trip as I usually did, I bought a round-the-world air ticket. With this type of ticket, you don't have to plan your trip ahead, you can call the airline at the last minute and get a seat to your next destination. The only restriction is that you can't backtrack. You have to keep moving either east or west. The trip took me a month, and I didn't book any of it ahead of time, not even any hotel rooms.

I went from my home in Los Angeles to Tahiti, on to Australia for the speaking engagement, and then to Singapore, Bangkok, Frankfurt, and Paris. I didn't have any trouble getting a taxi or renting a car when I needed it. I didn't have any trouble finding a hotel.

If you have an obsession with planning everything ahead of time, I recommend that exercise to you. Try taking off without any plans. Develop some confidence that you can handle whatever comes up. It will make you a better negotiator, and it will also raise your self-esteem.

Your self-esteem is directly related to your ability to handle things if they go wrong. Some people are devastated if their car won't start in the morning. Others have an enormous ability to plow through problems and not have the problems stop them.

Be Resilient

I love the adjective *resilient*. I always used to think that it means the ability to withstand damage, but it doesn't. It means the ability to recover from damage. If you squeeze a beer can, it stays squeezed. It is not resilient. If you squeeze a plastic water bottle, it pops back to its original shape because it is very resilient.

Resilience is a powerful characteristic for a negotiator. However much planning you do, it is unlikely that the negotiation will go the way you planned it. There will be unpleasant surprises. There will be difficulties that would force a lesser person to give up. If you have resilience, you have what it takes to bounce back from misfortune.

My wife, Gisela, is very resilient. She was born in Germany in the middle of World War II. It was bad enough being on the losing side of that war, but to compound the problem, she was in the Eastern side of the country, faced with brutal domination of the Soviet invasion. She, her parents, and her twin sister, Helga, managed to escape to West Germany and then, when she was 12 years old, migrated to Philadelphia. Psychologists tell us that much of our character is formed during those early years, and I certainly believe that all those early challenges made her as resilient as she is.

Resilience is a great characteristic for a speaker's wife. Very often, I have to tell Gisela that I'll be away in Florida all next week, giving seminars. She doesn't say, "What am I going to do while you're away?" She has her own friends and interests.

She showed a great ability to bounce back from misfortune when we were visiting Amalfi, a beautiful old town on the Amalfi Coastline that stretches from Naples, Italy, south to Sicily. Towering cliffs rise straight up from the Mediterranean, and over the centuries the Italians have found a way to build homes up those steep cliffs. It's an incredibly beautiful sight. In Roman times, the emperors would build their summer retreats on the top of those cliffs. If you haven't been there, be sure to add it to your bucket list. It's something you have to see before you die.

We were in Amalfi and wanted to visit Ravello, which is an artist's colony at the top of the cliff above Amalfi. We had fallen in love with Ravello when we rented a villa one summer in Positano, which is a beautiful town a few miles north, toward Sorrento and Pompeii. The only road to Ravello is a narrow two-lane road that miraculously climbs the cliffs with dozens of hairpin bends cuts into the rocks. It's a tough ride, but well worth it. If you can find a balcony in Ravello and get yourself a glass of Chianti Classico while you savor the view that has enchanted visitors for centuries, you'll agree with me that life doesn't get much better than that. You can search if you want, but you might as well take my word for it: Life doesn't get much better than that. Maybe it does with a bottle of Chianti Classico.

The problem was that we couldn't find a taxi to take us there. We waited at the taxi stand for 15 minutes, but none showed up. I saw a sign that said "Bus Tickets," and I said to Gisela, "Perhaps we could get a bus to Ravello?"

She said, "Have you ever ridden a bus?"

"Not since I moved to Los Angeles 35 years ago, but when I was a kid in London, I rode buses all the time. Let's give it a try." I bought a couple of tickets at the store, and they told me that I'd have 50 minutes to wait for the next bus." I suggested to Gisela that we have lunch and a bottle of wine at the restaurant on the beach where we could keep an eye on the bus stop. Soon we could see that more people were gathering for the bus than could possibly fit on it. I suggested that we line up with them. Gisela said, "It's so beautiful here, Roger. Why don't you line up and save me a seat? I'll finish the wine."

The bus pulled up and the crowd attacked it. I had to literally fight my way on to it, but managed to plunk myself down on two seats in the back row. The bus was jam-packed with people both sitting and standing. I frantically looked for Gisela but couldn't see her. The bus started to pull away, and I got a glimpse of her standing on the curb at the bus stop. I banged on the back window of the bus yelling, "I'm on the bus! I'm on the bus!" but I couldn't tell if she'd seen me.

The people next to me said, "Who was that?"

"That's my wife!"

They were incredulous. "You left your wife at a bus stop in a strange country! How could you?"

"Well, she's German and she's very resilient. She'll think of something," I told them, but in my heart I knew that I was in serious trouble. I would have to spend the rest of my life watching Emma Thompson movies to recover from that one.

As I contemplated my bleak future I could hear the other people on the bus talking about what had happened—sometimes in English ("Can you believe that idiot!"), sometimes in Italian ("Ci credi che idiota!"), and sometimes in French ("Mon dieu! Sacrebleu!"). Soon everyone on the bus knew that the idiot in the back row had left his wife at the bus stop in Amalfi, and I was sinking lower and lower in my seat.

Halfway up the corkscrew road, a taxi suddenly roared by the bus and cut it off. I saw Gisela get out of the cab and get on the front of the bus, yelling, "Roger, are you on this bus?" I said, "Yes, Dear. I'm back here!" The entire bus erupted in applause, and off we went to Ravello.

That's resilience. The ability to recover from misfortune. It's a great characteristic for a negotiator. When things don't go as planned, find a way to make it work.

A Competitive Spirit

Good negotiators have an intense desire to win when they're negotiating. Seeing negotiating as a game is a big part of what makes you good at it. It's fun to walk into the arena and pit your skills against the skills of the other person.

It always amazes me that salespeople can be so competitive in sports, but so cowardly when it comes to handling buyers. A salesperson may enjoy playing racquetball, so he sets up an early-morning game with a buyer before he's scheduled to make a presentation to him. On the racquetball court, he'll do everything he can—within the rules of the game—to beat the buyer. Then they shower off and go to the office to negotiate the sale, and, the moment the buyer mentions price, the salesperson rolls over and feels that he's at the buyer's mercy.

The more you think of negotiating as a game, the more competitive you'll become. The more competitive you become, the more courageous you become, and the better you'll do.

Don't Be Conflict-Averse

Power Negotiators are not restrained by the need to be liked. Abraham Maslow is famous for his pyramid of human needs, which showed our needs as:

1. Survival.
2. Security (the need to assure our continued survival).
3. Social (the need to be liked and accepted by others).
4. Self-esteem (the need to be respected by others).
5. Self-actualization (the need to feel fulfilled).

Power Negotiators are beyond stage three most of the time—they have surpassed the need to be liked. Negotiation, almost by definition, is the management of conflict or at least opposing viewpoints. People who have an exaggerated need to be liked will not be good negotiators because they fear conflict too much.

When I train physicians I frequently get the comment that they do not think it wise to be too tough a negotiator because they need to build long-term relationships with the people in their industry. I don't think that you build relationships by making concessions to people. Let me ask you this: If you had given your children everything they ever asked for, would you have a better or a worse relationship than you do now? I think that those physicians are confusing liking with respecting. When you're negotiating, you want the other side to respect you, not like you.

What these physicians are revealing is that they are conflict-averse. Physicians are the healers of the world, not the fighters. That's not a good characteristic for a negotiator. Learn to enjoy a good conflict as long as it produces a healthy result for both sides.

Does this mean that good negotiators are ruthless people who win because they don't care if the other person is losing? No, not at all. It does mean that the most important thing to them is to hammer away at the problem until a solution with which everyone can live is found.

Key Points to Remember

1. Learn to feel comfortable with ambiguity, because negotiating is the management of a fluid situation.
2. Be resilient. The negotiation will never go exactly as you planned. Learn to bounce back from misfortune.
3. Think of negotiating as a game to be won. Be vigorously competitive, but still play within the rules of the game.
4. Don't worry about being liked. You don't want the other side to like you; you want them to respect you.
5. Don't be conflict-averse. Learn to enjoy a good conflict, as long as it produces a healthy result for both sides.

Chapter 52

The Beliefs of a Power Negotiator

Negotiating Is Always a Two-Way Affair

Power Negotiating is always a two-way affair. The pressure is always on the other person to compromise in the negotiations just as much as it is on you. For example, when you're walking into a bank and applying for a business loan, you may get very intimidated. You tend to look at that big bank, and you start thinking, "Why on Earth would a big bank like this want to lend money to little old me?" You lose sight of the pressure that's on the other side. This bank spends millions of dollars a year in advertising to entice you to come in for a loan. There is tremendous pressure on the bank to get those deposits out in the form of loans. Many people at that bank have jobs that are dependent on their making loans.

A good negotiator learns to mentally compensate for the fact that we always think we have the weaker side in the negotiations. As she strides up to that loan officer's desk, she thinks to herself, "I bet that loan officer just got a royal chewing out from his boss, who told him, 'If you can't find somebody to lend money to today, we don't need you around here anymore.'"

Remember when you've had a key employee come to you to ask for a raise in pay? What are you sitting there thinking? You're thinking, "I hope I don't lose him over this. He has done so well for me, all these years. He's so skilled in what he's doing. I have no idea where I'd find a replacement for him."

He's probably sitting there thinking, "I hope this doesn't affect my career plan with the company. They've really been good to me over the years. Maybe I shouldn't push so hard. She's been so nice to me." You're both sitting there thinking that you have the weaker hand in the negotiation. Power negotiators learn to mentally compensate for that.

Why does this happen? Because each side knows about the pressure that is on him or her, but doesn't know about the pressure that is on the other side. For that reason, each side typically thinks that it has the weaker hand.

Don't buy into it when a potential customer says to you, "I've got half a dozen other guys that will do it for less money and do it just as well." Don't buy into that. Something brought the other side to the negotiating table. The customer has pressure, just as much as you have it on you. The minute you believe that and learn to mentally compensate for it, you become a more powerful negotiator.

Negotiating Is Played by a Set of Rules

The second belief that makes you a good negotiator is that negotiating is a game that is played by a set of rules, just like the game of chess. Perhaps when you read some of the Gambits in Section One, you thought, "Roger, you've never met some of the guys I have to deal with in my business. They make Attila the Hun look like Katie Couric. They're never going to fall for that kind of thing."

That's fair enough, but I want you to buy a little blue sky from me until you've had a chance to try them out. Repeatedly, students of mine have told me: "I never thought that it would work, but it did. It's amazing." The first time you Flinch, Nibble, or use the Vise on the other person, and walk out of the negotiations with $1,000 in your pocket that you didn't expect to get, you'll be a believer too.

The Vise in Action

I remember training the employees of a large savings and loan in Southern California. At a local hotel, they arranged an afternoon seminar followed by a cocktail party and a dinner. During the cocktail party, I was talking to the president of the savings and loan when the maitre d' from the hotel came up with two bottles of wine in his arms. He asked the president if he would like wine served with the dinner. When asked, he told the president that the wine cost $22.50 per bottle. The president was about to say okay when I said, "You'll have to do better than that." The maitre d' looked irritated, and the president looked shocked. The maitre d' said, "I tell you what. If you'll serve it for everybody, I'll give it to you for $15 a bottle." The president's face lit up and he was about to give his okay when I said, "We were thinking more like $10 a bottle."

This caused the maitre d' to say, "I'm not going to negotiate the price of wine with you—$13.50 is absolutely the best I can do." Remember that the president had been in the seminar that afternoon and had heard me talk about the Vise Gambit, but until he saw it in action, I don't think he thought that it would work.

Please buy some blue sky from me until you get a chance to get out there and try out these Gambits. The most important belief to have is that negotiating is a game that is played by a set of rules. If you learn the rules well, you can play the game well.

"No" Is Simply an Opening Negotiating Position

To Power Negotiators, the word *no* is never a refusal. It is simply an opening negotiating position. Remember that the next time you take a proposal to somebody—perhaps your boss or a potential customer—and he explodes with rage and says, "Not you again, with another of your crazy ideas. How many times do I have to tell you that we're never going to do it? Get out of my office, and quit wasting my time." When that happens, remember that a Power Negotiator doesn't take it as a refusal (I know—it's close); she takes it only to be an opening negotiating position. She thinks to herself, "Isn't that an interesting opening negotiating position? I wonder why he decided to start with that approach."

Your children know this, don't they? You can tell your child, "I am sick of hearing about this! Go to your room! I don't want to see you until the morning! And if you ever bring this up again, I will ground you for a month!" Do they hear a refusal? No! They're up in their room thinking, "Wasn't that an interesting opening negotiating position?"

☑ Key Points to Remember

1. Each side typically thinks that they have the weaker hand because each side knows about the pressure that is on them, but doesn't know about the pressure that is on the other side. For that reason, you always have a stronger hand than you think you do.
2. Negotiating is a game that is played by a set of rules, just like the game of chess. You will be pleasantly surprised by how well the gambits work!
3. The word *no* is never a refusal to a negotiator; it is only an opening negotiating position.

Section Six

Developing Power Over the Other Side

Power. Control. Influence. That's really at the heart of any interpersonal situation, isn't it? In negotiating, the person with the most influence or power will gain the most concessions. If you allow other people to manipulate and intimidate you, it is your fault if you're not getting what you want out of life. If, on the other hand, you learn what influences people and how to use and counter specific methods, you can take control of any situation.

Developing personal power over the other side is an issue that is so critical to Power Negotiating that I'm going to devote all of this section to it.

In any negotiation, one person always feels he's either the intimidator or the person being intimidated. You always feel that you either have control of the other person, or the other person has control over you. In this section, I'm going to explain where that feeling comes from and how to deal with it.

At a seminar in Iowa, a man approached me and said, "Roger, my wife took your Power Negotiating course, and I've never seen such a personality change in all my life. She has her own small business, and it wasn't doing that well. But once she studied up on personal power and your Negotiating Gambits, it's amazing to see the difference in her. She turned into a tiger, and she really turned that business around."

I have always been fascinated by what causes one person to be influenced by another, and, for the last decade, I have been absorbed with studying personal power. I'm going to teach you the essential things that give you power over people. In every situation in which one person exercises control over another, one or more of these factors have been called into play. Whether it is a drill sergeant harassing a private in boot camp, or a parent trying to maintain control over an errant child, one or more of these basic power factors is being used.

Power has earned a nasty reputation, hasn't it? In a letter to Bishop Creighton, Lord Acton said, "Power tends to corrupt and absolute power corrupts absolutely." Charles Colton said, "Power will intoxicate the best hearts, as wine the strongest heads. No man is wise enough, nor good enough to be trusted with unlimited power." However, I don't believe that power is inherently evil. It really isn't power that corrupts, is it? It's the abuse of power. You wouldn't say that water is bad because occasionally we have floods and people drown. You wouldn't say that air is bad because we occasionally have hurricanes and homes are destroyed. It's not power; it's the abuse of power that corrupts. There is tremendous power in the ocean's waves, and yet, every day, hundreds of eager surfers ride the towering crests. Electricity has the power to light a child's room at night, and the power to electrocute a convicted murderer. The power itself is independent of its use. The pope has power over millions of people and so did Adolf Hitler. As George Bernard Shaw said, "Power does not corrupt man; fools, however, if they get into a position of power, corrupt power."

Power can be a very constructive force. When I talk about power, I am not referring to the wanton ruthlessness of a dictator, whether he is in politics or industry; I simply mean the ability to influence other people.

What I'm going to cover in this section are the things that people can do when they're negotiating with you to cause you to blink first at the negotiating table. Of course, these things are also what can give you power over the other side. Where does that ability come from? It comes from one or more of these eight elements.

Chapter 53

Legitimate Power

Legitimate Power goes to anyone who has a title. I think you'll agree that you are always a little more intimidated by someone who has the title of vice president or doctor than you would be by someone who has no title. We gain Legitimate Power instantly, because it goes to us the moment that the title is conferred upon us.

For example, the moment the chief justice swears in the president of the United States, the president receives the full power of the presidency, independent of any personal power that may have existed moments before. What a president does with that power from that point on makes all the difference. Striking a balance between appearing presidential and appearing close to the people—just a regular guy (or gal!)—is difficult to do.

Titles influence people, so if you have a title, don't be afraid to use it. Don't be bashful about putting your title on your business cards and on your nameplate. If the title on your business card says vice president, you already have a head start over someone whose card says salesperson. When I ran the real estate company, I would let the agents who were farming a territory put *area manager* on their business cards. (Farming means that they had staked out an area of 500 homes, and they were knocking on doors and mailing newsletters to those homeowners to establish themselves as an expert in that community.) They told me that having the title area manager on their cards made a dramatic difference to the way people accepted them.

If you don't have an impressive title on your business card, this may be something your company should review. The standard designations for territories are that an area manager reports to a district manager who reports to a regional manager, so regional vice president appears to be the more impressive title. Occasionally, I run into a company that designates titles the other way and the area manager is in charge of the Western

United States. I don't suggest that they change, but because it's traditionally done the other way, area manager tends to be a less impressive title than regional manager.

Legitimate Power also tells you that you should have them come to you if possible, rather than negotiating in their territory, where their trappings of power surround them. If you're taking them somewhere, it should always be in your car because that gives you more control. If you're taking them to lunch, it should be to your choice of restaurant, not to their favorite place where they would feel in control.

Here are five small things that Power Negotiators can do to build their Title Power:

1. Use your title if you have one. If you don't have a title, see if you can get one.
2. Use your initials. For example, describe yourself as J.R. Doe, rather than John Doe. People who don't know you must then call you Mr. Doe rather than calling you by your first name.
3. If possible, negotiate in your office, or in your surroundings, rather than in theirs. That way you're in your power base, surrounded by the trappings of your title.
4. Always use your automobile when you're negotiating with people; don't let them drive. Real estate people always do that, don't they? When they're in your car, you have control over them.
5. Have an assistant place and screen your calls. I personally don't like administrative assistants who place calls for people, but it does convey Legitimate Power.

Other Forms of Legitimate Power

There are other forms of Legitimate Power. Positioning in the marketplace is a form of Legitimate Power. If you can claim that your company is the biggest (or smallest), or if you claim that it's the oldest (or the newest), you have authority in the marketplace. You can claim to be the most global company, or you can claim to specialize. You can tell people that you're brand new, so you're trying harder, or that you've been in the business for 40 years. It really doesn't matter how you position yourself; any kind of positioning gives you Legitimate Power.

Respect for the law is a form of Legitimate Power. Some people obey the law only because of fear of punishment, but most of us also respect the law and follow it because of that respect. There is almost no chance of us getting into trouble if we drive without a driver's license in our possession, but most of the time, we take pains to see that we have it in our pocket. It's very hard to enforce seat belt laws, but I started wearing mine when California passed a seat belt law, simply because I take pride in showing respect for the law. Do you zoom through red lights in the middle of the night if there's nobody around? Probably not, because we see the benefit of everyone obeying traffic laws.

Tradition is a form of Legitimate Power. (Until the start of the 20th century, tradition and law were thought to be the only main influences on people's behavior.) If you can establish in the other person's mind that you have been doing something for a long time, you can convince him or her that it's valid without giving any other reason for doing it.

An established procedure is another form of Legitimate Power. "We have always done it this way" has power. That's why price tags have Legitimate Power. Because they say, "Here's the way this works. We put a price tag on the merchandise. You pick what you want and bring it to the cash register. We charge you what is on the price tag." Simply because of this established procedure, few people question price tags in this country.

Conversely, the procedure on a car lot has been established differently. "You look at the price sticker and then you make us an offer" is the established procedure, and even people who hate to haggle will follow procedure. Power Negotiators know to use "standard contracts" when getting the other person to do what we want them to do. "This is our standard contract. This is the one that everybody signs" is simply conveying the power of procedure that is a form of Legitimate Power.

The first element of personal power is Legitimate Power, which goes to anybody who has a title, or has positioned himself or herself in the marketplace, or who has projected that an established way of doing things exists.

Legitimate Power as an Intimidation Factor

On the other hand, when you negotiate with other people, don't be intimidated by a title. We all tend to be more intimidated by someone who's a vice president of a bank or the president of a corporation than we would by someone who didn't have a title. For example, let's say that you're looking for a particular make and model of car.

One day, in the parking lot at a golf course, you find just the car for which you've been looking, and it has a "for sale" sign in the window. As you're peering into the driver's side window, trying to get a look at the mileage, the owner walks up. He tells you that he is selling it for $10,000. That seems a little overpriced, but you promise to think about it and get back to him. He scribbles his name and telephone number on a scrap of paper and tells you to give him a call at the office if you're interested.

You decide that you would love to have the car, if you can get him down to $6,000 or $7,000. You call him and say, "I want to make an offer on your car. When can we get together and talk about it?"

"I'm really busy this week," he responds. "But my office is downtown. If you'd like to meet me here, I can give you a few minutes." Later that day, you locate his office building, and the lobby directory guides you to the 24th floor, where a secretary ushers you into a penthouse suite through doors bearing large, gold-engraved signs that say "President."

Inside the large office, the walls are covered with plaques and diplomas, all extolling the great achievements and accomplishments of the man behind the desk—the same man that you met in the golf course parking lot. He stands up when you enter, shakes your hand, and then returns to his conversation, motioning you to a chair facing the desk. He's talking about selling some shares of stock on the Swiss Exchange, and it sounds like a multi-million-dollar deal. Finally, he hangs up the phone, smiles, and says, "Now how about that car? You're not going to ask me to come down on my price, are you?"

Now how do you feel about presenting your $6,000 offer? You're likely so intimidated that you will want to either excuse yourself politely, saying that you've decided not to buy the car at all, or say, "You'd let me have it for $9,000, wouldn't you?" At that point, you probably wish you were buying the car from a factory worker.

What does the seller's position have to do with the value you place on the car? Absolutely nothing. If the car is worth $6,000 or $7,000 to you, it is worth the same whether you are buying it from a person who puts caps on toothpaste tubes or the president of the United States.

In fact, if you analyze the situation more, you have assumed that this corporation's president would be unwilling to take a low offer because he's not under any pressure to sell his car. That could be wrong. He may be much more willing to accept less money, because he doesn't need the money or doesn't want to spend much time selling the car. On the other hand, that blue-collar worker may be under financial pressure and may need every penny of his asking price. Don't let a title intimidate you so you're blind to the other factors that should take precedence in your consideration of what price to offer.

Some Titles Don't Mean a Thing

A good reason not to let titles intimidate you is that some of them are meaningless. When I first came to this country in 1962, I had only $400, so I had to get a job quickly. I went to work for Bank of America, which was willing to train me on the teller line. That didn't make sense to me because I hadn't even learned the money yet. American money is very confusing to non-Americans. We have coins that don't have numbers on them. A dime doesn't read 10 and a nickel doesn't read five. The slots on a telephone don't read dime and nickel; they read five and 10. To further confuse me, all the bills were the same color and size.

It was confusing for me, but I needed a job and I wasn't going to question their judgment. There I was on the teller line, chanting to myself, "A nickel is bigger than a dime even though it's worth only half as much," when a lady approached me to get a check cashed. I said, "I'm sorry, but that check is above my limit. Would you mind taking it over to the platform to get it okayed by an officer?"

She said, "Don't you know who I am? My uncle is a vice president of Bank of America."

Bank of America was, at the time, the largest bank in the world and it had 500 or 600 branches, so this information immediately intimidated me. I took the standard Nuremberg defense and explained that I was just doing what my superiors had told me to do. Off she went in a real huff. I turned to the teller beside me and told her, "I think I just got myself into a lot of trouble. I've just upset the niece of the vice president of Bank of America."

The other teller laughed and said, "Don't you realize how many vice presidents Bank of America has?" She pulled out the directory that was like a telephone book. It listed hundreds of vice presidents. Titles are sometimes meaningless.

Some Titles Don't Mean Much

My daughter, Julia, graduated from the University of Southern California with a business-finance degree and went to work for Dean Witter, the New York stockbroker, in their Beverly Hills office. One day, she was talking about becoming a vice president there. I told her, "Julia, you must set realistic goals in life. That's a huge corporation, and it may take you years and years to become a vice president."

She replied, "Oh, no. I think I'll be a vice president by the end of the year."

I asked her, "How many vice presidents does Dean Witter have?"

She told me, "I don't know; it must be thousands. We have 35 in this one office." That company understands that titles influence people.

It's like the two people arguing that General Motors has so many vice presidents, they even have a vice president in charge of headrests. To settle the argument, they finally called General Motors and said to the operator, "May we speak to your vice president in charge of headrests?"

The operator asked, "Certainly, Sir. Is that passenger side or driver's side?"

Don't be influenced by titles, but understand that titles do influence people.

☑ Key Points to Remember

1. The first of eight types of influencing power, Legitimate Power goes to anyone who has a title.
2. We find it harder to negotiate with a vice president than we do a salesperson or a buyer.
3. Positioning in the marketplace, by saying we are the oldest, newest, or biggest, gives you Legitimate Power.
4. Respect for the law is another form. When you say, "Our mission statement precludes that possibility," you are appealing to their respect for the law.
5. Tradition is another form of Legitimate Power. "We have always done it that way" is an example.
6. Don't be intimidated by titles or other trappings of position, such as a fancy office.
7. Remember that some titles don't mean a thing.

Chapter 54

Reward Power

The second element of personal power is Reward Power. Power Negotiators know that if you can convince the other side that you would reward them, you have given yourself the power to influence them. Unfortunately, many people who are trying to sell their product or service never develop the self-confidence to project to the other side that they would be rewarding the buyer. These people think that the buyer is rewarding them by placing the order with them.

Reward Power takes on many forms. Money is the obvious one, but there are many more. Some other forms of reward power include praising the other person, forgiving the other person, the power to assign titles (manager, vice president, captain), the authority to assign work or vacation schedules, and making recommendations to others who have power.

If your company has grown to the point where you've delegated the task of selecting which worker goes to a job and which doesn't, you may have delegated away your personal power. Some presidents will relinquish power to their personnel director when they give the personnel director the right to make promotional moves and give increases in pay, and this gives the personnel director control.

Why do defense attorneys earn such incredible fees from their clients? It is because they have convinced the client that only they can secure an acquittal. They have convinced the defendant that they would be lucky to be represented by them. They have the client thinking, "If I could get this attorney to represent me, that would be really something, because he's the best in the business. You can't do any better than that." Attorneys who seek out clients and try to persuade those clients to hire them are relegated to the status of ambulance chasers.

How Defense Attorneys Operate

I once had a successful criminal defense attorney in my seminar and afterward I got to ask him a question that I'd always wanted to ask. "Do you ask your clients if they are guilty or not?" He told me, "Oh absolutely! I can't defend someone unless I know if they did it or not. I might spend a fortune trying to get evidence to support a client's alibi only to find that out that it never happened."

"How many of your clients are guilty?"

"I've been defending clients for over 25 years and I've only once had a client who was innocent. The rest all said, 'Sure, I did it. Just get me off and out of jail.' Remember that my fees are enormous. It's almost a given that anyone who would pay my fees is guilty and that the evidence against them is overwhelming."

You want to have power over your customers? Just convince them that you're the only one who can solve their problem. Don't sell on price! Selling by offering the best price is saying, "There are lots of people out there who can solve your problem but I'll do it for less."

If you're selling a product or service, you must believe that you're the best in the business. Then you must know how to convince your customers of that. They can't do any better than you. If you're willing to put your personal reputation and expertise, and those of your company, on the line to solve those buyers' problems, they are not rewarding you—you are rewarding them.

Of course, you can't push that too far because it quickly becomes arrogance, but don't roll over the other way, thinking that your customers would be rewarding you by giving you an order. I've heard rumors that some salespeople will actually beg a buyer to give them just a small part of the company's business. Can you believe that? Doesn't it sound like a dog begging for table scraps? When you truly believe that you are rewarding the buyer, not the other way around, you will feel confident in demanding all of their business.

Take a moment and jot down three reasons why someone with whom you negotiate would be rewarded by dealing with you. If you're in sales, think of the reasons why picking you over one of your competitors would reward her. If you're applying for a job or a promotion, think of three ways in which picking you would reward that company.

1. ______________________________

2. ______________________________

3. ______________________________

I wonder if one of the reasons you wrote was that "They get me." That should be the number-one reason that they pick you and not your competitor—not because of the quality of the product or service that you sell, but because they get you. To be successful at projecting reward power, you must add value to the product or service; they must see value in buying it from you. You probably have some legitimate competition in your industry—companies that can deliver the very similar product at a very competitive price. The difference has to be you, and your knowledge of your product and service, your knowledge of their problems and opportunities, and your ability to be creative in solving their problems and seizing their opportunities.

I wonder how many competitors you have for what you do? Two, three, or perhaps half a dozen? Guess how many competitors I have as a professional speaker? There are 3,500 members of my association, the National Speakers Association. Whenever I book a speaking engagement, there are 3,499 other speakers with whom I had to compete for the privilege of being in front of that audience. Meeting planners say to me, "Roger, with all that competition, how can you charge as much as you do?" I tell them, "Because I'm good!" That may sound very arrogant and egotistical to you, but you need to have that much confidence in what you do. You need to have that much confidence that you do what you do better than anyone else. The number-one reason they should pick you is that they get you and the only way they get you is to pick you.

Reward Power as an Intimidation Factor

Power Negotiators understand that anytime you perceive someone as able to reward you, you have given him the power to intimidate you. If you think that buyer is rewarding you by giving you an order, you've given him the power to intimidate you. This is why you feel intimidated when you're making a big sale than you do when you're making a small one. The potential reward is greater, so you feel intimidated. Of course, that's entirely subjective, isn't it? When you're first getting started, you may feel that sense of reward over a $1,000 sale. Later, it will take a $100,000 sale to get you excited.

When the other side starts using Reward Power on you, recognize it and don't let it intimidate you. Some people are absolute masters at using Reward Power. When they're asking you for a concession, they just happen to mention that they have a big project coming on line next week, for which you might be in the running, or they'll talk about their yacht down at the harbor, or their ski cabin up in the mountains. They don't even have to come out and tell you that if you did business together you'd get to use them; it's just implied Reward Power. Don't let it irritate you, but recognize it for what it is and don't let it throw you off-base in the negotiations.

Once you recognize Reward Power and understand what they're trying to do to you, their ability to control you with it goes away, and you become a lot more self-confident as a negotiator.

Key Points to Remember

1. You are rewarding the buyer by allowing him to buy your fine product or service. He is not rewarding you by buying from you.
2. Successful purveyors of services, such as defense attorneys, are skilled at projecting that you are lucky to have them on your side.
3. Don't sell on price! Selling by offering the best price is saying, "There are lots of people out there who can solve your problem, but I'll do it for less."
4. The number-one reason that they pick you and not your competitor is because they get you.
5. Look out for people using Reward Power on you.

Chapter 55

Coercive Power

The opposite side of Reward Power is Coercive Power. Any time you perceive someone as able to punish you, he has power over you. You know how awful you feel when the state trooper pulls you over to the side of the road and he's standing there and can write you, or not write you, a ticket. The penalty may not be very great, but the level of intimidation is very great indeed.

Incidentally, in the real estate industry in California, there's a joke about this. California has more 532,000 licensed real estate agents, which means every 50th person is either a broker or an agent. If you think you have competition in your industry, try California real estate. The joke is that a highway patrol officer pulls you over to the side of the road and says, "Okay buddy. Let me see your real estate license."

You say, "Officer, don't you mean my driver's license?"

He says, "No, not everybody in California has a driver's license."

It's hard for us to think about using coercive power on other people, but it's always present in any negotiation. If you're asking a clerk at the store to take an item back and give you a refund, both Reward Power and Coercive Power will influence that clerk's decision. If he gives you the refund graciously, you will reward him by thanking him, and it will be a pleasant experience. If he refuses to give you the refund, you might get angry, and it will be an unpleasant experience.

Here are some other forms of Coercive Power: the power to ridicule or embarrass; the power to affect a reputation by revealing a secret; the power to cause emotional pain by bringing up painful experiences; giving out difficult or painful assignments; the power to waste your time; make you repeat an assignment; or take a class again, and the power to limit your future.

Let's look at how Power Negotiators make Reward Power and Coercive Power work together as a powerful influencing force. Parents use Reward Power and Coercive Power with their children: "If you go to bed now, I'll read you a story." "If you don't eat your carrots, you can't watch television." Salespeople stress benefits to their customers to persuade them to buy, and try gently to imply the dangers of not investing: "Making this investment will do wonders for your bottom line." "Do it now before the competition gets the jump on you."

Managers use the carrot and stick approach to motivate their employees: "Do a good job on this one, and it'll really make you look good." "Joe, watch my lips. Don't mess up on this one." Politicians use it to maintain the balance of world peace: "Maintain a democratic government, and we'll give you favored nation status." "Mess with us, and we've got 10,000 nuclear warheads ready to take off on 15 seconds' notice."

In any persuasion situation, the elements of reward and punishment are always present. Let's say that your car is in the shop. They're telling you it won't be ready until tomorrow, but you must have it tonight. You let them know specifically how you feel.

What's going on in the repair shop manager's mind as he listens to you? If he goes along with your request, you'll reward him with your gratitude and a pleasant, warm environment. If he doesn't, he's apprehensive that things will turn nasty. Power Negotiators understand these two elements and know how to apply both of them skillfully.

People who don't understand Power Negotiation use one, but not the other. They threaten Coercive Power, but don't understand that it can be much more powerful when coupled with Reward Power. You've seen people make this mistake, I'm sure. When the car isn't ready, poor negotiators get angry and try to force the other person to give in against their wishes. "If my car isn't ready by 5 p.m., I'm going to sue you for everything you've got. I'll own this place." Applying fear tactics is an effective persuader, but it's often done so crudely that it backfires. Then, if the other side does cave in, they often compound the error by gloating over their victory.

Let's take a look at how a master persuader uses both reward and punishment to influence a nation. This is Winston Churchill ending a speech in the House of Commons on June 4, 1940, when the war with Germany looked to be lost.

> *We shall not flag nor fail. We shall go on to the end. We shall fight in France and on the seas and oceans; we shall fight with growing confidence and growing strength in the air. We shall defend our island*

whatever the cost may be; we shall fight on beaches, landing grounds, in fields, in streets and on the hills. We shall never surrender and even if, which I do not for the moment believe, this island or a large part of it were subjugated and starving, then our empire beyond the seas, armed and guarded by the British Fleet, will carry on the struggle until in God's good time the New World with all its power and might, sets forth to the liberation and rescue of the Old.

It's the last sentence that illustrates Winston Churchill's genius as an influencer of public opinion. A lesser person would have been content to cheer the English on and present a good old motivational speech about how "Britons never will be slaves," to quote Rule Britannia, a popular patriotic refrain. Churchill was smarter than that. He not only used Reward Power, but he also used Coercive Power by telling the country that they could well lose the battle and be occupied by Germany.

Power Negotiators know the subtle application of both Reward Power and Coercive Power is much more effective. They imply that things will get unpleasant if they don't get what they want. When the other side looks as though they're going to give in, however, they quickly switch to Reward Power by showing their gratitude. "That's great, I really appreciate it. You're very nice."

Take a moment now and jot down three reasons why someone with whom you negotiate would be punished by not consummating a deal with you. If you're in sales, think of the reasons why picking one of your competitors over you would punish a customer. If you're applying for a job or a promotion, think of three ways in which picking anyone else would punish the company.

1. ______________________________

2. ______________________________

3. ______________________________

Hopefully, one of the reasons you wrote was that they don't "get" you. That should be the number-one reason that they avoid choosing your competitor—not because of the quality of the product or service that you sell, but because they don't get you if they do that. To be successful at projecting Coercive Power you must add so much value to your product or service—that they fear not buying it from you. As with Reward Power, the difference has to be you: your knowledge of your product and service. Your knowledge of their problems and opportunities. Your ability to be creative in solving their problems and seizing their opportunities.

Remember when we talked about the Bracketing Gambit in Chapter 1? I told you that you should make your initial proposal so high that it brackets your real objective. Sometimes that's intimidating for you to do. You simply don't have the courage to make those way-out proposals, because you're afraid the other side will laugh at you. In my book *The 13 Secrets of Power Performance* (Prentice Hall), I gave you the answer to this: You must figure out what you fear the most and do it. As with Reward Power, the answer lies in experience. Although a neophyte businessperson may be uptight about a $1,000 negotiation, a more experienced businessperson will be philosophical about losing a $100,000 negotiation. Although a new salesperson may fear losing a $1,000 sale, the experienced salesperson will not let the loss of a $100,000 sale intimidate him.

New salespeople always have trouble with Reward Power and Coercive Power. When they first make sales calls, they see every buyer as being able to reward them by giving them the order, or punishing them by turning them down, or worse yet, ridiculing them for what they have proposed. Once they've been at it for a while, they recognize that selling is a numbers game just like anything else. If they're working hard at it and talking to a great number of people, there always will be a high percentage of people who will turn them down. Once they understand that it's a numbers game, their perception that people can reward or punish them goes away, and they become a lot more self-confident in what they're doing.

Any time that you perceive someone as able to coerce you, he has the power to intimidate you; and one of the greatest coercive forces we know is the power to embarrass people by ridiculing them.

Fear on a Mountaintop

The fear of ridicule can stop us from accomplishing many of the things we'd like to accomplish with our lives. Many years ago, when I was learning to ski, I was skiing at Mammoth Mountain in California with Ron and Marty Meripol, who skied much better than I did. They said, "Roger, we're going to take you up to the cornice today."

I said, "I don't think I'm ready for the cornice yet."

They said, "Oh, come on, Roger. You can make it. Let's go."

We rode the gondola up to the top of the mountain, which is just over 11,000 feet above sea level. I can still feel the tension in that tiny gondola as we drifted silently up the snow-covered face of this almost vertical cliff. It's such a daunting run that even the most experienced skiers won't talk as they approach the top. They sit there in silence, deep in their private thoughts, forcing themselves to overcome the fear of what lies ahead.

Finally, we slid into the terminal and stepped outside into the icy wind. I nervously put on my skis and skied down about 300 yards with my friends, until we were standing at the top of the cornice. A cornice is an overhang of snow, blown over the corner of the cliff by the snow. The skiers had cut a V-shape through this cornice, out onto the cliff. I would have to shoot down this V-shape chute, onto the face of the cliff, which is almost vertical. If I made just one slip, I'd go down the next 1,000 feet on my head.

I stood there, looking down through this chute, and as I saw it, I had two options. Option number one was to hike back up to the gondola and ride down, but if I did that, my friends would laugh at me. Option number two was to die! I chose to die, rather than be ridiculed. That's how strong that type of fear of punishment can be.

Recently, I skied down the cornice again with my children, and now they have a sign at the top that says "When your friends say go—don't be afraid to say no."

Understand and feel comfortable using Coercive Power. Whether you approve or not, it's always present in the negotiation, and your ability to use it effectively is critical to your success as a negotiator.

Key Points to Remember

1. Coercive Power is subjective.
2. Coercive Power is present in any communication.
3. Costing money is a big one, but there are many other forms of Coercive Power.
4. The number-one reason that customers avoid choosing your competitor should be because they don't get you if they do that.

Chapter 56

Reverent Power

The fourth element of personal power is Reverent Power. This power can be said of anybody who has a consistent set of values. An obvious example of this is a religious leader, who is saying, "You can trust me because I have a set of values, and I am not going to deviate from those values."

You like and admire consistent behavior in your customers. They like and admire it in you. If you're willing to take a stand for your principles, especially if it appears you're risking financial loss, it builds trust in other people, and they love you for it. For example, you might sell computers and you have the courage to say to your customers, "Of course, you'd like to save money. And I'd favor it, too, if it were the right thing for you to do—but it isn't. I know that you won't be completely happy unless you get the model with the two-terabyte hard drive. I'm sorry, but I won't sell you anything less."

They love you for that. Of course, it'll raise a few eyebrows, but if you've done your homework and you're right, you'll have power with that customer. If you back down, how are they going to respect you?

Suppose your doctor told you that you needed quadruple bypass heart surgery, and you said, "I think I can get by with a triple bypass." If he said, "Okay, let's try a triple bypass and see how it works," how would you feel about him then? Would you let that person come near you with a scalpel? I don't think so.

When you project Reverent Power, the other negotiators notice it; they admire and respect the consistent set of values, and it gives you a great deal of influence over them. When you're negotiating, and you indicate a willingness to cut corners, or in some way pull some strings that you shouldn't be pulling, you may get a short-term gain in your ability to make that sale. However, you get a long-term loss in your ability to influence that buyer over a long period.

Be careful that you're not setting up standards and then breaking your own standards. Don't tell that buyer that you would never cut prices and then go ahead and do it. That's worse than not setting up the standards in the first place.

Reverent Power is the most powerful influencing factor of all. Being able to project successfully that you have a consistent set of standards and that you'll never deviate from them has an awesome affect on people. Here's why it's more powerful than the obvious influencing factors of reward and coercion. Although those two may have an immediate and dramatic effect on people, you cannot sustain them. They eventually tend to backfire on you.

The parent who's always persuading his child by offering her rewards quickly finds out the child learns to expect those rewards and will rebel if she doesn't get them. You can pay a corporate executive $20 million a year, and in the early stages, it will be a tremendous motivating factor for him. He will do anything to assure the continuation of that reward. However, year by year, the value of that reward starts to diminish.

You can motivate a person with Coercive Power by threatening to fire him, for example. However, it always backfires if you keep it up too long. When you keep on threatening, he'll either find a way to get out from under the pressure, or he'll learn to live with it. Yet, Reverent Power just grows and grows. The longer you project that you have a consistent set of standards from which you'll never deviate, the more people learn to trust you. From that trust grows a tremendous ability to influence people in a negotiation.

Reverent Power as an Intimidating Factor

When people use Reverent Power on you, it can be daunting because we admire that characteristic. When they say to you, "Yes, but we don't do business that way. Our founder, God rest his soul, said when he first started this business 28 years ago, 'Let's establish a fair list price for our products and never deviate from that.'" When we heard such high-flown words, we hate to go against it because we admire people who have principles and don't like to oppose them.

When someone is using Reverent Power on you in that way, you have two alternatives:

1. Establish that, although they're telling you that they have never made an exception to the rule, there have indeed been exceptions. The power of precedent is a remarkable thing. If

you can establish that there has been an exception somewhere down the line, it negates Reverent Power entirely. If you are in a Holiday Inn in Florida asking for a special concession, and if you can establish that the Holiday Inn in Seattle once made that concession for you, it gives you great power in dealing with that desk clerk in Florida.

2. Establish that, although it may have been a good rule in the past, it's no longer the smart thing to do. I know of one Fortune 50 company that for years got away with saying "Our founder established a policy when he first started this company that we would never deviate from list prices. We should have a fair price and everyone should pay the same." The company was able to maintain that for decades, but finally their competition started discounting and they had to follow them. Just because it has been their policy for years, it doesn't mean that it should be their policy today.

Key Points to Remember

1. We want to be led by people with a consistent set of values.
2. Have the courage to decide what is best for your customers and never deviate from that.
3. Reverent Power is stronger than Reward Power or Coercive Power. Those powers may decrease with time, but Reverent Power continues to increase.
4. Reverent Power can be intimidating when it is used on you because we admire people who do things consistently.
5. Do enough information gathering that you can challenge statements such as "We've never made an exception to that rule."
6. If you can't find exceptions, convince them that it's time to be more flexible and make exceptions to the rule.

Chapter 57

Charismatic Power

The fifth element of personal power is Charismatic Power. It's probably the hardest one to analyze and explain. What is charisma? We've all heard of charismatic religions, of course. In that sense, charisma means a gift from God of a special talent, such as the ability to heal, or to prophesize. In popular usage, charisma means this: a special quality that gives a person the ability to capture the imagination of another person, inspiring support and devotion.

German sociologist Max Weber was the first person to bring the term into modern-day usage and present it as a learnable persuasion skill. He called it a form of authority. Until the start of the 20th century, we thought of authority as either law or tradition. Max Weber introduced charisma as the third form of authority. That, simply with their personalities, people could influence another person.

Max Weber also introduced the theory that charismatic leaders are elected in troubled times. That is certainly true of Adolf Hitler in Germany and Juan Peron in Argentina. Look at recent American politics and you'll see that phenomena also. Franklin Roosevelt was first elected in the middle of the Great Depression. Barack Obama was elected during the worst recession since the great one.

Obama is a charismatic president because of his congenial nature and his self-confidence. His forceful way of projecting his vision for the country inspires his followers.

Dean Simonton, a psychologist at the University of California–Davis, determined the elements that a presidential candidate must project if he is to be perceived as charismatic. He must have a flair for the dramatic, consciously refine his own public image, use rhetoric effectively, exhibit artistry in manipulation, convey a clear-cut, highly visible personality, have the ability to maintain popularity, enjoy the ceremonial aspects of the presidential office, and be a dynamo of energy and determination.

If you'll apply those characteristics to the president you think is or was most charismatic, you'll see that charisma is not a mysterious characteristic that you must be born with, but more a skill that you can develop. In my book *Secrets of Power Persuasion*, I spend two entire chapters explaining how to develop personal charisma. For now, let's just recognize its power and its limitations.

Meet the Master: William Jefferson Clinton

I'm sure you've had the experience of meeting a celebrity who has an overwhelmingly charismatic personality. When I met President Clinton, I was uncomfortable because I'm at the opposite end of the political spectrum, and I'm sure he could sense that. I didn't want to say anything that would constitute an endorsement, so I said, "Good luck, Mr. President. Don't let them get you down." Guess what he did. He looked me in the eye and said, "Roger, if you'll stay with me, I'll be there." I said, "I'll be there, Mr. President." Within 15 seconds, he'd gotten a commitment of support from me strictly based on the power of his personality.

In Tucson, I found myself talking to someone who had just met Bill Clinton at political event. She told me, "There were about 40 of us who had been chosen to meet him, and we were gathered in a hotel meeting room. He came in and spent about 20 minutes shaking hands as he went around the room. When he left, everyone of us was convinced that he had come into the room especially to meet them."

That's charismatic power!

Charisma is very hard to explain. We know it when we see, it but we have trouble explaining it. When you are having trouble understanding something, it helps to think of the opposite. What characteristics would you ascribe to the least charismatic person on earth? With whom would you least like to spend the rest of your life on a desert island? I think it would be a person who is totally self-centered, someone who only thinks of him or herself.

Take John Paul Getty, for example. When he was the richest man in the world, many people wanted to own what he owned, but nobody wanted to be who he was. Aristotle Onassis had the greatest difficulty in doing business with him until, as he explained in his autobiography, he accepted that anything Getty would do would be totally self serving.

If the opposite of charisma is being self-centered, it becomes clear that charisma is the ability to project that you care about everyone with whom you come in contact. You don't have to be a Mother Theresa, caring about every poor person on the planet, or a Martin Luther King, Jr., caring about everyone suffering racial prejudice, but you do need to care about everyone you meet.

Dale Carnegie, in his iconic book, *How to Win Friends and Influence People*, gave us this important advice: Treat everyone you meet as the most important person you will meet that day. That's well said, isn't it? Not the most important person you'll ever meet or even the most important person you'll meet that week—that would be over the top. Treat everyone you meet as if he is the most important person you'll meet that day. You can't get away with treating the vice president with respect, but treating the secretary as a servant.

Salespeople tend to overemphasize Charismatic Power. Many an old-time salesperson has told me, "The only reason my people do business with me is because they like me." Well, not nowadays. Don't fall into the Willie Loman trap. Even 60 years ago, when Arthur Miller wrote *Death of a Salesman* and had Willie Loman saying, "The most important thing is to be liked," he was making fun of it. Sure, that buyer is more likely to give you an order if he or she likes you, but don't think it gives you much control. Buyers are much too sophisticated for that today. It's a long way from control of the negotiations.

Charismatic Power as an Intimidating Factor

Some people are very astute about using Charismatic Power on you. Without realizing it, you can find yourself making concessions to them simply because you like them so much. Whenever you find yourself drawn to the other person, you should stop yourself and think, "Would I be making this concession if I couldn't stand this person?"

Key Points to Remember

1. Charisma is a special quality that gives a person the ability to capture the imagination of another person, inspiring support and devotion.

2. It is just as powerful and the two traditional ways of influencing people: the law (we have all agreed that we will obey these laws) and tradition (this is the way we've always done it).
3. Charismatic leaders have greater power during troubled times.
4. Charisma grows as you learn to project concern for other people.
5. Treat everyone you meet as the most important person you will meet that day.
6. Don't give concessions to people because you like them. Stop yourself and think, "Would I be making this concession if I couldn't stand this person?"

Chapter 58

Expertise Power

The sixth element of personal power is Expertise Power. When you project to people that you have more expertise than they do in a particular area, you develop power over them. Think of the people to whom you defer because of Expertise Power: your doctor, your auto-mechanic, and your plumber. I even defer to the maid who cleans my home when she tells me that I need to buy a particular type of cleaner for a special surface.

I think that Expertise Power is becoming increasingly more important as the world in which we live becomes more complex. I think that the trouble started back in 1965 when Sony marketed the first VCR machine. Until then, life was difficult, but manageable. We could turn on the oven, and switch on the radio and the television set. The moment we conceded that we couldn't figure out how to program our VCRs, we conceded that from that point on, there were going to be a great many things for which we'd have to call in an expert. Perhaps it started before that. I remember standing in front of a new car that my father had bought back in the mid-1950s. "Where's the hole for the hand crank?" I asked him.

"Doesn't have one," he told me.

"That doesn't make any sense. How will you get it started when the battery won't start it?" I was used to a car that I'd have to hand crank for 15 minutes on a cold morning when my mother wanted to go in to town for supplies.

"I'm not sure about that, either," my father told me. "They say that if the battery won't start it, you've got a serious problem that you should get fixed."

"That still doesn't make sense," I repeated. However, I got used to that, and I resigned myself to VCRs. The first time I saw a home computer, I thought that I'd never figure out how to use it. I still have trouble with my iPhone. If I can't figure out how it works, I get my 13-year-old granddaughter, Astrid, to explain it to me. Reluctantly, I concede that there's going to be a lot more compromising before I get to my horizon. With technology leapfrogging over itself year by year, month by month, and, soon, week by week, the expert is going to be king. Every one of us should realize that if we don't keep on frantically becoming more of an expert in our field, the avalanche of new technology will run over us.

Today, expertise is not something that you study and acquire, because what you knew last year is not enough to sustain you this year. You must be on a constant, never-ending quest for most expertise. All you have to do to lose Expertise Power these days is to refuse to believe that you must continually work on upgrading your skills.

The three big factors in having the ability to affect the actions of others are:

1. Reward Power or Wealth.
2. Coercive Power or Violence. That makes us squirm, doesn't it? But if you have the bigger army, you have power. If the drug cartels in Mexico have more and better firearms than the police, they have power. I described it as Coercive Power, which is a more delicate term than violence, but it refers to the same thing.
3. Expertise Power or Knowledge. If you know more, you have the ability to influence others. Before the printing press, the ability to read and write was considered expertise power. Now it's far more complex. It's what I call Expertise Power.

Here's a key point: Expertise Power trumps both Reward Power and Coercive Power. The least versatile is Coercive Power. You can only use it in rare cases. Reward Power is powerful because it loses its value. Expertise Power just grows and grows.

Think of this in the context of a corporation hiring an entry-level employee. At first, threats to fire that person will motivate him to work harder. Put him into management, and that $100,000 pay package you give him will motivate him—until his expertise grows to the point where a competitor will pay him $500,000 to run their company.

Expertise Power as an Intimidating Factor

Don't let people intimidate you with Expertise Power. Remember when you first started in your business, and you studied the technical side of what you do, but you weren't confident about it yet? Then you ran into someone who appeared to know more than you did. Remember how intimidating that was? Don't let them do it to you. When they question your expertise, don't be afraid to say, "That's not my area of expertise, but our experts are the finest in the business. You can have complete confidence in them."

Attorneys and doctors really play this one up, don't they? They develop a whole new language that you can't understand to project to you that they have expertise that you don't have.

There's not a reason in the world why doctors couldn't write prescriptions in English, but if they did, it would take away a little of that mystique—a little of that Expertise Power. Attorneys are the same way. They develop a whole new language that we can't understand so that they project Expertise Power.

Key Points to Remember

1. We defer to people who have more expertise than we do.
2. We must be on a never-ending daily quest for more Expertise Power. If we don't, technology and our changing world will swamp us.
3. The three big factors in having the ability to affect the actions of others are: violence (Coercive Power), wealth (Reward Power), and knowledge (Expertise Power).
4. Expertise Power trumps wealth and knowledge.
5. Don't let people intimidate you with their Expertise Power.

Chapter 59

Situation Power

The seventh element of personal power is Situation Power. We're all familiar with this one. This is the person down at the post office, someone who is normally powerless in any other area of his life, but in this particular situation, he can accept or reject your package. He has power over you, and he loves to use it.

It's prevalent in large organizations or government agencies where the people don't have much latitude in the way they perform their jobs. When they do get some latitude, and when they have some power over you, they're eager to use it.

Don't They Love to Use Situation Power!

I remember speaking to a huge sales rally in Halifax, Nova Scotia. The night before I got there, this group had put on the party to end all parties. These people all got bombed out of their minds. One of them got undressed to go to bed at 3 a.m. and then decided he'd like to have some ice in his room. He was standing there in his dazed state, trying to figure out whether it was worthwhile getting some clothes on to go get the ice. Finally he thought, "It's 3 in the morning. The ice machine is just around the corner from my door. Who's going to see me? I'll slip out the way I am," forgetting, of course, that the door would lock behind him the minute he got into the hallway.

Soon, he's outside his door with his bucket of ice and nothing else, mentally debating his options. He finally decided he didn't have many options, so he set his bucket of ice down and headed down, across the lobby of the Halifax Sheraton, and up to the young woman behind the desk. He asked for another key to his room. She looked straight at him and said, "Sir, before I can give you another key, I need to see some identification." That's Situation Power and don't they love to use it?

The key issue in negotiating is that sometimes you get to a point where people have so much Situation Power over you that you're going to lose this one, regardless of how good a negotiator you are. If you're going to have to make the concession anyway, regardless of what you do, you might as well make the concession as gracefully as you possibly can. It doesn't make any sense to get so upset about it that you lose the goodwill of the other person—and still have to make the concession.

How many times have we been into a department store to get a refund on something and the clerk says to us, "All right, we'll do it this one time. But it's not our normal policy"? What sense does that make? If you're going to have to make the concession anyway, you might as well make it as gracefully as you possibly can, so that you maintain the goodwill of the other person.

Many years ago, when I was a real estate broker, our company built four new homes at one location. In California, we typically build with poured slabs. Just as we finished pouring the slabs, the city building inspector pulled up, walked over, and casually asked, "What are you doing?"

That seemed self-evident to us, but he wasn't known for his sense of humor, so we simply replied, "We're pouring the slabs."

"Not until I've signed off on the plumbing you're not," he said, and we could swear that he was enjoying every minute of this. What followed must have looked like a Keystone Cops routine. Everybody was running around, trying to find the signed-off building permit card. With growing horror, we realized that he was right. Somebody had goofed, and the inspector had enough Situation Power that we were going to have to get a crew out there with shovels, digging out the concrete before it set, so that the building inspector could glance at the plumbing and sign it off. The point is this: Don't let it upset you. Power Negotiators recognize Situation Power for what it is and move into an area where they do have some control.

Key Points to Remember

1. Sometimes people who are not powerful have power over you because of the situation.
2. It is prevalent in government agencies and huge corporations where the people have little latitude in the way they do things. They are expected to do it by the book. When a situation gives them power over you, they love to use it.
3. Recognize Situation Power for what it is and don't let it upset you.

Chapter 60

Information Power

The final element of personal power is Information Power. Sharing information forms a bond. Any time that you share information with someone, you get closer to that person. This is why, in the old days, before members of Congress passed laws to restrain themselves, they were big on the lecture circuit. An association that might be penalized greatly by congressional legislation could hire a representative or senator to be the speaker at its annual convention.

The association could afford to pay that person a large honorarium. There wouldn't have to be any quid pro quo involved—just the fact that the lawmaker had mingled with the membership would cause him or her to bond with this industry. Pharmaceutical salespeople, who have a terrible time getting physicians to meet with them, know that they should always show up with some new piece of information, perhaps the results of a new study, because sharing information with the physician bonds them to the physician.

Information as a personal power has lost much of its ability to influence in this cyber age. The old adage that "information is power" has worn a little thin. Now that information is so freely available with a few search engine clicks, it is much harder to withhold.

Information Power as an Intimation Factor

Withholding information tends to intimidate. Large companies are skillful about doing this. They'll develop information at the executive level that they won't share with the workers. It's not because it's that secretive. It's not because it would do any harm. It's because these large corporations know that a level of secrecy at the executive level gives them control over the workers.

Here's an interesting quote from the Navy training manual:

Informational power depends on your giving or withholding of information or having knowledge that others do not have. Use informational power when giving orders to subordinates. Give orders in such a manner that your subordinates presume the order originated at your level. When forced to comply with orders you do not agree with, don't introduce the order by saying, "The division officer said." *Phrase and present the order in a manner that leaves no doubt you initiated it.*

When you're negotiating, don't tell the other side that you were told to do something. Make it your suggestion, and let them ponder why you decided that way.

The human race has a tremendous natural desire to know what's going on. We can't stand a mystery. You can put a cow in a field, and it will stay in that field all its life and never wonder what's on the other side of that hill. NASA plans to spend billions of dollars to fly to Mars because we have such a strong need to know if there is microscopic life on Mars.

Withheld information can be very intimidating. Let's imagine that you've made an extensive presentation to a buying committee and the members say to you, "We need to talk about this for a moment. Would you mind waiting outside in the lobby? We'll call you when we're ready for you." Is it any wonder you feel uncomfortable sitting outside in the lobby? We hate it when people withhold information from us.

The moment we realize they may just be doing this to us as a negotiating Gambit, they can no longer intimidate us with it. Realize that they may be in there talking about football scores for all we know, so that when we walk back into the negotiations, our level of self-confidence has gone down, and their level of power has gone up. Once we realize that it's just a ploy, they can no longer intimidate us with this Gambit.

☑ Key Points to Remember

1. Sharing information forms a bond with the other negotiator.
2. Withholding information intimidates.
3. In this cyber age, the old adage that information is power may still be true, but access to information is so universal that withholding information is hard to do and it has lost its power.

4. Don't tell the other side that you were told to do something. Make it your suggestion and let them ponder why you decided that way.
5. Don't be intimidated when the other side asks for time to discuss the negotiations. It may just be a ploy designed to intimidate you.
6. When you understand the dynamics of the negotiating ploy, you will not be intimidated by it.

Chapter 61

Combinations of Power

Now you know the eight elements that give you power over the other person. To recap, they are the following:

1. Legitimate Power (the power of your title or your position in the marketplace).
2. Reward Power (the ability to reward the other person).
3. Coercive Power (nearly always perception, not reality).
4. Reverent Power (the ability to project a consistent set of values).
5. Charismatic Power (the power of the personality).
6. Expertise Power (an ability that the other person does not have).
7. Situation Power (power that stems from circumstances).
8. Information Power (knowledge that the other person lacks).

Take the time to rate yourself in each of those elements—not as you see yourself, or maybe not even as you really are, but as you think other people see you. How do people with whom you negotiate perceive you in each of these eight areas? Give yourself a score from one to 10 in each area, with one being very weak and 10 being very strong. The potential maximum score is 80. If your score comes out in the 60s, that's a very good number for a Power Negotiator. You have Power, but you still have empathy for the other side. If your score is higher than 70, I'd be concerned that you're too intimidating when you're dealing with people. Less than 60, and you have some weak spots. Examine those elements for which you gave yourself a low rating, and see what you can do to get yourself close to a 10.

As you review this list, remember that these eight power elements are also the ways that the other side can intimidate you into thinking that you don't have any power. The next time you're negotiating and you feel that you've lost control—that they're beginning to intimidate you—identify which of those elements is getting to you. Identifying it will help you handle it.

Now let's look at special combinations of these eight powers. First begin with Reverent Power, Charismatic Power, and Expertise Power. Power Negotiators know that a combination of those three are critical if you are to control the negotiations. Do you know somebody who seems to have a much easier time persuading people to go along with his suggestions? Perhaps you've sat in on a negotiation with your boss and he made it look so easy. He sat down with the other person and chatted with her for 15 or 20 minutes. He didn't appear to be talking about anything of consequence, but at the end of that time, the other person said, "What do we have to do here? Do we need to go with the top of the line, or can we get by with the standard? You tell us. You're the expert."

Here's how he got that much power over the other side: He did a good job of projecting Reverent Power, Charismatic Power, and Expertise Power. Reverent Power: "I won't do anything that is not in your best interest, regardless of the gain to me." That builds trust, doesn't it? Charismatic Power: He has a likable personality. And Expertise Power: Your manager projected to the other side, without it becoming overbearing, that he knew more about it than she did. When you put those three together, you're very close to controlling the negotiations. You're very close to the point at which the other side will defer the decision. "Well," she'll say, "What do you think we should do?" She has surrendered control of the negotiation to your side.

Another combination of the eight components of personal power is of particular importance to Power Negotiators. The effects of these critical elements together are overwhelming. When these four come together in one person, what happens is incredible. The four are: Legitimate Power (the power of the title), Reward Power (the ability to reward people), Reverent Power (the consistent set of values: I'm not going to deviate from this regardless of what happens), and Charismatic Power (the personality: the pizzazz with which to put it across).

When these four come together in one person, the effect is phenomenal, whether it is used for good or evil. This is what gave Adolf Hitler control of Germany in the 1930s. He kept stressing the title—Fuhrer! Fuhrer!

Fuhrer! He kept stressing Reward Power. He kept saying to the German people: If we do this, if we invade Czechoslovakia and Poland, this is what we'll get. The dictatorial Reverent Power—we'll never deviate from this. Hitler also had hypnotic Charismatic Power. He could hold tens of thousands of people mesmerized with his oratory.

You Can't Get Any More Consistent Than This

It is fascinating to me that Adolf Hitler, who completed his autobiography, *Mein Kampf (My Struggle)*, in 1926, wrote in it every detail of what would follow, including the expansion of Germany through Czechoslovakia and Poland into the Ukraine. Although more than five million copies had been circulated in Germany before the start of World War II, it was never translated into any other language. Hitler tightly controlled circulation of his book to within the borders of Germany, but it is hard for me to believe that some copies were not smuggled out of the country and translated. Perhaps the people who translated it simply could not believe the enormity of what he planned to do. Perhaps we needed Hitler too much as a bulwark against communism. Perhaps they dismissed it as the ravings of a mad man. But had we have taken it seriously, we would have known every detail of his plans. Because he never deviated from his original intent.

This was also the way that David Koresh got control over the Branch Davidians in Waco, Texas, and had so much control over them that they wanted him to tell them not only where to live, what to think, and what to say, but also when to die. David Koresh told his people that he was God. That's a pretty good title—you can't do much better than that! He kept stressing Reward Power: If you stay with me, you're going to heaven. If you go with them, you're going to jail. Reverent Power: We don't care what the rest of the world thinks. This is what we believe. Charismatic Power: He had the hypnotic personality that is the trademark of all cult leaders.

On the good side of the coin is when you get a John F. Kennedy. Every president has the power of the title. Every president is able to reward, but not every president is able to project the consistent set of values. This was Jimmy Carter's undoing and was Bill Clinton's albatross, because they appeared to vacillate. It was Richard Nixon's undoing at the end.

Not every president is able to project Charismatic Power. This was Gerald Ford's problem. He had the other three elements in abundance, but he didn't have the personality with which to put it across. Throughout his career, Richard Nixon, although he was brilliant, was dogged by the fact that few people liked him. I think that it was George Bush Sr.'s downfall also, particularly because he followed Ronald Reagan, who was so charismatic.

John F. Kennedy and Ronald Reagan both had these four powers in great abundance, which made them the most popular presidents in modern history. Look at Barack Obama's remarkable rise to power and how well he rated in these four characteristics. You can have that kind of power if you concentrate on developing those four elements of personal power. When you do, I promise you that you'll see a remarkable transformation in your ability to influence people.

Key Points to Remember

1. Rate yourself on a scale of one to 10 as other people see you in these areas. If your total score is in the 60s, that's good for a negotiator.
2. Combinations of these powers are very potent.
3. Combining Reverent Power, Charismatic Power, and Expertise Power is especially potent.
4. If you are a 10 for Legitimate Power, Reward Power, Reverent Power, and Charismatic Power, you will have an enormous ability to influence people.

Chapter 62

Other Forms of Power

Another form of personal power is the power of crazy. I don't think that you'll want to use it very often, but you should know about it. It's the power of crazy: If you can convince the other side that you're crazy, you can have power over them.

Just after communist Vietnam opened its borders to non-Americans again, I spent a week in Ho Chi Min City (formerly named Saigon) and Hanoi. In Hanoi, I hired a guide to show me around. She had lived through the war, and I was eager to get her impressions. When I asked her who she thought was the best American president, I was aware that she was a government employee (as everyone is under communism) and would only say what she had been authorized to say.

She thought about it for a while and then said, "I not know who best president is, but I know the worst. Richard Nixon, he was the worst president. He wanted to drop nuclear bomb on us. He is crazy. He is the worst president of all." I'm confident that even Richard Nixon did not intend to drop a nuclear bomb on Hanoi. He and Henry Kissinger cooked up a strategy. They felt that if they could convince the North Vietnamese government that they were crazy, that they could force them to the negotiating table, which is what they did remarkably effectively.

In business, the power of crazy translates into the person who is so inconsistent in the way he reacts that you never know how he's going to treat you. One day you can walk into his office, and he'll throw his arms around you. The next time you walk into his office, he might throw you out. If you can convince someone that you're crazy, you can have power over him.

The Power of Risk Sharing

Another form of personal power is the power of risk sharing. You can have power over the other side if you convey to them that others are sharing their risk. This is the power of a syndicated investment: The more people you can get to invest, the easier it is to get others to sign up.

If I asked you to bet me $5,000 to my $20,000 on the flip of a coin, you ought to be eager to take the bet. I'm offering you four-to-one odds on two-to-one chance. (Professional gamblers will tell you that it doesn't matter what you bet on, as long as the odds are better than they should be.) However, the risk of losing $5,000 on the flip of a coin may be too great for you, and you would turn me down. Consider this: If you could get 100 people who were all willing to risk $50, would you then go ahead? Chances are you would, because although the potential gain is the same, you perceive that others are sharing the risk.

The same principle applies in investment syndication. If I asked you to invest $100,000 in a real estate syndication, you would be reluctant to risk that much. Even if I asked you to invest $5,000, you might consider the risk too great. However, if I told you that I have 19 other investors ready to put up $5,000 and you would be the 20th, you would be far more likely to go along with my proposal. Also, if I suggested that you invest $100,000 in 20 different syndications, you would be far more likely to do that than invest the entire $100,000 in one syndication because you feel that you are lowering your risk.

What can we learn from this? Anytime that you can demonstrate that the risk you are asking the other side to take is being shared, you develop the power to influence them.

The Power of Confusion

There is power in confusion. This may not sound right to you because you have always understood that a confused mind will say no. That is true—it is important to be sure that the person with whom you're dealing understands what he or she is getting into. However, it is also true that a confused mind can be more easily led.

If you're negotiating with someone and tell her, "There are two possible options for you, and they are very simple to understand. Let me explain them to you, and you'll be able to make a choice." With that approach, you have little ability to influence her because she can readily perceive the benefits of each option and make her own choice.

However, if you said to her, "There are many ways to go here and this can be very confusing. There are 25 different options open to you and, unless you are very familiar with them all, you will have a tough time knowing which one is best for you. Fortunately, I'm very familiar with the options, and I have successfully guided many people who are in exactly the same position as you…," she would be more pliable. The more confused I can get her, the better the chance I have that she will ask me for guidance, provided I can get her to do one thing, and that is trust me. A confused mind can be more easily led, but only if the person to be led trusts the leader.

As you can see, there is great power in confusion. The best defense that you have is just to keep your wits about you and don't let the other person confuse the issue so that you surrender to their ideas. When he starts sailing off on tangents say, "I don't see how all of these details are germane to my choices. Instead of confusing the situation, let's just stick to the key issues. Fair enough?"

The Power of Communicating Options

You can gain influence in negotiations if you advertise that you have many options and don't need to make a deal here and now. If you point out that there is competition for your product or services, chances are that the buyer will raise their offer—especially if you tell them that you don't need to sell, and certainly not for less than you are asking. For example, you could say to prospective buyer, "I wish that I could give you more time to make a decision, but I need to know right now, because I have two other bids already, and it's not fair for me to keep the other buyers waiting."

If you are buying, any seller finds it sobering to learn that you have many other choices and at lower prices. If you are responding to a classified ad for a boat or a car, for example, you might say, "I have two others to look at this evening, at 7 o'clock and at eight. They're not asking as much as you are, but I'd like to consider yours anyway. Could I come by and see yours at six?"

In any negotiation, the side with the most options has the most power. The more you can service the perception that you have options, the more power you will have as a negotiator.

☑ Key Points to Remember

1. If you can convince the other side that you're crazy, you can have power over them.

2. In business, this is the boss whose responses are unpredictable.
3. You can persuade people if you can illustrate that others are sharing the risk.
4. A confused mind says no, but a confused mind is more easily led.
5. The most important power in negotiating is the power of communicating that you have options.

Chapter 63

Negotiating Drives

Not often does someone other than a professional negotiator think about what is driving the other negotiator, because we all tend to assume that what drives the other person is the same thing that drives us. Sociologists call this "socio-centrism." This means we think that the other person wants what we would want, if we were they.

Power Negotiators know that what we would want, if we were them, may have nothing to do with what they want. Power Negotiators know that the better we can understand what is driving the other side—what they really want to accomplish—the better we can fulfill their needs without taking away from our position. Poor negotiators get into trouble because they fear that they will be vulnerable to the other side's tricks if they let the other side know too much about them. Instead of wanting to find out what is driving the other side and revealing their drives to the other side, the poor negotiator lets his fears stop him from being that open.

Peter Pestillo, executive vice president of corporate relations for Ford Motor Co. and a leading labor negotiator, points out that you must evaluate the negotiation and determine what is most important to you. "What kind of a negotiation is it?" he says. "If it's only a one-time event, you can concentrate on the result. But if there's an ongoing relationship involved, victory is making both sides feel satisfied. Take only what you need and don't try to make anybody look bad." In this chapter, we'll look at the different things that drive the other side when they're negotiating with you. Recognizing and understanding these drives is the secret to win-win negotiating.

The Competitive Drive

The Competitive Drive is what neophyte negotiators know best and it's why they see negotiating as challenging. If you assume the other side is out to beat you, by any means, you will fear meeting someone who may be a better negotiator than you, or someone who is more ruthless. This drive exists at car dealerships. The car dealer attracts customers by offering "the lowest prices in town" but pays its salespeople based on the amount of profit they can build into the sale. The customer wants the lowest price, even if the dealer loses money, or the salesperson loses his commission. The salesperson wants to drive the price up because it's the only way he can make any money.

Negotiators using the Competitive Drive believe you should find out all you can about the other side, but let the other side know nothing about you. Knowledge is power, but competitive drive negotiators believe that because of this, the more you find out and the less you reveal, the better off you'll be. When gathering information he distrusts anything the other side's negotiators might tell him because it may be a trick. He gathers information covertly by approaching the other side's employees or associates.

This approach is counter to the win-win philosophy that says the way to make both sides happy is to expand the negotiation to look for things beyond the main issues where concessions can be made without detracting from each side's basic needs. Competitive negotiating is not helpful to a win-win approach because neither side trusts the other side enough to share information.

Because he assumes that the other side is doing the same to him, he works assiduously to prevent the leaking of information from his side. What's causing this approach is the assumption that there has to be a winner and there has to be a loser. What's missing is the possibility that both sides could win because they are not out for exactly the same thing, and, by knowing more about the other side, each side can concede issues that are important to the other side, but may not be significant to their side.

The Solutional Drive

The Solutional Drive is the best negotiating situation to be in. This is when the other side is eager to find a solution and is willing to discuss the best way to do that. It means nobody threatens the other side, and both will negotiate in good faith to find a win-win solution. Solutional Drive negotiators are wide open to creative solutions because they feel there must be a better solution somewhere that hasn't occurred to them. It takes an open mind to be creative. Look at the variables buyers and sellers could propose in as simple a transaction as buying a house. The cost of financing to the buyer could be adjusted by letting the buyer assume an underlying loan. The seller could carry back all the financing and remain liable for the underlying loan (called wrapping the underlying).

The buyer could accommodate the seller by giving the seller additional time to find another home. The seller could lease back the house from the buyer for an extended term. The price could include all or some of the furnishings. The sellers could retain a life estate in the house that would enable them to stay in the house until they died. This is a great idea for elderly people who need cash, but don't want to move. The broker's fee could be eliminated, or the broker could be asked to take his fee as a note, rather than in cash. The buyer could move in, but delay the closing to help the seller with their income taxes.

The great thing about negotiating with someone who is in the Solutional Drive is he has cast nothing in stone. He is not restricted by company policy or tradition, feeling that everything is negotiable because everything was negotiated. Short of breaking the law or their personal principles, he will listen to any suggestion you care to propose because he does not see you as in competition with him.

It sounds like the perfect solution, doesn't it? Both sides cooperating to find the perfect and fair solution. However, there is one caveat. The other side could be feigning when they appear to be in the Solutional Drive. Once you have put your cards on the table and told them exactly what you are prepared to do, they may revert to Competitive Drive negotiating. If it seems too good to be true, be wary.

The Personal Drive

You may encounter situations where the main drive of the other negotiator is not to win for winning's sake, or to find the perfect solution. Their main drive may be for their personal profit or aggrandizement. A case that quickly comes to mind is that of an attorney who is working on a fee basis rather than a contingency basis. It would be in that attorney's best interest not to find a solution too quickly. When you run into this, you should see what you could do to satisfy that personal need for more fees. It may be in your best interest to threaten to take your solution over the attorney's head to his client. He won't appreciate that, of course, but if he feels that his client would accept the compromise if you went over his head, you may force him to accept your solution.

Another example may be a young corporate negotiator who wants to look good to his company. The last thing he wants to do is go back empty-handed, so your best strategy may be to establish that he has a deadline and stall the negotiations. You might be able to reach a terrific settlement in the limousine on the way to the airport if he'd rather agree to anything than go home empty-handed.

A further example would be a union negotiator who wants to look good to his members. In that case, it may be in both your best interests to make an outrageous initial demand. Then he can go back to his members and say, "I wasn't able to get you everything you wanted, but just listen to their opening negotiating position. I was able to get them all the way down from that for you." If you made a more modest opening negotiating position it might have been difficult for him to sell it to his members because they didn't feel that their union fought hard enough for them.

The Organizational Drive

You may find yourself in a situation where the other negotiator seems to have a fine Solutional Drive. She really wants to find the best solution, but the problem is that it has to be a solution that she can sell to her organization. This happens a great deal in Congress, where the senator or representative is eager for a sensible compromise, but knows that he would get pilloried by the voters in his state or district. In close votes, you'll see this all the time.

On both sides of the house, the politicians who have the support of their voters will commit quickly. Those who will be in trouble back home may want to support their party, but are reluctant to toe the line. In this case, the party leadership counts noses to see how many votes they need to win by one vote. Then they let their members who would be most hurt by voting for the bill vote no. The ones who would be least hurt are led, like lambs to slaughter it always seems to me, and made to vote for the bill.

It's hard for me to believe that any intelligent senator would oppose a ban of assault weapons on our streets, but many of them were forced by their more radical voters to oppose a gun control bill.

When you're negotiating with someone who must please an organization, he may be reluctant to spell out his problem for you because it would seem too much like collusion. You need to be proactive and be in the Organizational Drive by thinking, "Who could be giving him heartburn over this one?" Is it his stockholders, this legal department, or perhaps government regulators, whom he would have to circumvent to implement the best solution? If you understand his problem, you may be able to do things to make the solution more palatable to his organization. For example, you might take a more radical position in public than you do at the negotiating table. In this way, your compromise gives the appearance of making major concessions.

A company hired me once to help them when their assembly worker's union went on strike. The union negotiators felt that the solution they had negotiated was reasonable, but they couldn't sell it to their members, who were out for blood. We developed a solution in which the local newspaper interviewed the president of the company. During the interview, he expressed sincere regrets that he was caught in a difficult situation.

The union couldn't sell the plan to its members and the president couldn't sell anything better to his board of directors and stockholders. It appeared that the strike would soon force him to move production from that factory to their assembly plant in Mexico. The next day, the worker's spouses opened the newspaper to headlines that read "Plant to Close—Jobs Going South."

By the afternoon of that day, the spouses had put enough pressure on the workers that they clamored to accept the deal that they had previously turned down. If you're dealing with someone who has to sell the plan to his or her organization, you should always be looking for ways to make it easier to do that.

The Attitudinal Drive

The attitudinal negotiator believes that if both sides trust and like each other, they can resolve their differences. The Attitudinal Drive negotiator would never resolve a problem by telephone, e-mail, text message, or fax, or through an intermediary. They want to be facing the other person so they can get a feel for who that person is, believing that, and "If we know each other well enough, we can find a solution."

Jimmy Carter is an attitudinal negotiator. He initiated contact with the North Koreans when they were refusing to back down on their nuclear weapons program. He met with Haitian General Cedras until the brink of war and pleaded with President Clinton for a few more minutes to reason with the general. When he finally reached a settlement, he invited the dictator to come to his church in Plains, Georgia, to teach a Sunday-school class. The problem with that kind of negotiating is that it can easily lead to appeasement of the other side.

The Attitudinal Drive negotiator is so eager to find good in the other side that they can be easily deceived. A good example of this was when Prime Minister Neville Chamberlain of England made a last-minute effort to avoid war with Adolf Hitler. He returned to England, proclaiming that he had averted war by giving away only part of Czechoslovakia. Adolf Hitler had already figured out that he was a chump, and it didn't take the rest of the world long to agree with Hitler's assessment.

It helps that both negotiators know and like each other because it's hard to create a win-win solution unless they trust each other. However, Power Negotiators know that you must create a solution that is in the best interest of both sides. Then, it is mutually beneficial for both to support the agreement and see that it is implemented.

Key Points to Remember

1. Don't be guilty of socio-centrism. What we would want, if we were they, may have nothing to do with what they want.
2. The more you understand what is driving the other side the more likely you are to produce a win-win solution.
3. Competitive Drive negotiators won't share information that might be helpful to the other side and don't trust information given to them by the other side.
4. Solutional Drive is when both sides trust each other to work for a mutually acceptable solution.
5. Beware of Competitive Drive negotiators masquerading as Solutional Drive negotiators.
6. Sometimes the needs of the Personal Drive negotiator may be more important than finding the best solution.
7. Organizational Drive negotiators may be happy with the solution but can't sell it to their people and think of ways that could help them convince their organization.
8. Attitudinal Drive negotiators put too much confidence in gaining the friendship of the other. Instead, work for a solution that benefits both sides. Then it doesn't matter if you like each other.

Chapter 64

Win-Win Negotiating

Finally, let's talk about win-win negotiating. Instead of trying to dominate the other person and trick him into doing things he wouldn't normally do, I believe you should work with the other person to figure out your problems and develop a solution with which you can both win. Your reaction to that may be, "Roger, you obviously don't know much about my industry. The people with whom I negotiate don't take any prisoners. There's no such thing as win-win in my industry. When I'm selling, I'm obviously trying to get the highest price I possibly can, and the buyer is obviously trying to get the lowest possible price. When I'm buying, the reverse is true. How on Earth can we both win?"

Let's look at the most important issue here. What do we mean when we say win-win? Does it really mean that both sides win? Or does it mean that both sides lose equally so that it's fair? What if each side thinks that they won and the other side lost—would that be win-win? Before you dismiss that possibility, think about it more. What if you're selling something and leave the negotiation thinking, "I won. I would have dropped the price even more if the other person had been a better negotiator"?

However, the other person is thinking that she won and that she would have paid more if you had been a better negotiator. Both of you think that you won and the other person lost. Is that win-win? Yes, I believe it is, as long as it's a permanent feeling. As long as neither of you wake up tomorrow morning thinking, "Son of a gun, now I know what he did to me. Wait until I see him again."

That's why I stress doing the things that service the perception that the other side has won, such as the following:

- Not jumping at the first offer.
- Asking for more than you expect to get.

- Flinching at the other side's proposal.
- Avoiding confrontation.
- Playing Reluctant Buyer or Reluctant Seller.
- Using the Vise Gambit.
- Using Higher Authority and Good Guy/Bad Guy.
- Never offering to split the difference.
- Setting aside impasse issues.
- Always asking for a trade-off.
- Tapering down your concessions.
- Positioning the other side for easy acceptance.

Rule 1 of Win-Win Negotiating

The first thing to learn is: Don't narrow the negotiation down to one issue. If, for example, you resolve all the other issues, and the only thing left to negotiate is price, somebody does have to win and lose. As long as you keep more than one issue on the table, you can always work trade-offs so that the other person doesn't mind conceding on price because you are able to offer something in return.

Sometimes buyers try to treat your product as a commodity by saying, "We buy this stuff by the ton. As long as it meets our specifications we don't mind who made it or where it comes from." They are trying to treat this as a one-issue negotiation to persuade you that the only way you can make a meaningful concession is to lower your price. When that's the case, you should do everything possible to put other issues, such as delivery, terms, packaging, and guarantees, onto the table so that you can use these items for trade-offs and get away from the perception that this is a one-issue negotiation.

At a seminar, a real estate salesperson came up to me. He was excited because he'd almost completed negotiating a contract for a large commercial building. "We've been working on it now for over a year," he said. "And we've almost got it resolved. In fact, we've resolved everything except price, and we're only $72,000 apart." I flinched because I knew that, now that he'd narrowed it down to one issue, then there had to be a winner and there had to be a loser. However close they may be, they were probably heading for trouble. In a one-issue negotiation, you should add other elements so that you can trade them off later and appear to be making concessions.

A Spy for a Spy

During the cold war, FBI agents arrested Gennady Zakharov, a physicist who was a member of the Soviet delegation to the United Nations. The FBI had caught him red-handed (pardon the pun) as he paid cash for classified documents on a New York City subway platform. A week later, the KGB arrested Nicholas Daniloff, the Moscow correspondent for *U.S. News and World Report*. Nine months earlier they had set up Daniloff for just such an opportunity by having a KGB agent dressed as a priest ask him to deliver a letter to the U.S. embassy.

Now the Soviets were demanding the release of Zakharov in exchange for the release of Daniloff, whom they had branded as a spy. Outraged by the blatancy of their move, Reagan refused, and the incident began to threaten the upcoming arms control summit. Everybody knew that the fate of Zakharov and Daniloff was insignificant compared to the potential for world peace, but by now, both sides had dug into their positions and were blind to their mutual interests. It was a one-issue negotiation: Would we trade Zakharov for Daniloff or wouldn't we? President Reagan was adamant that he wouldn't be a patsy for the KGB.

To the rescue came Armand Hammer, the chairperson of Occidental Petroleum, who had been doing business in Russia since the revolution. He knew that the way to break the deadlock was to introduce another issue into the negotiations so that the Russians could offer a more palatable trade-off. He suggested to the Russians that they also agree to release dissident Yuri Orlov and his wife, Irina Valitova. This broke the deadlock because Reagan, who had dug into his position of not trading a Russian spy for an American journalist, could find the new trade acceptable because it didn't violate his previously stated position.

If you find yourself deadlocked with a one-issue negotiation, you should try adding other issues into the mix. This is called expanding the pie, rather than slicing the pie. Fortunately, usually many more elements than just the one main issue are important in negotiations. The art of win-win negotiating is to piece together those elements, like putting together a jigsaw puzzle, so both people can win.

Rule one is: Do not narrow down the negotiations to just one issue. Although we may resolve impasses by finding a common ground that we have on small issues, to keep the negotiation moving as I taught you in Chapter 10, you should never narrow it down to one issue.

Rule 2 of Win-Win Negotiating

People are not out for the same thing. We all have an overriding tendency to assume that other people want what we want, and because of this, we believe that what's important to us will be important to them. But that's not true.

The biggest trap into which neophyte negotiators fall is assuming that price is the dominant issue in a negotiation. Many other elements other than price are important to the other person. You must convince her of the quality of your product or service. She needs to know that you will deliver on time. She wants to know that you will give adequate management supervision to their account. How flexible are you on payment terms? Does your company have the financial strength to be a partner of theirs? Do you have the support of a well-trained and motivated workforce?

These all come into play, along with half a dozen other factors. When you have satisfied the other person that you can meet all those requirements, then, and only then, does price become a deciding factor. The second key to win-win negotiating is this: Don't assume that they want what you want. If you do, you further make the assumption that anything you do in the negotiations to help them get what they want helps them and hurts you.

Win-win negotiating can come about only when you understand that people don't want the same things in the negotiation. Power Negotiating becomes not just a matter of getting what you want, but also being concerned about the other person getting what he or she wants. One of the most powerful thoughts you can have when you're negotiating with someone is not "what can I get from them?" but "what can I give them that won't take away from my position?" Because when you give people what they want, they will give you what you want in a negotiation.

Rule 3 of Win-Win Negotiating

Don't be too greedy. Don't try to get the last dollar off the table. You may feel that you triumphed, but does that help you if the other person felt that you vanquished him? That last dollar left on the table is a very expensive dollar to pick up. A man who attended my seminar in Tucson told me that he was able to buy the company that he owned because the other potential buyer made that mistake. The other person had negotiated hard and pushed the seller to the brink of frustration. As a final nibble, the buyer said, “You are going to put new tires on that pickup truck before you transfer the title, aren’t you?” That straw broke the proverbial camel’s back. The owner reacted angrily, refused to sell his company to him, and instead sold it to the man at my seminar. Don’t try to get it all. Leave something on the table so that the other person feels that she won, also.

Rule 4 of Win-Win Negotiating

Put something back on the table when the negotiation is over. I don’t mean by telling them that you’ll give them a discount over and above what they negotiated. I mean do something more than you promised to do. Give them a little extra service. Care about them a little more than you have to. Then you’ll find that the little extra for which they didn’t have to negotiate means more to them than everything for which they did have to negotiate.

Now let me recap what I’ve taught you about win-win negotiating: People have different personality styles, and because of this, they negotiate differently. You must understand your personality style, and, if it’s different from the other person, you must adapt your style of negotiating to theirs. The different styles mean that in a negotiation, different people have different goals, relationships, styles, faults, and different methods of getting what they want.

Winning is a perception, and by constantly servicing the perception that the other person is winning, you can convince him that he has won without having to make any concessions to him. Don’t narrow the negotiation down to just one issue. Don’t assume that helping the other person get what he wants takes away from your position. You’re not out for the same thing. Poor negotiators try to force the other person to get off the positions that they’ve taken. Power negotiators know that, even when positions are 180 degrees apart the interests of both sides can be identical, so they work to get people off their positions and to concentrate on their interests. Don’t be greedy. Don’t try to get the last dollar off the table. Put something back on the table. Do more than they bargained for.

Remember the Power Negotiators’ Creed:

The most important thought you can have when you are negotiating is not “what can I get them to give me?” It is “what can I give them that would not take away from my position, but may be of value to them?” When you give people what they want, they will give you what you want.

Key Points to Remember

1. Win-win doesn't mean that both sides conceded equally, or that both sides gained equally.
2. It's win-win as long as each side feels that they won, even if each side feels that the other lost.
3. Power Negotiating means that from the way that you negotiate, you can get what you want and still have the other side feeling that they won.
4. If you narrow the negotiation down to just one issue, there must be a winner and a loser. Keep enough issues open that both sides can feel that they won.
5. If you're dealing with a one-issue negotiation, introduce other issues. This is called expanding the pie, rather than slicing the pie.
6. Don't assume that they want what you want. If you do, you further make the assumption that anything you do in the negotiations to help them get what they want helps them and hurts you.
7. Don't try to get the last dollar off the table.
8. Do a little more than you bargained for.
9. Remember the Power Negotiators' Creed:
   The most important thought you can have when you are negotiating is not "what can I get them to give me?" It is "what can I give them that would not take away from my position but may be of value to them?" When you give people what they want, they will give you what you want.

Conclusion

Final Thoughts

Throughout this book on negotiating, I've always tried to emphasize the win-win philosophy—that the answer to negotiations is not to dominate the other person, but to achieve a win for them, too. Always remember that people will give you what you want, not when you dominate them—and not when you over power them—but they'll give you what you want when you're able to give them what they want.

I've tried to stress my conviction that in any negotiation, the object is not to beat your opponent, but rather to creatively reach an agreement in which each negotiator can feel that he's a winner. I maintain that in every negotiation, no matter what the object of the negotiation is, both sides can win. More than that, I've been saying that both sides should win.

Negotiating Benchmarks

I've talked about some of the standards of good negotiation, those benchmarks by which the value of a negotiation may be judged. These standards shouldn't be any less lenient than those used by the silver craftsmen in old England, as they hammered their mark into their wares. These standards can help you determine not only whether you won or lost, but how you played the game as well.

↳ **Everyone must feel like a winner.** The first standard that you should consider is whether everyone involved in the negotiation emerged feeling like a winner. You've probably not completed a good negotiation if the other party walks away from the table thinking he or she isn't a great negotiator, muttering something like, "I can't believe it. He talked me out of everything." Rather, a good negotiation has been completed when both parties can walk away from the deal feeling as though they had accomplished something important.

- **Both care about the other's objectives.** The second benchmark is the feeling that both sides care about the objectives of the other. If you felt that the other party was listening to you and, if not being gratuitous, then at least they were taking your needs into consideration. If the other side had the same feeling about you, then, as a negotiator, you probably succeeded in creating an atmosphere of communication, in which a win-win settlement could be reached.
- **It was fair to both sides.** The third benchmark to watch for is the belief (which both sides should hold) that the other side was fair in the way in which it conducted the negotiations. For instance, a football team doesn't mind losing the game nearly so much if they know that the other side was playing by the rules. Nobody minds a tough fight, as long as it's a fair fight.

  A political candidate doesn't mind his loss so much if he believes that his opponent has waged a fair and reasonable campaign. It's when there's foul play, a rule is being broken, or something sneaky is going on. That's when the negotiators will hold feelings of betrayal. The attitudes of both negotiating teams, as they conclude the negotiations, should be, "Well, they were tough, and they fought hard. But they did listen to my point of view. I believe that they were fair in the way that they conducted the negotiations."
- **The process was enjoyable.** Benchmark number four is that each negotiator should feel as if he or she would enjoy dealing with the other party or parties at some time in the future. We could assume that this is how two chess players would feel, leaving a match, if the game was conducted fairly and well. Each would want to play the other again, not to out-do the other or get revenge, but simply because the process of playing one another was enjoyable and challenging.
- **Both sides are eager to follow the agreement.** The fifth standard of judgment is the belief held by each party that the other party is determined to keep the commitments made in the contract. Each side should have a good reason to believe that the other will uphold the conditions of the agreement.

If either side feels that, given the opportunity, the other side would back down from its promises, then that negotiation was not a win-win negotiation. Therefore, my definition of a win-win negotiator is a person who can get what he wants out of negotiation and still bring himself or herself up to the standards established by these five benchmarks. And a losing negotiator is someone who has not fulfilled the requirements of those benchmarks, no matter how many of his or her own objectives he or she gained in the negotiation.

Needs Negotiating

It's important to understand that every person acts only in his or her own self-interest, and must therefore be motivated from that standpoint. International negotiators call this "needs negotiating." Underpinning this philosophy is the concept that people will only act in order to meet their own needs. In doing so, they need not necessarily meet the needs of someone else in order to reach a workable agreement. The winning negotiator respects the needs and values of his or her opponent, and actively works to satisfy those needs, as well as his or her own.

Spend some time with the ideas that we've discussed. If you'll work to apply them in everyday situations, you'll acquire a surprising amount of control in any situation in which you're dealing with other people. Use these techniques to help you reach the level of success that you desire for yourself. And remember that everything that you need or want is currently owned or controlled by someone else.

Now you have the skills that you'll need to deal with these people more effectively. It's up to you to use them in an ethical manner to reach an agreement that is advantageous to everyone concerned—a win-win solution.

Now you are ready to graduate as a Power Negotiator. The skills you have learned will give you the power to command any business situation so that you can smoothly get the best deal for you and your company. Far more importantly, these skills will give you the power to manage conflict in your life. Starting now, there should never be a time when you lose control of a situation because of anger or frustration.

Starting now, you will be in control of your life. Starting now, you may appear upset or angry, but you're doing this as a specific negotiating technique—you will never be out of control. Even when it's only a simple matter, such as getting your son to clean up his room or getting your daughter to go to bed on time, you will be in control.

From now on, you will understand that any time you see conflict it is because one or more of the participants does not understand Power Negotiating. Whether it's a husband and wife in an argument, a boss firing an employee, a worker going on strike, a crime being committed, or an ugly international incident, Power Negotiators know that it happened because the participants did not know how to get what they wanted without resorting to conflict. I look forward to the day when all conflicts are avoided because people know how to get what they want with good negotiating skills. I invite you to share this vision with me by pledging now to remove conflict from your life and the lives of those around you by always practicing good negotiating skills. Then the example that you set will help lead us into a bright new future where violence, crime, and wars become an anachronism.

Index

About the Author

Roger Dawson was born in England, migrated to California in 1962, and became a United States citizen 10 years later. Formerly the president of one of California's largest real estate companies, he became a full-time author and professional speaker in 1982.

His Nightingale-Conant cassette program, *Secrets of Power Negotiating*, is the largest-selling business cassette audio program ever published. Several of his books have been main selections of major book clubs. He is the founder of The Power Negotiating Institute, a California-based organization.

Companies and associations throughout North America call on him for his expertise in negotiation, persuasion, and decision-making.

He was inducted into the Speaker Hall of Fame in 1991. His seminar company conducts seminars on Power Negotiating, Power Persuasion, Confident Decision Making, and High Achievement throughout the country and around the world.

The Power Negotiating Institute

1045 East Road

La Habra Heights, California 90631 USA

Tel: 800–YDAWSON [932–9766] (from the United States or Canada only)

International telephone number 1–562–694–5306.

For more information see his Website: *www.RogerDawson.com*.
You are welcome to e-mail comments, questions, complaints, and suggestions to *Roger@RogerDawson.com.*

Also by Roger Dawson

Books

You Can Get Anything You Want
Secrets of Power Negotiating
Secrets of Power Persuasion
The Confident Decision Maker
The 13 Secrets of Power Performance
Secrets of Power Negotiating for Salespeople
Secrets of Power Persuasion for Salespeople
Secrets of Power Problem Solving (coming Spring 2011)

(with Mike Summey)
The Weekend Millionaires Guide to Real Estate Investing
Weekend Millionaire Mindset
Weekend Millionaire FAQ
Weekend Millionaire Secrets to Negotiating Real Estate

Audio Programs

Secrets of Power Negotiating
Secrets of Power Persuasion
Secrets of Power Performance
Confident Decision Making
The Personality of Achievers
Power Negotiating for Salespeople

Video Training Programs

Guide to Everyday Negotiating
Guide to Business Negotiating
Guide to Advanced Negotiating Power
Power Negotiating for Salespeople (a 12-part series)

Speeches and Seminars

If you hire speakers for your company, or influence the selection of speakers at your association, you should learn more about Roger Dawson's speeches and seminars. He will customize his presentation to your company or industry so that you get a unique presentation tailored to your needs. You can also arrange to audio or videotape the presentation for use as a continuous training resource.

Roger Dawson's Presentations Include:

Secrets of Power Negotiating

Secrets of Power Persuasion

Confident Decision Making

The 13 Secrets of Power Performance

To get more information and receive a complimentary press kit, please call, write, e-mail, or fax:

The Power Negotiating Institute
1045 East Road
La Habra Heights, CA 90631 USA

Phone: 800–YDAWSON (932–9766)
Fax: 562–697–1397
E-mail: *Dawsonprod@aol.com*
Website: *www.RogerDawson.com*

Audio CD and Video Programs

Following is a listing of Roger Dawson's audio and video programs that you can order from the following:

The Power Negotiating Institute
1045 East Road
La Habra Heights, CA 90631 USA
Phone: 800–YDAWSON (932–9766)
Fax: 562–697–1397
E-mail: *Dawsonprod@aol.com*
Website: *www.RogerDawson.com*

Audio CD Programs

Secrets of Power Negotiating **$69.95**

Six hours of great training on 6 audio CDs. This is one of the largest-selling business audio programs ever published, with sales of more than $38 million. You'll learn 20 negotiating gambits that are sure-fire winners. Going beyond the mere mechanics of the power negotiating process, Roger Dawson helps you learn what influences people, and how to recognize and adjust to different negotiating styles, so you can get what you want, regardless of the situation.

Also, you'll learn:

- A new way of pressuring people without confrontation.
- The one unconscious decision you must never make in a negotiation.
- The five standards by which every negotiation should be judged.
- Why saying yes too soon is always a mistake.
- How to gather the information you need without the other side knowing.
- The three stages terrorist negotiators use to defuse crisis situations, and much, much more.

Power Negotiating for Salespeople **$69.95**

Six hours of great training on 6 audio CDs. This program that supplements and enhances Roger Dawson's famous generic negotiating program *Secrets of Power Negotiating,* teaches salespeople how to negotiate with buyers and get higher prices without having to give away extras, such as freight and extended payment terms. It's the most in-depth program ever created for selling at higher prices than your competition and still maintaining long-term relationships with your customers. It's guaranteed to dramatically improve your profit margins, or we'll give your money back.

Special Offer. Invest in both *Secrets of Power Negotiating* and *Power Negotiating for Salespeople* and save $30.
Both for only $110.

Secrets of Power Persuasion **$69.95**

Six hours of great training on 6 audio CDs. In this program, Roger Dawson shows you the strategies and tactics that will enable you to persuade people in virtually any situation. Not by using threats or phony promises, but because they perceive that it's in their best interest to do what you say.

You'll learn:

- Why credibility and above all, consistency are the cornerstones of getting what you want.
- You'll learn verbal persuasion techniques that defuse resistance and demonstrate the validity of your thinking.
- To develop an overwhelming aura of personal *charisma* that will naturally cause people to like you, respect you, and gladly agree with you.
- It's just a matter of mastering the specific, practical behavioral techniques that Roger Dawson presents in a highly entertaining manner.

Secrets of Power Performance **$69.95**

Six hours of great training on 6 audio CDs. With this program, you'll learn how to get the best from yourself and those around you! Roger Dawson believes that we are all capable of doing more than we think we're capable of. Isn't that true for you? Aren't you doing far more now than you thought you could do five years ago? With the life-changing secrets revealed in this best selling program, you'll be able to transform your world in the next five years!

Confident Decision Making **$69.95**

Six hours of great training on 6 audio CDs. Decisions are the building blocks of your life. The decisions you've made have given you everything you now have. The decisions you'll make from this point on will be responsible for everything that happens to you for the rest of your life. Wouldn't it be wonderful to know that, from this point on, you'll always be making the right choice? All you have to do is listen to this landmark program.

You'll learn:

- How to quickly and accurately categorize your decision.
- How to expand your options with a 10-step creative thinking process.
- How to find the right answer with reaction tables and decision trees.
- How to harness the power of synergism with the principle of huddling.
- How to know exactly what and how your boss, customer, or employee will decide, and dozens more powerful techniques.

Video Training Programs

Guide to Business Negotiating **One hour DVD video $55**
Guide to Everyday Negotiating **One hour DVD video $55**
Guide to Advanced Negotiating Power **One hour DVD video $55**

If you're in any way responsible for training or supervising other people, these videos will liven up your staff meetings and turn your people into master negotiators. Your sales and profits will soar as you build new win-win relationships with your customers. Then use these programs to develop a training library for your employees' review, and for training new hires.

Power Negotiating for Salespeople **12-Part Video Series $499**

Think how your sales and your profit margins would soar, if you could have Roger Dawson speak at your sales meetings once a month! Now you can, with this new series of twelve 30-minute videotapes designed just for this purpose. Dawson goes one-on-one with your salespeople to show them how to out-negotiate your buyers. Play one a month at your sales meetings and watch your people become masterful negotiators!

Special Prices for Career Press readers. Mention this book when you place your order and receive a 20-percent discount. All major credit cards accepted.